Prologue to Provocations

Prologue to Provocations

A Search for Truth in Christian Anthropology

Compiler
Romero D'Souza SDB

CWI
Christian World Imprints™

First Published in 2016 by

Christian World Imprints™
Christian Publishing & Books from India
H-12 Bali Nagar, **New Delhi-110015**
info@christianworldimprints.com
www.ChristianWorldImprints.com
Phone: +91 11 25465925

ISBN: 978-93-5148-103-4 (HB)

ISBN: 978-93-5148-139-3 (PB)

Digitally Printed at Replika Press Pvt. Ltd.

Printed in India.

Acknowledgement

At this juncture, I express my profoundest gratitude to all those who have accompanied me in my philosophical venture to reach this 'moment of life.' This is the task of authentic philosophy. I wish your openness as you (reader) journey this way of contemplation and participation, more especially the risk of being provoked to search for truth in the Christian Anthropological view as expressed by contributors in this work.

Me being gratuitous is in the grace of God and due to the support of my parents and brother, my Salesian family, my friends and family. I owe my sincere gratitude to the Salesian Provincial of the Mumbai Province, Rev. Fr. Godfrey D'Souza SDB for enabling me to publish this book. Also, my gratitude is due to the Salesian Province of Mumbai and especially to ex-Provincials, Rev. Fr. Ivo Coelho SDB and Rev. Fr. Michael Fernandes SDB, who accepted me in the Salesian congregation, to continue in this way of life; and who gave me an opportunity to do my further studies in philosophy.

I have journeyed the Salesian way of life, thus far and in a special way, I am grateful to *Divyadaan* – the institute, its teaching staff, co-staff members, my its companions and all the brothers pursuing their philosophical studies.

In a very special way, I am indebted to Rev. Fr. Biju Michael SDB, the President of *Studium Theologicum Salesianum* (*STS*), who encouraged me to walk this journey. I appreciate the good will and patience of Rev. Fr. Stephen Kuncherakatt SDB, Rev. Fr. Matthew Coutinho SDB, Paul Chou SDB and Rev. Fr. Aloysius Hembrom SDB, Cl. John Paul Vemo Soro SDB for their meticulous corrections, microscopic observations and insightful suggestions that has enriched and enhanced the quality of this research work.

In the journey of explicating and being provoked in search for truth, I was blessed with the richness and profundity of this academic venture that has surfaced in the outcome of these contributors: **Manu Michael, Moses Wanjala, Cara Judea Alhadeff, Thomas Storck, Joanna Golec, Marina D'costa, Benedikt Paul Göcke, Albert Kumar, James Schall, and Kevin Otieno Mwandha** who have willingly and earnestly shared their knowledge and wisdom, experience and judgment, by way of their scholarly and well-researched essays.

I wish to thank the Rector Rev. Fr. Andrew Wong SDB and the community – Salesian Monastery Ratisbonne, Jerusalem – Israel; the President Rev. Fr. Biju Michael SDB and the teaching staff of *Studium Theologicum Salesianum* (*STS*), Salesian Pontifical University, Faculty of Theology in Rome – Jerusalem Campus, Israel of the last few months that I have been blest and privileged to live at (to grow in wisdom and knowledge of Christ), for their love, understanding and all the help received by way of encouragement and support, inspite of all the time it took me away from them. I also take this opportunity to thank the Salesian Provincial of the Middle East Province (MOR). Rev. Fr. Munir El Rai SDB and the Province.

Thanks to the *Christian World Imprints* in a special way, Sudhanshu Kanda - without whom this book would never have taken its form and be available for persons and institutions, libraries and bookshelves.

Last and not least, I humbly ask pardon of all those who have been with me over the course of the years and whose names I have failed to mention.

Romero D'Souza, SDB
Feast of Mary Help of Christians
Jerusalem - Israel, 24th May 2016

Preface

Prologue to Provocation: Search for Truth in Christian Anthropology intends to showcase the exciting, world-benefiting, faith-deepening, political, cultural, and ecological engaging reality. This book will assist one to understand our present age – a pluriform postmodern world – and to deal with some of its challenges in a rational manner. My *companions* – contributors/authors have probed and coped with diverse situations and from their expertise have presented their valuable and thought-provoking insights in these papers. The process for this complied work began when I was thinking of pressing the most impatient question asked by Pontius Pilate to Jesus: "What is Truth?"(John 18:38).

The idea of "Prologue to Provocations" implies before we search for truth we need to tackle issues (problems, probabilities, pluralism, paradoxes, parapraxis). Therefore, this book will deal with a pansophical view in search for truth from varied perspectives and paradigms. It presents a powerful challenge to the fashionable belief of truth in the present day, here and now.

What motivated me to take this step is the movement to life crisis, the challenge to life, and those who choose to live a life of compromise, convenience and consensus - concern*less* human beings. Along with the contributors, I am also concerned of issues with regard to anthropology in the postmodern and globalized era.The unsettling questions also promote new discoveries and insights about humanity, divinity and Christianity which is a light of promise as well as has the darkness of problems. Therefore, there is a gap that grows with ubiquitous challenges and complexities caused often by the relational problem we face in the nature of humanity – human thinking and human living. There is an urgent need to reflect on contemporary intercommunicating realities.

Allow me, to caution you at the very beginning that the thoughts and ideas produced in this compiled work are not infallible pronouncements that claim a monopoly on the ultimate truth. However, they deal with and *search for truth* in unique and creative ways.

The intended audience of this book are researchers, research students in the field of anthropology and philosophy. Also, it is a must have for the institutes and readers interested in general philosophy and its relation to inter-related disciplines such as sociology, culture, politics, ecology, anthropology, and theology.

I would like to convey my appreciation to all the contributors (companions) who submitted their papers (chapters of the book). This complied work contains original contributions researched by: **Manu Michael**, **Moses Wanjala**, **Cara Judea Alhadeff**, **Thomas Storck**, **James Schall**, **Kevin Otieno Mwandha, Benedikt Paul Göcke, Marina D'costa, Joanna Golec, and Albert Kumar**. The authors have expressed their views and opinions with convictions, provocations, and questions to be further studied and critiqued. These are and I would like to believe, truly philosophical in nature. They 'carry us beyond' the first meaning of a sentence and allows us to land on unknown shores where perhaps even risk getting lost, to experience an adventurous journey in search for truth.

Each chapter contains a detailed account of issues dealt with according to the author's expertise in their respective field in relation to philosophy. Their presentations are enriched by critical observation and practical insights. There has been a persistent and consistent examination, in the light of experiences that reveal a search for truth. Their opinions and conclusions after an in-depth reflection and research lead us to a precarious venture as we move from subjective understanding to an objective outlook. Above all, perhaps, their interpretation present a practical and pragmatic proposal for understanding the context and claims in search for truth.

I sincerely hope that the publication of this work will lead to further analysis of the subjects researched and presented. This book will not only serve as useful groundwork for further in-depth research but also make an inspiring contribution to a significant understanding of the nature of man in search for truth: A Prologue to Provocation in Christian Anthropology.

Introductory Note

"*And you shall know the truth and the truth shall set you free*" **(John 8:32)**

Prologue to Provocations

Prologue to Provocations is the title of this book emerging in the course of the evolution of this collection of well-researched scholarly papers. It is a productive prefix to deal with the critical and creative standpoints in the present project. My purposeful and playful intention to name this book *Prologue to Provocations* is to show the active and dynamic relation of philosophy with the other sciences. The idea of "prologue to provocations" implies that before we search for truth we need to tackle issues like problems, probabilities, pluralism, paradoxes, parapraxis. Therefore, this book will deal with a pansophical view in search for truth from varied perspectives and paradigms. The papers featured in this book present a – "phenomenological pedagogical" outlook in the search for truth. They present a powerful challenge to the fashionable belief of truth in the present day, here and now.

Search for Truth

One might be curious and begin to wonder when one is posed with a question such as *What is truth?* Along with this question the most essential and necessary questions are: *Why* does one search for truth and *How* does one arrive at the truth? I think these are essential questions. Almost everyone (scientists, religionists, philosophers, historians, archaeologist, theologians, and others) is engaged in a noble search for truth. *Truth* can be defined or described as conformity to reality or actuality, and in order for something to be "true" it must be objective, public, eternal, independent, absolute, transcendental, meaningful, beautiful, and accessible; therefore the search for truth is inevitable. I am concerned with the truth in which we live (why) and grow (how). What motivated me to take this step were the movement to life crisis, and the challenge to life; and those who choose to live a life of compromise, convenience and consensus - concern*less* human beings. I am also concerned with the world and therefore the issue and situation of politics, culture, society and religion in the globalized era.

The 21st century postmodern world has increasingly sophisticated the reality of truth. It therefore exhibits attitudes such as prejudices and problems, pluralism and paradoxes which lead to the danger of humanities. Thus, the essential need for suggested probabilities and possibilities have been provoked in the impetus for the project of which this book has been compelled to respond to the quest in *Search of Truth* in relation to Philosophy and other fields of human expertise. The contributions made by intellectuals – academic researchers, deal with erroneous assumptions and suggest praxis-theory implications to the search for truth. I think they have been self-conscious and self-critical in studying and presenting, in articulating and philosophizing from their perspective the subject matter researched. They have intentionally engaged in reflecting on the meaning and value in search for truth. They have expanded our horizon to achieve a breakthrough in our understanding of reality. They have effectively paved an analytical process through which we can attain conclusive responses. The study of sciences led by my companions involves embracing particular and specific ontological, epistemological and metaphysical realities that are different from each other. However, they all accompany the reader in the *Search for Truth* with accuracy and sincerity, consistency and contingency, theoretical and practical ways. We shall seemingly read and reflect in *search for truth*, the accountability, the flexibility, the visibility – a care-confrontation of truth.

Christian Anthropology

A worldview is a philosophy of living that enables us to make sense of life and our daily experiences. It affects the way we process ideas, and allows us to understand society and our place in it. It is important in the context of society today – this is because the contemporary world has had a huge effect on human beings (Man – *Anthropos*). We seem unable to deal with unpredictable change and increased complexity of life – culture, politics, economics, ecology, digital reality, morality, education, religion, intellectual realm, and others. It helps us to make the critical decisions that will shape our future and our own selves, and it aids us in providing a picture of the whole, as opposed to a fragmented reality.

Our worldview will be that of *"Christian" Anthropology*: It is the study of humanity in a very speculative, normative and critical perspective. It is primarily focused on the nature of humanity – the *how* and the *why* of our relatedness to God and the World. It seeks to define and answer in a classical way: Who is man? What is man? Why man is called a man? How can we define or describe man? I think in the course of history varied sciences have treated these fundamental questions in relation to Anthropology.

Allow me, to caution you at the very beginning that the thoughts and ideas produced in this compiled work is not an infallible production that claims ultimate truth. However, it will surely deal with and remain in the *search for truth* in unique and creative ways. One might come to think that the complied work is a step forward that is too radical and revolutionary or one might tend to think that it is regressive – conservative and fundamental. Being judgmental is not our concern here and therefore, I humbly ask you not to judge but rather ask these questions: Is there hope for truth in a world where humanity is more concerned with power and pleasure, with selfish and individualistic pessimism on one hand and on the other where many are struggling with poverty and problems, with willful ignorance and wishful optimism?

In reviewing what I have said thus far, we note that "*Prologue to Provocation - A Search for Truth in Christian Anthropology*" is a philosophical endeavour, necessary to humanities. I take this opportunity to acknowledge my companions – the contributors/authors of the scholarly papers presented in this book hoping earnestly that you (the readers) may follow in our footsteps, finishing that which we may not have completed, and correcting any errors of our judgment by careful and impartial investigation, and thorough enquiry into the *search for truth*. My humble intention was to bring together thinkers from across the globe to voice their thoughts for the sake of the common good, the common search, and to arrive at communion, that is, to engage in a relational and philosophical outcome that will be a prologue that provokes a search for truth in Christian anthropology.

Therefore, the prologue to provoke productive essays and the search for truth in a critical constructive way has been paved by the contributors to journey in a lateral and creative style.

Chapters of the Book

Manu Michael in Chapter one: ***Relationship: A Levinasian Reading*** deals with "I" the subject related to the Other *not based on any moral principle rather steered by* one's response to the encounter. Every encounter according to the Levinasian understanding commences the ethical nature of relationship which is an asymmetry that is never an equal relationship but a relation between bigger and smaller, high and low, God and man, infinite and finite. The subject never dominates the Other, instead it responds to the epiphany of the face. Every relationship is not a call to understand but to respond – a response made by the subject as an answer to the summoning of the face of the Other, which often commands, making the subject a hostage. Thus, the vulnerable subject is in an asymmetrical relationship. I am responsible before the Other in his alterity, responsible before all the Others for all the Others. The condition of being hostage is an authentic figure of responsibility, a true model of relationship for Levinas.

Moses Wanjala in Chapter two: ***Faith Formation and Maturation Experience in the Family: An Anthropological, Biblical, Liturgical and Spiritual Treasure*** makes a study of the nuclei of life, that is, family. He presents both the flourishing experiences as well as the fragmented and forced challenges that often result in moments of crisis. Inspired by the life of the first Christian community in the Acts of the Apostles, he attempts to rediscover *our journey* *towards a continuous growth in an authentic family spirit* and to contribute to the *actualization of a true home* where the beauty of our faith is experienced and shared freely, peacefully and fruitfully. The study takes the anthropological-biblical-liturgical step to facilitate our faith maturation experience within the family-ecclesial-societal domain. This enables us to interpret, to rediscover and appreciate individual and community gifts, so as to be living credible witnesses to today's world permeated by a secularized, globalized, pessimistic and individualistic mentality.

Cara Judea Alhadeff in Chapter three: ***Convenience Culture and the Violence of the Everyday*** proceeds to disentangle the roots of systemic psychic and social violence. The article investigates how the forces of misogyny, racial hygiene, and anti-intellectualism reconfigure the troubled, yet vital concept of equality. Political and ethical analyses of the interstices of cultural studies and corporeal politics that enable a rhizomatic re-conceptualization of community rooted in difference and vulnerability. Her research offers a constructive strategy to challenge the inertia that perpetuates insidious body-phobic, convenience-culture hegemonies inscribed in the current crisis of agency in the United States, and lays the groundwork for an emancipatory pedagogy. A radical democracy requires that theory becomes practice. By examining the lived intersections of technology, aesthetics, eroticism, and ethnicity through the lens of vulnerability, this essay offers citizen-subjects an opportunity to recognize their potential for transformative action. Although, vulnerability is conventionally understood to mean *being susceptible to harm*, the foundation of this practice is rooted in encountering vulnerability and difference *as* physical and emotional strength—an enfoldment of ambiguity, the unknown, and the uncanny. She is proposing an embodied democracy in which social models become a practice based protomodel on recognition of the absolute necessity of difference: an infinite potential of our bodies as contingent modes of relation.

Thomas Storck in Chapter four: ***What account can Philosophy give of Culture?*** unleashes the anthropological concept of culture which is presented together with the idea of the philosophy of culture. He further discusses the relationship between culture and nature, and argues that, although any particular cultural expression is always arbitrary, without culture the capacities and demands of human nature can hardly be expressed. Next, he answers the question of whether any ideas can rightly be termed transcultural, with particular attention to philosophic ideas, to which he proposes that in principle philosophy can offer universal truths which perforce apply to all cultures. Finally, in his essay he returns to the idea that the modern scientific enterprise is the best example of transcultural knowledge which is critiqued. His analytic approach states that in fact science has been shaped by particular cultural trends of the modern West.

James Schall in Chapter five: ***The Nature of Political Philosophy*** attempts to make a conclusion based on his research by suggesting that "political philosophy" is not merely a "branch" of philosophy. Rather it looks to the politician's understanding of the things that are not political and how one must deal with them. In a regime where everything is politicized, no room is left for philosophy or revelation. Politics deals with human beings organized to achieve their potential good. However, this good requires thought about what man (human being) is. His paper introduces the thought of political philosophy beginning with the deaths of Socrates and Christ, on whether it is always necessary that the city killed its best men. The problem of the politician is what to do with the aberrant philosopher. The problem of the philosopher is how to convince by speech that something greater than the city must exist in the city if human beings are to be what they are by nature.

Kevin Otieno Mwandha in Chapter six: ***Philosophy and Jurisprudence: Some Parallels and Challenges*** draws an inter-intra contrast and similarity that Philosophy and jurisprudence may seem two separate and diverse sciences without parallels. However, philosophy, in its depth and richness, is an important *instrumentum laboris,* extremely necessary for interpretations of law without prejudice to the existential challenges that occur between these disciplines. Philosophy as a science has various branches or schools of thought. The science of law – *jurisprudence* – also has its branches. He provides a general overview of the converging and diverging elements existent between philosophy and jurisprudence without taking delight in the faults and follies of these sciences. Taking into account the numerous schools of thought that exist in both sciences (philosophy and jurisprudence), it would be impossible to treat each school as a separate entity. Therefore, in the article (apart from the introductory notes and some concluding remarks) he focuses primarily on the contributions and challenges of some philosophies in jurisprudence and vice versa. The philosophical schools of thought he examines are focus on methodological scepticism, existentialism, utilitarianism, pragmatism, positivism and realism.

In Chapter seven, Benedikt Paul Göcke discusses ***Challenges for a Christian Worldview*** writing about the plausibility of a Christian worldview which is highly contested in the academia. Whether it is the existence of God, the affirmation of objective moral truth, or life after death – almost every core feature of Christian faith is heavily disputed. In the well-articulated essay, Benedikt briefly clarifies the essential features related to the concept of a worldview and then proceeds to specify some of the most important assumptions of a Christian worldview. Analytically he continues to formulate some of the most popular arguments against the plausibility of a Christian worldview. And thereby, suggests with logical reasoning by way of arguing that none of the arguments is decisive. His concluding premise is: One can affirm a Christian worldview without contradiction.

Joanna Golec in Chapter eight presents: ***The Great Escape – Remarks on Anachoresis Then and Today*** shows the period of Late Antiquity and the group called anachoresis which lasts till today and fascinates people despite their religious beliefs. In this article, Golec observes the historical and present state of the understanding and living of the anachoresis. She further develops archaeological data from authentic Egyptian hermitage and modern eremites, to seek an answer to given questions thus answering many doubts.

Chapter nine authored by Marina D'Costa entitled: ***Death Inspires Life – A Perspective in Medical Anthropology,*** has in an ironically critical way presented her topic "death inspires life" inspired by death where Christian Anthropology tries to understand how human beings are connected to God (pre and post life), often having its base in the bible. Keeping her focus on the aspects of Christian Anthropology she speaks about the human body as a creation in the image and likeness of God. In the following sections of her article she claims that the essence of the human body is health, which is understood in the context of medical anthropology. Her main focus is health which she deals with very decisively from both the perspectives of Medical Anthropology and Christian Anthropology, highlighting how the fear of death has caused humans to seek pro-life measures in the arena of health systems and health services. She concludes the article by responding to the issue of death in the context of health as the human response and human phenomena.

Albert Kumar in Chapter ten: ***Certitude in Newman's Grammer of Assent*** begins, in its first part by explaining the term assent as it is necessary in order to understand Newman's argument to certitude. It explains clearly what certitude is and how it is distinguished from assent. The second part deals with the essentials of Certitude: It follows investigation and proof, and is indefectible, and causes a sense of repose and triumph. The other parts of the article answer the question, How do we arrive at certitude in the concrete? Certitude in concrete matters, according Newman is preceded by informal inference whose conclusions are conditional to the extent that they are probabilities converging toward a truth. This happens through the natural faculty called illative sense as by which the mind arrives at truth in concrete matters. The whole argument of Newman for certitude ends with the clear understanding of the faculty 'Illative Sense'. In conclusion, the study is evaluated and proved significant in the study of epistemology.

Romero D'Souza in Chapter eleven: ***Paradigm Shift – Ecological Crisis to Ecosophical Care*** recognizes the urgent need of the present times in the life of human beings. It precisely deals with the significant role of a paradigm shift from the ecological crisis to ecosophical care and the wisdom in accomplishing such a transition. The article unfolds in two parts: The first part deals with the *2014 Faith and Ecology Conference in Jerusalem* and the second part reflects on *the paradigm shift from the ecological crisis to ecosophical care*. This is the shift in understanding that needs to be implemented for a better future. He further examines how wisdom – the quintessence of the knowledge and praxis of ecosophy - is a step to care. Along these lines, he intends to offer a path forward for humanity in terms of a rediscovery of a harmonious and sustainable relationship with the physical world, a re-emphasis of understanding human existence in terms of interrelatedness and interdependence, and a reawakening to the sacred dimension of all creation. He concludes his reflection using snippets of articles collected from the encyclical "Laudato Si" on the topics of creation, ecosophy, and care for creation. He goes on to make some critical comments and practical suggestions for a paradigm shift in ecosophical care.

In the epilogue, we shall reflect on the understanding of ***Christian Anthropology*** according to Karol Wojtyla/ Saint Pope John Paul II.[1] We shall see the guiding principles that are fundamental in the *Christian Anthropology* of Karol Wojtyla/Saint Pope John Paul II: *Definition, Meaning and Centrality of the Human Person; The Human Person as Unity of Body and Spirit, as a Rational Being which has a Spiritual Nature, as Subject and as Object, as a Concrete and Unique Subject, as the Imago Dei and as a Gift; and Human Person in relation to Subjectivity, Transcendence, Truth and Love.* The whole truth about the person is based on a ***rich synthesis of faith and reason***, of a ***lived reality-experience***, that gives the human person a centrality in the universe. His recurrent and insistent emphasis on each and every '***real***,' '***concrete***,' and '***historical***' outlook of person intends to promulgate an understanding of man as a ***unique*** person. In this forceful declaration we gain an insight into the ***Personalism*** that enlightens both his philosophy and in particular his anthropology. These are the basic principles of 'the truth about man' so often articulated in the writings of Karol Wojtyla/ Saint Pope John Paul II.

1 Thomas McGovern, "The Christian Anthropology of John Paul II: An Overview," *Josephinum Journal of Theology*, 8/1 (2001): 132-147.

Contents

Chapter 1

Relationship
A Levinasian Reading

Manu Michael

1. Introduction

Emmanuel Levinas, one of the most important continental philosophers of the twentieth century clarifies the concept of the Same and the Other in the traditional western philosophy. The division between the Same and the Other becomes one of the most fundamental concepts in Levinas' thought and is one of the keys to the rest of his works.[1] Discussing the same in *Totality and Infinity* (1961) Levinas asserts that being produces itself as multiples and split itself into the Same and the Other.[2] Further he says, the Same and the Other, at the same time, *maintain* themselves in relationship and *absolve* themselves from this relation, and thus remain absolutely separated. He ponders that this absolute separation is essential for the idea of Infinity.[3] Hence, Levinas remain opposed to the philosophical

1 The concept of the Same and the Other are found in the dialogues of Plato, '*The Sophist*' and they also play a key role in the metaphysics of Hegel. In the Levinasian use of the term the Same is associated with the 'I' of subjectivity and the Other with the other person and in the form of *illeity*, with God. From a logical perspective, these terms are directly opposed. The possibility of interchangeableness would be in the sense that the Same can be defined as the Other of the Other. According to Levinas the natural egoistic self '*moi*' on the ethical demands of the Other transforms into what Levinas calls '*soi*' (*soi* is used in French to denote self but not strictly myself as into the use of '*moi*'). Cf. Michael B. Smith, *Toward the Outside: Concepts and Themes in Emmanuel Levinas* (Pennsylvania: Duquesne University Press Pittsburgh, 2005), 37.

2 Emmanuel Levinas, *Totality and Infinity: An Essay on Exteriority*, translated by A. Lingis (Pittsburgh: Martinus Nijhoff Publishers, 1979), 269.

3 Levinas, *Totality and Infinity*, 102.

tradition which was started by Parmenides (c. 515 - c. 445 BCE) and continued by Benedictus Spinoza (1632-1677) and George Hegel (1770-1831). Levinas interpret their philosophies as misguided attempts to reconcile the Same and the Other by incorporating them into a larger whole. He opposes this because it spoils the transcendental relation which keeps the identity of the Same and the alterity of the Other.[4]

The Same and the Other are in relationship, at the same time they are absolutely separated. The infinity requires this separation as an ultimate source of being.[5] For, Levinas says "Without separation there would not have been truth; there would have been only being."[6] Totality or ontology, do not contain the final secret of being; as the idea of infinity, it proceeds from what is thought not from the thinker.[7] The relationship subsists between the Same and the Other despite the impossibility of the whole in the ultimate structure.[8] When we say that truth is a modality of relation between the Same and the Other we do not oppose intellectualism, rather we ensure its fundamental aspiration. In knowledge the knower doesn't become part of the known being. The relation of truth involves interiority. This rests on language; a relation in which the terms remain absolute within the relation.[9]

> We are the same *and* the other. The conjunction *and* here designates neither addition nor power of one term over the other. We shall try to show that the *relation* between the same and the other—upon which we seem to impose such extraordinary conditions—is language. For language accomplishes a relation such that the terms are not limitrophe within this relation, such that the other, despite the relationship with the same, remains transcendent to the same. The relation between the same and the other, metaphysics, is primordially enacted as conversation, where the same, gathered up in its ipseity as an "I," as a particular existent unique and autochthonous, leaves itself.[10]

"It is in order that alterity be produced *in being* that a 'thought' is needed and that an I is needed."[11] So alterity is possible only starting from me. However, the Absolutely Other is the Other. There is no commonality between 'He' and 'I.' Nothing is common between I, and the stranger who disturbs the being at

4 Cf. Adriaan Peperzak, *To the Other* (Indiana: Purdue University Press, 1993), 13.

5 Cf. Emmanuel Levinas, *Totality and Infinity: An Essay on Exteriority*, translated by A. Lingis (Pittsburgh: Martinus Nijhoff Publishers, 1979), 102.

6 Levinas, *Totality and Infinity*, 60.

7 *Ibid.*, 61.

8 *Ibid.*, 80.

9 *Ibid.*, 61-62.

10 *Ibid.*, 39.

11 *Ibid.*, 39.

home with oneself. But the stranger also means the free one. Over him I have no power.[12] The primordial sphere, which corresponds to what we call the Same, turns to the Absolutely Other only on call from the Other. The Absolutely Other does not limit the freedom of the Same. Calling it to responsibility justifies it. The relation with the absolute alterity is always maintained in peace.[13]

2. Time and Relation

Man's ethical relation is prior to his ontological relation and to the totality of things (World Cosmology). The relationship with the Other is time.[14] Time means the Other is forever beyond me, irreducible to the synchrony of the Same. Time can be seen as a general term for any relation to otherness that is reducible to comprehension or understanding.[15] For Levinas sees, there are always people who move from the ethical perspective of alterity to the ontological perspective of alterity. Time fashions man's relation to the Other, and to the Absolutely Other, or God, as a diachronic relation irreducible to correlation. Levinas gives importance to the future. He sees the future as absolutely new, and so Absolutely Other. The future is still more mysterious. It is a relationship with the Other where the Other is radically Other. Truth requires as its ultimate condition, infinite time, the condition for both goodness and the transcendence of the face.[16]

3. Face-to-Face Relationship

Being convinced that ethics must be first philosophy, Levinas lays the ground for his objection to the fundamental moves, and privileges granted therein, found in Heidegger's fundamental ontology. To establish ethics as first philosophy, emphasis and priority is given to the face-to-face encounter and infinity of the Other. If the essence of philosophy consists in going back from all certainties toward a principle, if it lives from critique, the face of the Other would be the starting point of philosophy.

3.1 The Face

The face itself is a presence. When it manifests itself, the face breaks through its own plastic image. The face is not simply an aspect of the body. The face enters

12 Cf. Levinas, *Totality and Infinity*, 39.

13 *Ibid.*, 97.

14 Cf. Alain P. Toumayan, *Encountering the Other: The Artwork and Problem of Difference in Blanchot and Levinas* (Pittsburgh: Duquesne University Press, 2004), 112.

15 Cf. Simon Critchley, "Introduction," in *The Cambridge Companion to Levinas*, edited by Simon Crichley and Robert Bernasconi (Cambridge: Cambridge University Press 2004), 11.

16 Cf. *Levinas, "Martin Buber and the Theory of Knowledge,"* in *The Levinas Reader*, edited by Sean Hand (Oxford: Basil Blackwell, 1989), 65.

into our world from a sphere absolutely foreign, from an absolute. Though his face becomes visible he remains Absolutely Other than the I and Other to the I.[17]

However, the face is not merely an image, or a portrait. Insofar as the face manifests the Other, and not the projection of oneself, it is truly the epiphany of the Other. Yet, the Other that is manifested through the face is totally exterior to me; there is a 'radical heterogeneity' that creates an 'infinite' distance between the I and the Other. The face, thus, manifests the uniqueness of the Other.[18]

"The face resists possession, resists my powers."[19] The face due to its epiphany, and expression, turns into total resistance to the grasp. This resistance to the grasp is not produced as an insurmountable resistance like that of a start in the immensity of space. Rather the expression of the face defies my ability for power, and not just the feebleness of my power.[20] That is to say "the face speaks to me and thereby invites me to a relation incommensurable with a power exercised, be it enjoyment or knowledge."[21] So, "the face arrests totalization."[22]

3.2 Exteriority

Levinas considered exteriority as the property of space which brings subject back into himself.[23] The Levinasian understanding of 'exteriority' takes a more essential meaning due to its essential search of 'the good,' that is beyond being.[24] However, separation makes possible a relation with the detached-absolute exteriority. This relation is brought about primordially by the epiphany of the Other in the face. We have sought to expose the epiphany of the face as the origin of exteriority. "The primary phenomenon of signification coincides with exteriority; exteriority is signifyingness itself. And only the face in its morality is exterior."[25] Exteriority defines the existence as existent, and the signification of the face due to an essential coinciding of the existent and the signifier.[26]

17 Cf. *Emmanuel Levinas, Ethics and Infinity: Conversations with Philippe Nemo*, translated by Richard. Cohen (Pittsburgh: Duquesne University Press, 1985), 85.

18 Cf. "Johnson J. Puthenpurackal, "Ethics of Responsibility: A Study Based on the Philosophy of Emmanuel Levinas," (a paper presented during the meeting of Association of Catholic Philosophers of India, held in 1997, at Nitika, Calcutta), 7.

19 Levinas, *Totality and Infinity*, 197.

20 *Ibid.*, 198.

21 *Ibid.*

22 *Ibid.*, 281.

23 Cf. Emmanuel Levinas, *Time and the Other*, translated by Richard Cohen (Pittsburgh: Duquesne University Press, 1987), 75-76.

24 From the point of view of hypotheses exteriority is considered as a precisely spatiality and light, since it is the movement from a less-than-full being to being of the world. Cf. Michael B. Smith, *Toward the Outside: Concepts and Themes in Emmanuel Levinas* (Pittsburgh: Duquesne University Press, 2005), 156.

25 Levinas, *Totality and Infinity*, 261-262.

26 *Ibid.*, 261-262.

3.3 Proximity

Levinas considers the closeness without distance as Proximity. "Proximity is not a failed coincidence, but an incessant, infinite, and glorious increase of alterity."[27] The subject is exposed to alterity before it can gather itself up and take a stand. "The relationship with alterity,... exceeds all comprehension, is infinitely remote, is, paradoxically enough, the most extreme immediacy, proximity closer than presence, obsessive contact."[28] Proximity *par excellence* is the proximity of the Other, the neighbour. And, Levinas' language has become the language of ethics. By ethics Levinas understands the relation of the subject to a pure regularity where the two are united neither by a synthesis of the understanding nor in subject-object correlation, but where one term of the relation is significant to the Other before any thought or meaning.

3.4 Face-to-Face

The Other presents himself in the face, but does not negate the Same or does it do violence to it.

> The relationship between men is certainly the non-synthesizable par excellence. One can also wonder if the idea of God, can be made part of a totality of being, or if it is not, much rather, transcendent to being. The term "transcendence" signifies precisely the fact that one cannot think God and being together. So too in interpersonal relationship it is not a matter of thinking the ego and the other together, but to be facing. The true union or true togetherness is not a togetherness of synthesis, but a togetherness of face to face.[29]

For Levinas face is pre-eminently self-expressive. The Other looks at me straight in the eyes, via the glance we stand 'eye-to-eye' with one another (face-to-face) in a totally immediate manner. In this way I experience the Other as the pre-eminent factthat 'traumatizes' and 'surprises' me.[30] The face expresses the presence and the absolute 'otherness' of the Other which cannot be reduced. As Roger Burggraeve sums up: "The face is ethical because it is simultaneously demanding and begging, or rather because it may beg only to the extent that it also demands and may only demand to the extent that it also begs."[31]

---

27 Smith, *Toward the Outside*, 27.

28 Cf. Alphonso Lingis, "Translator's Introduction," *Otherwise than Being or Beyond Essence*, translated by A. Lingis, (Dordrech: Kluwer Academic Publishers, 1978), xix.

29 Cf. *Levinas, Ethics and Infinity*, 77.

30 Puthenpurackal, "Ethics of Responsibility: A Study Based on the Philosophy of Emmanuel Levinas," 7.

31 Roger Burggraeve, *The Ethical Basis for a Humane Society According to Emmanuel Levinas*, translated by Catherine Vnahove-Romanik (Leuven: Centre for Metaphysics and Philosophy of God, Institute of Philosophy, 1981), 26.

In the face of the Other, "I see the reflection of my real self; the egocentric imperialism that drives me to work exclusively towards my own self-development, without even a glance from within my kingdom to the other-than-myself. This discovery throws me into shame."[32] The Other, in the rectitude of his face, is not a character within a context. The face is what one cannot kill, or at least it is that whose *meaning* consists in saying: 'thou shall not kill.' Murder, it is true, is a banal fact: one can kill the Other; the ethical exigency is not an ontological necessity.[33] What Levinas wants to establish is that, in our relationship with the Other, looking at the face of the Other, we cannot deny our responsibility to respond to the needs of the Other.

4. Asymmetrical Relationship

In his second major work *Otherwise than Being or Beyond Essence* (1974), Levinas considers responsibility as responsibility for the Other, that is to say, the subject is responsible for his very responsibility.[34] So he holds that the epiphany of the Other denotes at once the relation to the Other, which is fundamentally asymmetrical.[35] It is not an encounter between two people on equal footing, nor is it a friendship based on reciprocity.[36] Levinas agrees with Abraham Heschel (1907-1972) who claims that 'God is in search of man.' It is a relationship that is never an equal relationship but a relation between bigger and smaller, high and low, God and man, infinite and finite. This relationship is called asymmetrical relationship. It is true with regard to human relationship too. Levinas mentioning the face of the Other says that I do not grasp Other in order to dominate, instead respond to the epiphany of the face. And this relation is metaphysical in nature.

In an interview of Levinas by Tamra Wright, Peter Hunhes and Alison Ainley, he stresses:

> The idea of asymmetry seems very important to me; it is, perhaps, the most important way of conceiving of the relationship between the self and other which does not place them on the same level. The idea of asymmetry is another way of telling that in the perseverance in being we are all equal, but the idea that the death of the other is more important than my own in an

32 Cf. Puthenpurackal, "Ethics of Responsibility: A Study Based on the Philosophy of Emmanuel Levinas," 9.

33 Cf. *Levinas, Ethics and Infinity,* 86-87.

34 *Ibid.,* 96.

35 Cf. Emmanuel Levinas, "Meaning and Sense," in *Emmanuel Levinas: Basic Philosophical Writings*, edited by A. Peperzak, S. Critchley, and R. Bernasconi (Bloomington, Indiana: Indiana University Press, 1996), 53.

36 Cf. Sekar Sebastian, *Radical Responsibility for the Other: An Ethical Appraisal of Emmanuel Levinas* (Bangalore: Asian Trading Corporation, 2010), 73.

> affirmation that we are not being looked at from outside, but the essential difference between me and the other remains in my look.[37]

We are familiar with the saying of Aloysha Karamazov in *The Brothers Karamazov* by Dostoyevsky, "we are all responsible for everyone else - but I am more responsible than everyone else."[38] This essential asymmetry is the very basis of ethics, not only am I more responsible than the Other but I am even responsible for everyone else's responsibility.[39] The ethical rapport with the face is asymmetrical in that it subordinates my existence to the Other. I owe more to the Other than to myself. The Jewish proverb says, 'the other's material needs are my spiritual needs.' This is an asymmetry which is an ethical refusal of the first truth of ontology. "Ethics is therefore, *against nature* because it forbids the murderousness of my natural will to put my own existence first."[40]

Levinas underlines the Other's right as the basis of true humanism.

> The being that presents himself in the face comes from a dimension of height, a dimension of transcendence whereby he can present himself as a stranger without opposing me as obstacle or enemy. More, for my position as *I* consists in being able to respond to this essential destitution of the Other, finding resources for myself. The Other who dominates me in his transcendence is thus the stranger, the widow, and the orphan, to whom I am obligated.[41]

Levinas moves from the ethical to the juridical asymmetry, which means to say "that 'right' begins as inequality and heteronomy. 'Right' does not begin in my freedom, but in the Other himself: it is an-archic (pre-original)."[42] The only basis for a truly ethical 'right' is the unconditional responsibility that the face imposes on me. My responsibility for the Other becomes the Other's right and a demand of justice. Levinas considers 'justice' as superior to 'love' as the latter term

37 Tamra Wright, "The Paradox of Morality: An Interview with Emmanuel Levinas," in *The Provocation of Levinas*, edited by R. Bernasconi and D. Wood (London: Routledge Press, 1998), 179. As cited in Sebastian, *Radical Responsibility for the Other*, 91-92.

38 Emmanuel Levinas and Richard Kearney,"Dialogue with Emmanuel Levinas" in *Face to Face with Levinas,* edited by Richard Cohen (Albany: State University of New York Press, 1986), 31.

39 Cf. Levinas and Richard Kearney, "Dialogue with Emmanuel Levinas," *Face to Face with Levinas,* 31. *Levinas, Ethics and Infinity,* 96.

40 *Ibid.,* 24.

41 Levinas, *Totality and Infinity*, 215.

42 Roger Burggraeve, *From Self-development to Solidarity: An Ethical Reading of Human Desire in its Socio-Political Relevance according to Emmanuel Levinas* (Leuven: Centre for Metaphysics and Philosophy of God, 1985), 89.

is popularly linked with mere 'feeling.' But 'love' rightly understood, means "to recognize that the Other has rights over me."[43]

I am responsible for the other without waiting for reciprocity. Reciprocity is Other's affair.[44] It is precisely insofar as the relationship between the Other and me is not reciprocal that I am subjection to the Other; and I am 'subject' essentially in the sense that I am responsible for the Other without waiting for his response. Levinas quotes Dostoyevesky to say that 'we are all guilty of all and for all men before all, and I more than the others.' This is not owing to such or such a guilt which is really mine, or to offences that I might have committed; rather because I am responsible for a total responsibility, which enables me to answer for all the Others and for all in the Others, and even for their responsibility. "The I always has one responsibility *more* that all the others."[45] In short, the Other as Other is situated in a dimension of height and of glorious abasement.

5. The Responsible Relationship

Levinas feels that the approach of the ethical question must be one of moral height, of obligation and responsibility, not for what is, but for what it ought to be. Ethics is not merely different from thinking, rather it is absorbed by thinking's play of differences; it cuts across ontology, it is radically and irreducibly otherwise than being or beyond essence. The responsibility to respond to the Other is, for Levinas, precisely the inordinate responsibility, the infinite responsibility of being-for-other *before* oneself - the ethical relation.[46] Responsibility is enacted in giving one's own substance for the Other.[47] It is a bond between my present and what came to pass before it. I am responsible before the Other in his alterity, responsible before all the Others for all the Others. The condition of being hostage is an authentic figure of responsibility.[48]

Is not then my relationship with the Other a burden which would make me feel guilty of not performing to the full? Levinas does not leave anyone with a guilty conscience; he leads them out of it by calling for a 'conversion from within' in order to break the closed circle of my autonomy. *From* my narcissism, *through* my experience of shame and of guilt, I am led to my 'responsibility for the Other.' This profound experience of responsibility begins as an absolute *heteronomy*: I am no longer the law, but the Other is; I am not 'the measure of all things' but the one 'to be measured.' 'My responsibility for the Other' is not my freedom of choice; my responsibility is attributed to me even before I am in a position to make

43 Emmanuel Levinas, *Difficult Freedom: Essays on Judaism*, translated by Sean Hand (Baltimore: The Johns Hopkins University Press, 1990), 168.

44 Cf. *Levinas, Ethics and Infinity*, 98.

45 *Ibid.*, 98-99.

46 Cf. *Richard Cohen*, "Translator's Introduction," in *Ethics and Infinity*, 12.

47 The figure of maternity is an authentic figure of responsibility.

48 Cf. Lingis, "Translator's Introduction," *Otherwise than Being or Beyond Essence*, xiii-xiv.

a decision. Thus, the heteronomous responsibility is an-archic and pre-original. From 'responsibility as heteronomous substitution,' Levinas leads us to the notion of 'election'-my *privilege* of being *responsible.* I am specially and exclusively chosen for a mission, from which I cannot escape. Thus my responsibility for the Other is both *inevitable* and *irreplaceable.* I cannot run away from my responsibility, throwing it on to others. I have to act as the 'only one responsible.' I am set apart to be a *messiah,* and every ethical subject is called to be a *messiah.*[49]

6. Language Relationship

Levinas defines language as "an ethical relation, a responsibility to the Other person."[50] He gives much importance to language in his works. In his first major work *Totality and Infinity* (1961) he proposes a new theory of ethical relationship, which finds its foundation in language, where discourse is considered as a relationship. The second major work *Otherwise than Being or Beyond Essence* (1974) presents us with alterity in language.

6.1 Discourse

Levinas considers face and discourse as tied together. The face speaks. It speaks; it is this that renders the possibility for all discourse to begin. By the notion of vision it is difficult to describe the authentic relationship with the Other; it is discourse and, more exactly, response or responsibility which is this authentic relationship.[51] The incomprehensible nature of the presence of the Other is not to be described negatively. Discourse relates with what remains essentially transcendent which is better than comprehension. The fact that the face maintains a relation with me by discourse does not range the face in the same; he remains absolute within the relation. The ethical relationship which subtends discourse puts the I in question, which emanates from the Other.

> The presence of the face, the infinity of the other, is a destituteness, a presence of the third party, ... and a command that commands commanding. This is why the relation with the Other, discourse, is not only the putting in question of my freedom, the appeal coming from the other to call me to responsibility, is not only speech by which I divest myself of the possession that encircles me by setting forth an objective and common world, but is also sermon, exhortation, the prophetic word.[52]

---

49 Cf. Puthenpurackal, "Ethics of Responsibility: A Study Based on the Philosophy of Emmanuel Levinas," 10-11.

50 Emmanuel Levinas, *Otherwise than Being or Beyond Essence*, translated by A. Lingis (Pittsburgh: Martinus Nijhoff Publishers, 1981), 93.

51 Cf. *Levinas, Ethics and Infinity*, 88.

52 Levinas, *Totality and Infinity*, 213.

6.2 Saying and the Said

In Levinasian understanding the presence of the Other is very essential for ethical relationship, the 'Other' demands that 'I' act. Levinas wants to express the liveliness of relationship in explaining the elements of saying and the said. In any utterance Levinas explains 'what is said cannot be apart from the *saying* 'from' which it is said.' Saying, for Levinas, is a pre-thematic and pre-conscious expression of our being-with-the-other, a 'signification' which gives rise to an intention that results in a statement, a 'said.' Saying only occurs in relation with the Other. In Levinas' view it is in that relation that "the face opens the primordial discourse whose first word is obligation."[53] Saying is an ethical sincerity insofar as it is an exposition. This saying is irreducible. It is a way of giving everything. Language or saying is an ethical openness to the Other; as that which is said—reduced to a fixed identity or synchronized presence—it is an ontological closure to the Other.[54] In an interview with Philippe Nemo, Levinas emphatically expressed: "In fact, for me, the *said* [*le dit*] does not count as much as the *saying* [*le dire*] itself. The latter is important to me less through its informational contents than by the fact that it is addressed to an interlocutor."[55]

6.3 Language: The Basis of the Ethical Relationship

Levinas finds that language is the basis of the ethical relationship, because it enables links to be made between people. Language is defined as a potential break with representation and the totalizing impulse. The signifier becomes an opening-up to the Other. Language is the astonishment of the Other speaking to me. Language bears witness to an ethical relationship with alterity. In ethical relation we recognize language—produced in the face-to-face. In language we recognize teaching—a master teaching his student. Language establishes a relation between terms that breaks up the unity of a genus. Language is perhaps to be defined as the very power to break the continuity of being or of history.[56]

Language is the source of all significations. Language takes hold before the straightforwardness of the face, making murder possible or impossible. The expression adds value to our relation. This expression is irreducible to images. "The presence of the Other, or expression, source of all signification, is not contemplated as an intelligible essence, but is heard as language, and thereby is effectuated exteriorly. Expression, or the face, overflows images which are always immanent to my thought, as though they came from me."[57]

---

53 Cf. Levinas and Richard Kearney, "Dialogue with Emmanuel Levinas," *Face to Face with Levinas,* 28-29.

54 *Cf. Levinas, Ethics and Infinity,* 42.

55 Levinas, *Totality and Infinity*, 297.

56 *Ibid.,* 195.

57 *Ibid.,* 96.

6.4 Signification

Signification refers to the Other. Signification or intelligibility does not arise from the identity of the Same who remains in himself, but from the face of the Other who calls upon the Same. "In fact signification has always been envisaged on the level of relations."[58]

"The first instance of signification is produced in the face. The face would not receive a signification by *relation* to something. The face signifies by itself; its signification precedes *Sinngebung*."[59] Levinas considers language as protection against totalization. For he says the language manifested signification of beings. A relation between terms that resist totalization is possible only by language.[60] Signification arises from the Other stating or understanding the world. "A meaningful world is a world in which there is the Other through whom the world of my enjoyment becomes a theme having a signification."[61]

7. Conclusion

However, Levinas shifts the focus of philosophical thought away from the constitution of the Other and the Same in consciousness to a relationship between the Same and the Other.[62] He does not provide a stable set of moral principles to govern this encounter; rather he states that each one's response to the encounter defines one's ethical nature. He is not interested in giving ethical solutions to the relationship, but to challenge the Subject. Placing responsibility as the key to relationship, he says the other person is not so much someone to be understood, but someone to be responded to. The Other in his ethical making is different from other things because the expression of the Other is a solicitation, a summons to respond. "The face summons me";[63] the face is a summons to respond, it summons the subject to assume responsibility for the Other. [64]

The subject, who is indebted to the Other for its expression to the Other,[65] manifest the qualities of responsibility, substitution, docility and even as one striving for difficult justice. It is weak, and is a hostage. The ego of the subject, 'I,' undergoes transition at the demand of the Other and becomes an accusative 'me.' According to him, the subject is hostage to the other, a sort of hostage that

58 Levinas, *Totality and Infinity*, 95.

59 *Ibid.*, 261; *Sinngebung* means bestowing.

60 *Ibid.*, 97.

61 *Ibid.*, 209.

62 Cf. Robert John Sheffler Manning, *Interpreting Otherwise than Heidegger: Emmanuel Levinas Ethics as First Philosophy* (Pittsburgh: Duquesne University Press, 1993), 183.

63 Emmanuel Levinas, "Beyond Intentionality," in *Philosophy in France Today*, edited by A. Montefiore, translated by Kathleen McLaughlin (Cambridge: Cambridge University Press, 1983), 110.

64 Cf. Manning, *Interpreting Otherwise than Heidegger*, 183.

65 *Ibid.*, 184.

assumes responsibility to the Other, which comes prior to autonomy and freedom. Thus the subject becomes a humble self who loses oneself on the demands of the face of the Other in an asymmetrical relationship.

Bibliography

Levinas, Emmanuel. "Beyond Intentionality," in *Philosophy in France Today*, edited by A. Montefiore, translated by Kathleen McLaughlin (Cambridge: Cambridge University Press, 1983), 110.

_________. *Emmanuel Levinas: Basic Philosophical Writings.* Edited by A. Peperzak, S. Critchley and R. Bernasconi. Indiana: Indiana University Press, 1996.

_________. *Ethics and Infinity: Conversations with Philippe Nemo.* Translated by Richard Cohen. Pittsburgh: Duquesne University Press, 1985. (Originally, *Ethique et Infini. Dialogues avec Philippe Nemo*, 1982)

_________. *Otherwise than Being, or, Beyond Essence.* Translated by A. Lingis. The Hague: Martinus Nijhoff Publishers, 1981. (*Autrement qu'etre ou audela de l'essence*, 1974)

_________. *The Levinas Reader.* Edited by Sean Hand. Oxford: Basil Blackwell, 1989.

_________. *Time and the Other.* Translated by Richard Cohen. Pittsburgh: Duquesne University Press, 1987. (Originally, *Le Temps et l'Autre*, 1947)

_________. *Totality and Infinity: An Essay on Exteriority.* Translated by A. Lingis. Pittsburgh: Martinus Nijhoff Publishers, 1969. (Originally, *Totalite et Infini: Essai sur l'exteriorite*, 1961)

_________. *Difficult Freedom: Essays on Judaism.* Translated by Sean Hand. Baltimore: The Johns Hopkins University Press, 1990.

_________.*The Ethical Basis for a Humane Society According to Emmanuel Levinas.* Translated by Catherine Vnahove-Romanik. Leuven: Centre for Metaphysics and Philosophy of God, Institute of Philosophy, 1981.

Levinas, Emmanuel and Richard Kearney. "Dialogue with Emmanuel Levinas" in *Face to Face with Levinas,* edited by Richard Cohen, 13-14. Albany: State University of New York Press, 1986.

Manning, Robert John Sheffler. *Interpreting Otherwise than Heidegger: Emmanuel Levinas Ethics as First Philosophy.* Pittsburgh: Duquesne University Press, 1993.

Peperzak,Adriaan. *To the Other: An Introduction to the Philosophy of Emmanuel Levinas.* West Lafayette: Purdue University Press, 1993.

Sebastian, Sekar. *Radical Responsibility for the Other: An Ethical Appraisal of Emmanuel Levinas.* Bangalore: Asian Trading Corporation, 2010.

Smith, Michael B. *Toward the Outside: Concepts and Themes in Emmanuel Levinas.* Pittsburgh: Duquesne University Press, 2005.

Toumayan, Alain P. *Encountering the Other: The Artwork and Problem of Difference in Blanchot and Levinas.* Pittsburgh: Duquesne University Press, 2004.

Chapter 2

Faith Formation and Maturation Experience in the Family
An Anthropological, Biblical, Liturgical and Spiritual Treasure

Moses Wanjala

Often times, coming in contact with some families[1] and communities, one notices that there are great moments and opportunities of joy to treasure, to appreciate and to live for. At the same time, we notice the need to continuously grow in certain aspects in life so as to truly make our life more spontaneous, simple, joyful, meaningful, qualitative and worth living. In our families or communities, we unfortunately hear of: incomprehension; jealousy; un-constructive criticisms and prejudices; feelings of negative pride and superiority over other persons and cultures, characterized by the "show off mentality"; an increasing relational gap between the elders and the young, aggravated by a lack of time dedicated to each other and a limited amount of regular dialogue and communication with one another; capitalization and exaggeration of small issues and deliberate refusal to see the good in the other; indifferences; prolonged and built up anger; un-reflected and hasty conclusions over small or big issues, etc. We actually run the risk of burning out and spending our precious energies on negative and pessimistic issues which we can avoid, only if we are a little careful, patient, understanding and prudent in our family relations. All our energies can make miracles if utilized in a positive direction. It is a pity that sometimes the ones who "shout louder or make a lot of noise" in our families are often the ones who are heard and whose views

1 By the term *"Family,"* I intend to mean and also include the community, Church, consecrated persons, school, society or any group of persons who encounter, share their lives and journey together for the well being, dignity and common good of each other.

are considered as right, whereas the silent ones are seen as "stupid"! We know how people hide their true identity by making noise. On the other hand, we also notice how silence enables us to come face-to-face with our true selves and our true world.

In such an unhealthy atmosphere, the spirit and life of the family is without doubt, at a great risk if each individual, by virtue of his conscience, doesn't stand his ground to concretely make a prudent, responsible, positive, respectful and constructive criticism, for the betterment of the society. Why allow our conscience to sleep when sometimes we know where the truth lies? Why omission and indifference? Why not heal our society by facing the truth with respect, simplicity, humility and generosity? Could it be that our *familiarity* and *daily routine* sometimes make things appear monotonous to the extent of taking each other for granted in the family? In such a context we should examine ourselves if we really take time to discover, to know, to learn, to appreciate and to encourage the development and sharing of the underlying treasures within each person. Possibly we are obstacles to those who want to or are trying to progress!

In this article, we highlight the commitment to a *continuous growth in the spirit of family relationships* and also make an attempt to contribute to the *realization of a true home* where the goodness of our Faith in God is tasted, nurtured, lived, experienced, transmitted, and where everyone peacefully feels free, loved and at home with each other. Definitely this is the work of each individual person in a large human family, realized collectively and never in isolation.

1. Role of Anthropology in the Family-Building Experience

The call of the human person is an ongoing *life project* that insistently reminds him to *listen* to every situation with the eyes of his heart; *discover* the truth, goodness and beauty within and around him; *respond* to the promptings of his heart and the voice of his conscience, in view of the *fulfillment* of his goals and purpose in life. Our existence as human beings is a *gift and participation*. Every moment, each person with his internal and external faculties, is called upon to flourish and bloom where he is planted in life. The person sometimes finds himself interweaving the various forms of his inner confrontations with challenging and often "mixed up" family situations. No matter the situation, it is good to recall that the person is *never alone;* he is often strengthened and accompanied by *"the other"*. Even the solitude, suffering, worries that surprise him, are signs that inevitably manifest a call to an open *encounter* and to *communion with the other*, and with the *Creator*.

Each person has a unique story of life to narrate and offer to the world. It is made of not only enriching moments, but also with worries, anxieties, rejection and misunderstanding. This story is marked from our very beginning. It is part of us and we can say that it has made us what we are today no matter how challenging and tough it could have been before. Generally, the call and aspirations of the person's life are elaborated on the basis of a more usual, spontaneous and decisive interpersonal relationship. Given some fortunate cases in which the family experience gathers authentic, conscious, consistent and active members, the witness to life manifests and concretely enjoys positive memories of God's continuous interventions in the human story. The *family calls forth and nurtures the vocation of each individual.* It offers an atmosphere for a true encounter with oneself, where individuals learn to grow and live up to their own aspirations. The atmosphere ought to enhance an ambient where *the other,* no matter his state of life: freely confronts, communicates and solicits correspondence; *shares prayer and the meal at a common table*; feels welcome, forgiven, accompanied, understood and accepted as he is.

The presence of *the other* in the family is first of all for *communion of purpose, service and mutual sharing* of aspects that unify the various dimensions of the family life. Actually, it urges and supports their full realization. In moving towards the authenticity and fulfillment of each person's vocation, individuals, in the *spirit of faith and sacrifice*, are encouraged to learn how to empty themselves of obstacles that hinder their personal growth as well as the growth of the spirit of the family. *Faith and Sacrifice* celebrate hope over any form of death. The great and mysterious words of Jesus: *"Very truly I tell you, unless a grain of wheat falls to the ground and dies, it remains only a single seed. But if it dies, it produces many seeds"* (Jn 12:24), resound in all their illuminating transparency to the hearts of every family member, highlighting the fruits that come with the spirit of Sacrifice. Life has a way to freedom, quite demanding too. We do not realize ourselves without *emptying* ourselves of false images, *devoting* ourselves to others and *offering* ourselves to God who transcends everything. Jesus invites us to *"seek his kingdom, and these things will be given to us as well"* (Lk 12:31). God's kingdom is the basis on which the diversity of family plans finds its meaning and converging point.

Consequently, *faith and sacrifice* do not only become a proposal of life but rather a communitarian experience of solidarity with all, a concrete expression of love. Usually, *love involves sacrifice and sacrifice expresses concretely the spirit of love.* (Mt 5:43-48 exhorts us as God's family to the most perfect love of God as well as an invitation to pray for our enemies. The word *perfect* in the Hebrew and Aramaic sense means *wholeness, completeness* or *not lacking in what is basic, necessary and essential.* This implies that God intends and calls us to completeness. The *God who created us in His image and likeness* (Gen 1:26-27) continuously calls us as His people, to be like Him and to grow in *wholeness* and *maturity* so that we can love as the Father loves and choose to do good in rejecting what is evil (Eph 4:13-16). Jesus' invitation to *be perfect as the heavenly Father is perfect* continues to sound deeper into the hearts of our families, as the core of our human-Christian calling within. Since our perfect God is love, then we can equally deduce that the text reminds us to *be love* as *God is love* and when we truly love, then we already taste / experience the Divinity of God. In our family context, St. John's practical message on *God as love* inspires us when he challenges us to love as God loves:

> *Beloved, let us love one another, for love is from God; and everyone who loves is born of God and knows God. The one who does not love does not know God, for God is love. By this the love of God was manifested in us, that God has sent His only begotten Son into the world so that we might live through Him. In this is love, not that we loved God, but that He loved us and sent His Son to be the propitiation for our sins. Beloved, if God so loved us, we also ought to love one another. No one has seen God at any time; if we love one another, God abides in us, and His love is perfected in us. By this we know that we abide in Him and He in us, because He has given us of His Spirit [...]* (1Jn 4:7-21).

The Spirit reminds us that *love as a true Sacrifice in the family* context, is a concrete act to do (be) good to God by doing (being) good to others. Our practical and sacrificial acts of love, then, make the invisible God, visible. Here lies our personal fulfillment. We love not only for our own sake, but also for the sake of doing good to our neighbor, and as we continuously love our neighbor we mature as persons created in God's image and likeness. Our primary vocation as human beings is to Love. If we are to be truly human, we should fulfill our call to love as God loves. We cannot live without love and to live without love means to live without God, the author of life. Our lives lose meaning when we do not search, participate, practice, experience and live the love we receive from God, right from our simple daily sacrificial gestures of sharing our time, sensitivity, openness, sympathy, kindness, forgiveness, generosity within our families. Jesus promises an immense depth of love when he commands us to love one another as he has loved us, and to lay down our lives for our friends: *"As the Father has loved me, so I have loved you. Remain in my love"* (Jn 15:13).

Our *relationship as persons* in a family is thus about an anthropology: of *Communion (koinonia)*, availability, generosity, solidarity; of *Service (Diakonia)*; of *Self-emptying (Kenosis)*, sacrifice; of *Self-transcendence (Metanoia)*, with appeals to an *ontology of participation* in line with the basic concept of *Revelation* in the theological-liturgical perspective. It is about the interpretation of the voice of God in any *family situation*; *through the Church,* in an atmosphere of inter-relationships, communion and fraternity, which each individual is called to proclaim, reveal, share and witness to all.

While recognizing the good intentions and contributions of each individual in the family faith experience, we should at the same time rethink the basic assumption of anthropology! The *"I think"* mentality of the modern tradition, for instance, risks commanding only an individualistic vision of reality, in which the developments are influenced and oriented towards the horizon of a single individual and not the authentic needs of the family. In this way of individualistic thinking, the communitarian experience is seen as an external, accidental and even interrupting factor! In other words, it is about recovering the communitarian positive mentality of *"we think"* and not only relying on the *"I think" individualistic* attitude. Normally, the *"we think"* attitude ought to enable the community to discern, respond and realize its *real needs*.

The *family faith formation experience is a task, opportunity and responsibility of each individual.* The family that welcomes is not only a shelter to rest; a warm nest free from worries and from responsibility. No! As it welcomes us home, the family calls us to *act and offer our individual contribution to the ongoing holistic growth of its individual members as well as the entire society*. Finding ourselves together so as to share the same hope is beautiful and illumining. It constitutes an effort, some times more vigorous, to attempt together, as we move towards the community's positive goals; a call to verify without fear, the concrete conditions, reformulate, update and actualize them. The driving force of family life is a conscious effort towards personal, communitarian and structural renewal. The *common vocation and the faith shared experience in family life* are precious resources of human-spiritual enrichment and maturity. They stimulate the riches of a lived tradition and appeal to the past; live and treasure the present; elaborate the future events, for the good and actual growth of every person.

2. Biblical-Liturgical References to the Family Faith Experience

Besides the anthropological background, the family faith experience also finds in the biblical pages a privileged place that reveals the nature of the family as a home. Our point of departure is *liturgical Paschal experience*, characterized by the *Covenant and Liberation*. The Paschal facts evidence how the first intention of God, right from creation, *was to take the person to a life of communion with Him.* The *Covenant* is an expression of this journey that finds its fullness in Christ. It is first, situated in an experiential context of *social-anthropological life*, even before we call it religious. The mysterious invisible God becomes sacramentally and physically visible in Christ. God identifies Himself with us and becomes one of us so that we can experience eternity and happiness already right now as we await the recapitulation of everything at the end of time.

In the *"Covenant perspective,* God communicates His divinity through Israel as His own chosen people"[2]. It is an object of predilection and reservoir of a Promise. By virtue of this free initiative and choice of God, Israel is liberated from Egyptian slavery, and like this, it is invited to experience and *taste and live the goodness and faithfulness of its God.* This experience follows the revelation of God's design:

> "You yourselves have seen what I did to Egypt, and how I carried you on eagles' wings and brought you to myself. Now if you obey me fully and keep my covenant, then out of all nations you will be my treasured possession.

2 Cf. Moses, Wanjala SDB, Foretaste of Heavenly Liturgy: Commemorating, Celebrating and Living. *An Anthropological, Theological and Liturgical Reflection on African Sub-Saharan Music through Saint Augustine and Sacrosanctum Concilium.* Jerusalem: Studium Theologicum Salesianum Publications 2015, 63-76.

> Although the whole earth is mine, you will be for me a kingdom of priests and a holy nation" (Ex 19:4-6).

This revelation is *not only a guarantee of liberation for the Jewish nation, but it rather becomes a motivation for their past, present and future.* Like this, the Covenant signs a relationship between God and His people. Consequently, *the Law* becomes an *expression of the Covenant* among the Israel community. Its value is exactly that of approving the bond between God and His people who are also called to accept the law and its conditions, if they wish to live and be an object of the choice of God: *"We will do everything the Lord has said"* (Ex 19:8).

The *Covenant and the Law are followed by an organization* within the Israel community. Every time the people reformed themselves after dispersion, the Covenant was renewed; the will of Israel to accept the design of God was reconfirmed. Joshua renewed the Covenant at Shechem (Jos 24); David received again the Promise for his dynasty's everlasting reign (2 Sam 7:1-29).

With the *Prophets*, the unfaithfulness to the Pact is denounced. Israel becomes more conscious that the Covenant is not simply a juridical or legal bond, but it is an expression of a *concrete relationship of love.* The new Covenant, proclaimed by the prophets, is still a sign of the free love of God (Jer 31:35*ff*; 33: 20-26; Hos 2:20-24; Ez 16:60; 34:23*ff*; 36:26). Families, today, should always renew their covenant relationships among themselves and with God's law of love, through a daily sincere examination of conscience and forgiveness.

The prophetic proclamation is realized in the fullness of *Christ who becomes the realization and New Covenant for all.* The words of the Last Supper: *"This is My blood of the new Covenant, which is being poured out for many for the forgiveness of sins"* (Mt 26:28), testify that Jesus, by identifying himself with the Suffering Servant of Isaiah 53: 11*ff*, becomes the true Mediator of the Covenant, *with the power to forgive sins.* Jesus' blood effectively actualizes and realizes the definitive union between God and the one family of His own people, of every race, color, sex, language, religion, status, pre-announced by the Prophets Jeremiah and Ezekiel.

Strengthened by Jesus' continuous inspirations, consolations and interventions in our lives, the Church, through the family, has a task to witness and manifest a concrete life of communion, the presence of God's Kingdom to all. The newness of the relationships announced in the Old Testament, realized with the coming of Christ and the effusion of the Holy Spirit, find their response in the concrete gestures of the Christian family that takes care of *sharing the Good News in the spirit of dedicated generous service.* Looking at *Pasch as liberation and precisely the Exodus event,* we observe that at the origins of the faith of the Jews, there is no abstract revelation, but rather a concrete experience of a group of persons that, with the intervention of God, come out to freedom. It is the first act of faith for the Jews: *"I am the LORD your God, who brought you out of Egypt, out of the land of slavery"* (Ex 20:2). The theme of *liberation* is central to the Jewish experience and belief (Deut 26: 5-9), as well as for Christians.

The first encounter with God is the *history of liberation*. Biblically speaking, *salvation, liberty* or *coming out of slavery* are the same thing. God Himself *guarantees this liberation and freedom*, through the commandments. God remains the *unique God* and the *person* never becomes an object of manipulation. Freed from Pharaoh, Israel is called to *live in dignity and freedom*. The experience of the Exodus becomes a basic reason to denounce every situation of injustice. God commits Himself to persons that live together; for a community. *Sin* in general and even *liberation* are not understood if not in the life together; in the family. It is the people that are freed: "together" they can live this freedom; "together" they can lose it.

All the *works of Jesus Christ* have the *scope of giving freedom and life to the full*. The Pasch is a typical and concrete moment of this freedom and liberation from sin. Jesus addresses himself to those who are despised and excluded from society, i.e., the sick, lepers, publicans, little ones, women, Samaritans, etc., because they are more in need of liberation in every aspect, but especially the freedom of their Spirit from any entanglement of worldly pleasures. Jesus' mission was to reach out to as many people as possible and to share with them the Good News from God, the Father. He spent quality time with persons, respecting their dignity, listening and answering to their needs, with love and patience, e.g., the leper (Mt 8:2-13); the woman at the well who later confesses (Jn 4:5-42); the woman caught in adultery (Jn 8:1-11); the man born blind (Jn 9:1-41); the rich man, Dives and Lazarus: (Lk 16:19-31), etc.

When asked which is the greatest commandment of the Law, Jesus answered: *"You must love the Lord your God with all your heart, with all your soul and with all your mind"* (Mt 34-40). Quoting Deuteronomy 6:5, Jesus said that the second commandment resembles the first one: "*You must love your neighbor as yourself*" (Lev 19:18). Jesus explains who the neighbor is, through the parable of the Good Samaritan (Lk 10:29-37). Jesus himself, as a sign of contradiction, was a victim of hatred, violence, misunderstanding, death and in spite of all these evils, he says: *"Love your enemies, do good to those who hate you, bless those who curse you, pray for those who treat you badly" [...]; "Treat others as you would like them to treat you"* (Lk 6:27-31; cf. Tobit 4:16). It is also inspiring to learn from the convictions of St. Augustine and St. Francis of Sales, on love: *"the measure of love is to love without measure"*.

With Jesus, the Kingdom of love, service and liberation, becomes a reality or rather it becomes something and someone that we can touch. The Pentecost signs the first moment for the new life in the spirit of the community. The new people of God possess the Spirit. All the people are *promoted and freed*. The Spirit is not something that is reserved; it is a *gift for all*, and it overcomes all divisions (Acts 2: 1-4). Here we notice a true story of unity that ought to incarnate (take flesh) so that it becomes a credible and true sign, overcoming every form of division:

> *"[...]. There is neither Jew nor Gentile, neither slave nor free, nor is there male and female, for you are all one in Christ Jesus. [...]."* (Gal 3:26-29).

The first Christians who *shared everything in common and were of one heart and mind,* made this freedom-liberation realized by the Pasch of Christ, a reality in their community:

> *"Now the full number of those who believed were of one heart and soul, and no one said that any of the things that belonged to him was his own, but they had everything in common. And with great power the apostles were giving their testimony to the resurrection of the Lord Jesus, and great grace was upon them all. There was not a needy person among them, for as many as were owners of lands or houses sold them and brought the proceeds of what was sold and laid it at the apostles' feet, and it was distributed to each as any had need"* (Acts 4:32-35).

The *Paschal experience* has always been a culminating event of the communitarian life of Israel right through the first Christian community to today. Israel as a family often *lived and recalled the history of God's intervention in their lives, but also anticipated the joy and eternal happiness in the ever faithful promises of the Creator.* The *Promise* is realized whenever there is an encouraging thrust towards a more human, Christian and authentic life; and *Salvation,* for the hope and the courage that it raises before concrete challenges of liberation *from* everyday slavery of fear, sin, pain, addiction, injustice and death, *to* the freedom of the children of God.

3. Proposals for a Faith Formation and Maturation Experience within the Family-Ecclesial-Community Domain

Bearing in mind the above anthropological-biblical-liturgical perspectives, we acknowledge the great role that the *family as a cradle of life* plays in the holistic formation of persons, at all levels of their growth. Knowing well our family roots facilitates the *faith formation and maturation process.* It is in the family that the children first learn to be humans and to be divine. In order to *appreciate, treasure and develop the human-communitarian-ecclesial faith maturation process, we make some proposals, given the reality of diverse family life situations*:

a) Addressing and Interpreting Every Situation in the Light of the Good News that Frees

Since everything comes from and returns to our Creator, whatever exists and whatever happens should always be confronted within the perspective of the Word of God. It is up to the people of God, especially the Shepherds of souls and theologians, with the guide of the Holy Spirit, to analyze, discern and interpret the various happenings and family realities of our time and, interpret them in the divine light of the Good News. We are to take up this challenge so that all our activities do not only end at a superficial level, but that they lead all to a personal encounter with the liberating Person of Jesus, through a concrete service of the needy around us, just as our Lord reminds us: *"Whatever you did for one of the least of these brothers of mine, you did for me"* (Mt 25:40). Yes, it is good to remind ourselves that we do it *to / for Jesus.*

It is always fascinating and encouraging to note that *our God manifests Himself within the concrete moments of our lives.* Taking the example of the *Prodigal Son* (Lk 15:11-32), we observe that in our Christian lives, there are no static moments but rather continuous dynamic movements, especially the desire to move from evil to goodness, because Our Father is always there to welcome us in the family whenever we examine our consciences and come to our senses. Our past life prepares us to embrace a hopeful future and to appreciate a continuity of life which matures even in our brokenness, weakness and mistakes in life. Another instance to reflect upon is the *betrayal of Judas Iscariot* (Lk 22), where Judas himself is seen as evil because he betrayed Jesus. I put Judas in comparison with the betrayal of Peter who denies Jesus, and our own betrayals. Judas became thoughtless, egoistic, proud, greedy, insensitive, heartless and helpless in his own security. On the other hand, Peter was saved because he did not only admit his own sinful mistake, but also because he confessed it, making himself ready for a sincere conversion of heart. That explains why we should be bold enough to advise, but we should not judge the person because he has made a mistake, since the person himself, if he wishes, can change and be able to give a new sense/ beginning to his own life no matter the state of his previous story of life.

b) Accompaniment and Empowerment of Youth in the Faith Formation Experience

In speaking about the family, we emphasize youth formation because youngsters are the *present and future* of the Society. When the youth are educated right from their early stages, we are then sure of a fruitful present and future of the family and the society. Many youth risk creating their own world, if not accompanied and reminded of the beauty and value of our Christian faith. One can say that they could be somehow justified to act like this if there is no one bold enough to guide their minds, hearts and bodies in the right direction! Some youth do not have any idea of Christian life and are without good role models even in human life! They thus look for models outside the truly human-Christian-family sphere because their minds are easily exposed to this.

The good or bad ambient created among the youth themselves automatically influences them to grow into what they are; and the worst part of it is when their parents do not accompany or give a good example. We should remember that *the young learn not only from what the parents say to them but also from what the parents "do" or "do not do" to (with) them.* Parents or educators will lose control and respect from their children if they do not give full time paternal-fraternal attention and presence especially during their initial delicate moments of growth. We should never lose their trust in us. It is through consistent presence, appreciation and friendly dialogue that we know what their needs truly are; that they feel with us; we feel with them and we know when and how to accompany them. It is only when we win their heart that we can propose our human-Christian-religious values to them because they see us as part of them. We should *invite the young to be protagonists that are capable of transforming the world. They can do this only if they begin from personalizing their own good convictions in life.* By putting the young at the center, we create a family atmosphere of growth between adults and youth, that helps us discover that life is a call and a dream to fulfill together as individuals.

c) Journeying Together as one Family in the Faith Maturation Experience

Given the geographical vastness and growing numbers of Christian believers in some parts of the world especially in Africa and Asia, one feels an insistent need to propose, create and implement the sharing of the Good News and maturing in faith through consistent encounters among the small Christian communities or families that are open for all. This could take the form of living and sharing *Lectio Divina* so that the *"riches of God's Word may be easily accessible in more abundant measure"* [3], *especially to those in hopeless situations*. The ecclesial animation groups and movements like: Young Christian Students; Couples for Christ; Catholic Women Association; Catholic Men Association, etc., ought to be encouraged for their great work as bridges and points of references for the various respective groups in our society today. In such a reality, each person is encouraged to find a home within the group of his choice where he can freely grow and mature. It is more fruitful that these groups work out as a team and in harmony their general work plan and objectives, update them and carry out an ongoing formation, both for themselves as an animation team, as well as those they animate. It is also recommended that as a family, we strive to live together the significant moments of life; participate fully, actively, consciously and authentically in the Sacraments, e.g., the Eucharistic Liturgy, which is the *"summit toward which the activity of the Church is directed; at the same time it is the font from which all her power flows"*[4]; engage in charitable activities, because it is through these moments that we concretely experience and touch the presence of Christ among the needy. Another proposal is that of promoting *Family Centre units*, with an information-formation scope, so as to respond to the challenges that parents and children go through, in attempting to give authentic meaning to life.

3 *English Translation of the Cathechism of the Catholic Church for the United States of America © 1997, United States Catholic Conference, Inc. no. 1163*; Cf. *Sacrosanctum Concilium* 92 and 102; *Evangelli Nuntiandi* 45.

4 *Sacrosanctum Concilium* 10; cf. *Lumen Gentium* 11; cf. *Catechism of the Catholic Church* 1324-1327.

d) Rediscovering Charisms and Gifts within the Individual and the Community

Our families are comprised of unique persons with diverse gifts and charisms of the Holy Spirit. Following Christ in our various states of life and through the various expressions of service, and conscious that God is at work in us, every member ought to collaborate, cultivate and develop his gifts so as to build up and maintain the unity of the one body of Christ:

> "There are different kinds of gifts, but the same Spirit distributes them. There are different kinds of service, but the same Lord. There are different kinds of working, but in all of them and in everyone it is the same God at work" (1 Cor 12:4-11).

Right from the Primitive Church, the Apostles and later the founders of western Monastic life like St. Benedict, were prophetic signs of unity and persons ready for service to all Christians, the family of God. With the renewal of the Vatican II, where the various Congregations and Institutes of Apostolic life were asked to rediscover the roots and the spirit of their respective founders, the experience of consecrated life gets closer to the Primitive Apostolic model, thereby enabling us to taste already now, in today's context, the history as we await the unending joys with the Father of our one family, who is always at work in us.

e) Christian Faith Witness to Today's World

In our social, family, ecclesial, economic, political life contexts, the witness of Christ, through a proclamation of the liberation, takes up a relevant value and develops with another intimate certainty: *"The Kingdom of God is already among you"* (Lk 17:21) right there where we are. In our family life together, we attempt to manifest the renewal of relationships that the certainty of the liberating presence of God in our own story of life arouses in us as believers. In order for ours to be truly a Christian community, certain intense, consistent and sincere moments of friendship, of confrontation, of relaxation and amusement, and of evaluation in the light of the Word of God, are necessary. As we accept and be ready to live in any diversified and heterogeneous community, we ought to respect the various rhythms of growth of each individual. Unfortunately, sometimes we are obstacles to the Christian-community maturation, with our egoism, indifference, pride and selfishness. We should, instead, be attentive to the real needs in our world of work, at home, at school, in the Church, in the hospital, etc., where we exercise our service.

The Catholic Church, in protecting the human-Christian dignity of persons in God's family, has always kept a paternal, maternal and fraternal welcoming attention to all people within their various daily circumstances of life. This has precisely been expressed through some of its social teaching documents, which enhance the faith formation experience in the family and hence enrich the society at large. One major document which expresses the role of the Christian family in the modern world is the Apostolic Exhortation, *Familiaris Consortio.*[5] The other Church documents are: *Rerum Novarum*[6] (on the conditions of the poor); *Mater et Magistra*[7] (On Christianity and Social Progress); *Pacem in Terris*[8] (Peace on Earth);

5 This document issued by John Paul II in 1981, talks of the Church at the service of the family; Inculturation; Man the Image of the God who is Love; Marriage, Family and Communion between God and People; Jesus Christ Bridegroom of the Church; Children, the precious gift of Marriage; Family, Communion of Persons; Role of the Christian Family; Forming a Community of Persons; Love as the Principle and Power of Communion; Rights and Role of Women in Society; Men as Husbands and Fathers; Elderly in the Family; Serving and transmission of Life, Cooperators in the Love of God the Creator; Church stands for Life; Integral Vision of the Human Person and his/her Vocation; Church as Teacher and Mother for Couples in difficulty; Educating in the Essential Values of Human life; First experience of the Church; Participating in the Development of the Society; Family as the First and Vital cell of Society; Family life as an experience of Communion and Sharing; Society at the Service of the Family; Christian Family's Grace and Responsibility; Sharing in the Life and Mission of the Church; Family, within the mystery of the Church; to Preach the Gospel to all Creation; Church's Sanctuary in the Home; Marriage as a Sacrament of Mutual Sanctification and an Act of Worship; Marriage and the Eucharist; Sacrament of Conversion and Reconciliation; Family Prayer; Prayer and Life; New Commandment of Love; Discover the Image of God in each Brother and Sister; Church accompanies the Christian Family on its Journey through Life; Families for Families; Men and Women Religious.

6 This Encyclical addresses the dehumanizing conditions in which many workers labor and affirms workers' rights to just wages, rest, and fair treatment, to form unions, and to strike if necessary. Leo XIII upholds individuals' right to hold private property but also notes the role of the state in facilitating distributive justice so that workers can adequately support their families and someday own property of their own.

7 John XXIII: Comments on increases in workers' rights and social programs, and the decline of colonialism; Notes the world's global interdependence and expresses profound concern about the arms race and the growing inequalities between rich and poor nations, noting that gains in science and technology should not lead to economic disparity but should instead benefit the common good; Proposes that Christians should engage in observing, judging, and acting to put the Church's social doctrine into practice.

8 First Encyclical to be written to "all men of good will," instead of just the world's Catholics. In it, John XXIII lifts up a moral order that should prevail between humans; persons and states; and in the world community. He emphasizes basic human rights and responsibilities, calls for an end to the arms race based on trust and respect for human rights, and supports the creation of a world authority to protect the universal common good. He notes that the arms race impedes the development of societies and that under-development and injustice threaten peace.

Gaudium et Spes[9] (The Church in the Modern World); *Quadragesimo Anno*[10] (On Reconstructing the Social Order); *Evangelii Nutiandi*[11] (On Evangelization in the Modern World); *Redemptor Hominis*[12] (Redeemer of Man); *Laborem Exercens*[13] (On Human Work); *Evangelium Vitae*[14] (The Gospel of Life); *Sollicitudo Rei Socialis*[15] (On Social Concern); *Populorum Progressio*[16] (On the Development of Peoples);

---

9 Vatican II focuses on responding to "the joys and the hopes, the grief and the anguish of the people of our time," especially the poor. The Church must interpret the signs of the times in light of the Gospel. The Council emphasizes the Church's concern for human dignity, solidarity of the human community and the engagement of the Church in society and the world. The second part focuses on marriage and family, cultural diversity, social and economic life, political life, peace and war, international cooperation, and the need for integral human and spiritual development.

10 This Encyclical, written to celebrate the 40th anniversary of *Rerum Novarum*, reaffirms the Church's concern for workers and defends workers' rights, including just wages, and condemns the increasing disparities between the elite and suffering workers. Pius XI notes the need for state intervention but also introduces the idea of "subsidiarity".

11 Paul VI articulates a "new evangelization" that links social transformation with the Gospel. He calls for an evangelization that transforms both believers and social structures. Evangelization includes the development and liberation of peoples from oppressive structures that cause famine, disease, and poverty; injustices in trade and economic activities; and the oppression of cultural and political colonialism.

12 John Paul II examines human dignity and rights in the light of the mystery of redemption. He questions consumer attitudes and materialism. He notes degradation of the environment and economic structures that lead to inequality. He notes the connection between violations of human rights and war and the need for true progress based on respect.

13 Written on the 90th anniversary of the very first social encyclical, *Rerum Novarum*, John Paul II presents work as a fundamental dimension of human existence through which the person achieves fulfillment as a human being. He emphasizes the dignity of labor and notes that through work, the human person can share in the activity of the Creator. He reminds us that we must protect the rights of workers to employment and to just wages.

14 John Paul II affirms the gift of life and the need to protect it at all stages. He speaks of the value and dignity of life while decrying the culture of death and calling for a renewed culture of life. He addresses a wide range of old and new threats to life, especially abortion, euthanasia, experimentation on human embryos, and the death penalty. He argues that we must be people of life who stand "for all life and for the life of everyone". The culture of death, he says, is caused by an overemphasis on individual freedoms and a lack of recognition of relationship with others. This mentality, reflected in materialism's emphasis on "having" over "being," must be replaced by one of solidarity and seeing life as a responsibility. He notes that the family is the "sanctuary of life" and connects respect for life with the need for social and economic policies that support families and integral human development which promotes the dignity of the person.

15 John Paul II criticizes super development and consumerism, i.e., putting excessive value on material things, as false forms of development. He discusses the environment, noting the dignity of creation and humanity's misuse of it. He calls for solidarity between rich and poor in order to attain true development and peace.

16 Paul VI criticizes unjust economic structures that have led to inequality and underdevelopment, including the economic domination and exploitation of poor countries by rich ones, and the

Octogesima Adveniens[17] (A Call to Action); *Caritas in Veritate*[18] (Charity in Truth); *Deus Caritas Est*[19] (God is Love); *Centesimus Annus*[20] (On the Hundredth Year of *Rerum Novarum*).

In conclusion, the fellowship and witness of the first Christian community of believers is a great inspiration to our family spirit in our communities today:

> *"And they devoted themselves to the apostles' teaching and the fellowship, to the breaking of bread and the prayers. And awe came upon every soul, and many wonders and signs were being done through the apostles. And all who believed were together and had all things in common. And they were selling their possessions and belongings and distributing the proceeds to all, as any had need. And day by day, attending the temple together and breaking bread in their homes, they received*

prioritization of military spending and the arms race over development. He challenges the nations to focus on the "integral human development" of the poorest nations. This type of development includes much more than economic growth, requiring a true commitment to solidarity and genuinely human values.

17 On the 80th anniversary of *Rerum Novarum*, Paul VI urges local churches to develop responses to the social and economic problems facing their communities. He reminds Christians of their duty to participate in working for social and political reform to promote social justice. He identifies new societal problems related to urbanization, the situation of workers, women and youth, discrimination, and attitudes towards immigrants from poor countries and notes that "preferential respect" should be given to the poor. He urges changes in policies on issues affecting the poor such as trade, debt, and economic policy, and warns against basing progress on economic growth alone.

18 Benedict XVI lifts up love as the "extraordinary force" that leads people to faith inspired engagement in the world. He identifies justice as the "primary way of charity" and notes the obligation of "every Christian" to "take a stand for the common good" and work for institutional change. In the face of a global economic crisis, He writes about the need for "a new vision for the future" (no. 21) guided by love, truth, and solidarity. These values must inform all aspects of economic life, such as finance, trade, and globalization, which must be humanized and re-oriented to the common good. He links concern for life with the duty to care for creation, emphasizing environmental concern more than in any past encyclical.

19 Benedict XVI writes that the human person's ability to love is rooted in the Father's love for humankind and the person's identity as created in the image of God. God's love manifests itself in Christ, who gives of himself freely for the salvation of humankind. The call to love neighbor flows from God's love for humanity. He locates love for the poor at the center of Catholic life, noting that the "exercise of charity" is one of the Church's three "essential activities, along with the administration of the sacraments and the proclamation of the word" (no. 22). He writes that the Church must form the consciences of the laity so that they can work for a just ordering of society.

20 John Paul II writes to recognize the hundredth anniversary of *Rerum Novarum*. He examines the fall of communism, brought about by the struggles of workers and the inefficient economic system that failed to protect human rights, private property, and economic freedom. He points to the advantages and limitations of the market, which sometimes do not adequately respond to human needs and can prioritize profit at the expense of the dignity of the human person. He also restates themes of Leo XIII's Encyclical and calls for a just society based on the rights of workers, economic initiative, and participation.

> *their food with glad and generous hearts, praising God and having favor with all the people. [...]."* (Acts 2:42-47).

In any case, we can affirm that the first Christian communities frequently cultivated various practices in as far as power and possessions are concerned, i.e, whatever they did was for the good of the entire community. Life, possessions and every individual choice, are to enhance the good of the other. The good of the community ought to be the good of each individual and the good of each person is to be seen in the optic of the good of the community.

From the above highlights, we have noticed how the theme of the *family* is vividly, relevantly and curiously felt today, as a search for meaning, fulfillment and authenticity, and as a space of encounter. Our primary occupation in the faith formation and maturation in the family should not only be in the various works, however good they are, but rather, on persons created in God's image and likeness and God who invested us with dominion over the earth (Gen 1:24-31). Our precious time ought to be characterized more with *"fruitful moments lived with persons" in the family, than, with "things"*. Things are good in as much as they are at the service of persons. We cannot substitute persons in the family for anything.

Bibliography

1. Magisterial Sources

Concilium Vaticanum II, Constitutio de *Sacra Liturgia Sacrosanctum Concilium* (4 decembris 1963), *AAS* 56 (1964), 97-134.

———, Constitutio Dogmatica de Ecclesia *Lumen Gentium* (21 novembris 1964), *AAS* 57 (1965), 5-67.

———, *Constitutio* Dogmatica de Divina Revelatione *Dei Verbum* (18 novembris 1965), *AAS* 58 (1966), 817-830.

———, Constitutio Pastoralis de Ecclesia in mundo huius temporis *Gaudium et Spes* 53 (7 decembris 1965), *AAS* 58 (1966), 1025-1120.

———, Decretum de Presbyterorum Ministerio et vita *Presbyterorum Ordinis* (7 decembris 1965), *AAS* 58 (1966), 991-1024.

Sacra Congregatio de cultu divino et disciplina sacramentorum, Instructio *Inter Oecumenici* (26 septembris 1964), *AAS* 56 (1964), 877-900.

———, Instructio *Varietates Legitimae* 41 (25 ianuarii 1994), *AAS* 87 (1995), 288-314.

———, Instructio *Redemptionis Sacramentum* (25 martii 2004), *AAS* 96 (2004), 549-601.

Ioannes XXIII, Litterae Encyclicae Mater et Magistra (15 maii 1961), AAS 53 (1961), 401-464.

———, *Litterae Encyclicae Pacem in Terris (11 aprilis 1963), III: AAS* 55 (1963), 286-289.

Paulus VI, *Litterae Encyclicae Populorum Progressio (*26 martii 1967), *AAS* 59 (1967), 257-299.

———, *Litterae Encyclicae Humanae Vitae (25 iulii 1968), AAS* 60 (1968), 481-503.

———, Adhortatio Apostolica *Evangelii Nuntiandi* (8 decembris 1975), *AAS* 68 (1976), 5-76.

Ioannes Paulus II, Litterae Encyclicae *Redemptor hominis, "Pontificali eius ministerio ineunte"* (4 martii 1979), *AAS* 71 (1979), 314.

———, Adhortatio Apostolica *Familiaris Consortio* (22 novembris 1981), *AAS* 74 (1982), 81-191.

———, Litterae Encyclicae *Centesimus Annus*, (1 maii 1991), 43: *AAS* 83 (1991), 847.

———, Litterae encyclicae *Evangelium Vitae, "De vitae humanae inviolabili bono"* (25 martii 1995), *AAS* 87 (1995), 424-428.

———, Adhortatio Apostolica Post-synodalis *Ecclesia in Africa* (14 septembris 1995), *AAS* 88 (1996), 39-40.

———, Litterae encyclicae *Fides et Ratio* (14 Settembris 1998), *AAS* 91 (1999), 76-77.

———, Epistula Apostolica *Novo Millennio Ineunte* (*6* ianuarii 2001), *AAS* 93 (2001), 308.

———, Litterae Encyclicae *Ecclesia de Eucharistia* (17 aprilis 2003), *AAS* 95 (2003), 433-475.

Benedictus XVI, Litterae Encyclicae *Deus Caritas Est* (25 decembris 2005), *AAS* 98 (2006), 232.

———, Adhortatio Apostolica Post-synodalis *Sacramentum Caritatis* 64 (22 februarii, 2007), *AAS* 99 (2007), 111-112.

———, Litterae encyclicae *Caritas in Veritate* (29 iunius 2009), *AAS* 101 (2009), 643-647.

———, *Adhortatio Apostolica Post-synodalis Verbum Domini* (5 *novembris 2010), AAS* 11 (2010) 681-787.

———, *Adhortatio Apostolica Post-synodalis Africae Munus* (*19 mars 2009), AAS* 101 (2012), 907.

Franciscus, Adhortatio apostolica *Evangelii Gaudium* (24 novembris 2013), *AAS* 105 (2013), 1121.

2. Instruments

Catechismus Catholicae Ecclesiae. Editio typica latina. Città del Vaticano: LEV, 1997.

Enchiridion Symbolorum. Edited by Heinrich Denzinger and Peter Hünermann, Freiburg: Herder, [40]2009.

World Christian Encyclopedia, a Comparative Survey of Churches and Religions in the Modern World, A.D. 1900-2000. Edited by David B. Barrett. Oxford: University Press, 1982, 685-689.

3. General Studies

Bass, Diana Butler, *The Practicing Congregation: Imagining a New Old Church.* Herndon, Va.: Alban Institute, 2004.

Bass, Dorothy, C., and Don C. Richter. *Way to Live: Christian Practices for Teens.* Nashville, Tenn.: Upper Room Books, 2002.

Bass, Dorothy, C., *Practicing Our Faith: A Way of Life for a Searching People.* 1st ed. San Francisco, Calif.: Jossey-Bass, 1997.

Bunge, Marcia, J., *The Child in Christian Thought.* Religion, Marriage, and Family Series. Grand Rapids, Mich.: W.B. Eerdmans, 2001.

Dean, Kenda Creasy, *Practicing Passion: Youth and the Quest for a Passionate Church.* Grand Rapids, Mich.: Eerdmans Pub., 2004.

Dean, Kenda Creasy, and Ron Foster, *The Godbearing Life: The Art of Soul Tending for Youth Ministry.* Nashville: Upper Room Books, 1998.

Dykstra, Craig, R., *Growing in the Life of Faith: Education and Christian Practices.* 2nd ed. Louisville, Ky.: Westminster John Knox Press, 2005.

Everist, Norma Cook, *The Church as Learning Community: A Comprehensive Guide to Christian Education.* Nashville, TN: Abingdon Press, 2002.

Lubac, Henri de, *The Motherhood of the Church,* San Francisco: Ignatius Press 1982.

May, Scottie, *Children Matter: Celebrating Their Place in the Church, Family, and Community*. Grand Rapids, Mich.: William B. Eerdmans Pub., 2005.

Parks, Sharon Daloz, *Big Questions, Worthy Dreams: Mentoring Young Adults in their Search for Meaning, Purpose, and Faith*. 1st ed. San Francisco, Calif.: Jossey-Bass 2000.

Root, Andrew, *Revisiting Relational Youth Ministry*. Downers Grove: InterVarsity Press 2007.

Schillebeeckx, Edward, *Church: The Human Story of God*, New York: Crossroad Publishing Company 1993. Segundo, Juan Luis, *The Community Called Church*, Maryknoll, New York: Orbis Books 1973.

Stortz, Martha Ellen, *A World According to God: Practices for Putting Faith at the Center of Your Life*. 1st ed. San Francisco: Jossey-Bass 2004.

Strommen, Merton, P., and Dick Hardel. *Passing on the Faith: A Radical New Model for Youth and Family Ministry*. Winona, Minn.: Christian Brothers Publications, 2000.

Sullivan, Francis Aloysius, *The Church we Believe in: One, Holy, Catholic, and Apostolic*, New York / Mahwah, N. J.: Paulist Press 1988.

Tavard, George H., *The Church, Community of Salvation: An Ecumenical Ecclesiology*, Collegeville, MN: Liturgical Press 1992.

Thompson, Marjorie, J., *Family, the Forming Center*. Rev. and expanded. ed. Nashville: Upper Room Books, 1996.

Wanjala, Moses, SDB, *Foretaste of Heavenly Liturgy: Commemorating, Celebrating and Living.*

An Anthropological, Theological and Liturgical Reflection on African Sub-Saharan Music through Saint Augustine and Sacrosanctum Concilium. Jerusalem: Studium Theologicum Salesianum Publications 2015.

Chapter 3

Convenience Culture and the Violence of the Everyday

Cara Judea Alhadeff

1. Mediocrity, Morality, and The Sanctity of Normalcy

The system reproduces its existence because it goes unrecognized.
Pierre Bourdieu

Civilization requires the *perception* of conviviality,[1] proportionality, and balance in order to function efficiently, defending laws and mores maintaining the status quo—which, as Barthes states, are fundamental to the "maintenance of dominant identity" (Sandoval 118.9). Socially imposed assumptions of neutrality-as-universal dictate how we must conduct ourselves in public and in private.[2] Officially sanctioned abuses legislate how we encounter the body

1 See Ivan Illich's essays on proportionality in *Tools for Conviviality*, Marion Boyars, 1990. In the early 90s, Illich regularly lectured in Penn State University's Science, Technology, and Society Program. I had the privilege of attending many of his remarkably embodied lectures. He sat cross-legged without shoes on a table facing his rapt audience. I wrote frantically attempting to keep up with Illich's incalculable peregrinations. A massive cancerous tumor on the side of his face moved in concert with his empassioned gestures.

2 In her *Methodology of the Oppressed*, Sandoval presents Barthes' Rhetorical Figures cultural management categories: The Inoculation; The Privation of History; Identification; Tautology; Neither-Norism; The Qualification of Quality; and The Statement of Fact. Each of Barthes' rhetorical devices, "poses", "figures", "machines" become a "deputy for the real that works to erase difference" (Sandoval, 118.9). Congruently, the activists/scholars writing for *The Development Dictionary: A Guide to Knowledge and Power* scrutinize the most basic terms that we take for granted as humanitarian and just, i.e., naturalized and normalized universalization *doing* the real through the lens of contemporary Euro-American superstructures.

politic. Neutrality, like transcendence, by necessity is static, sanitized, absolute, relentlessly homogeneous. Experientially, neutrality is a fiction-a vast mythology proselytized to maintain order with the purpose of appropriating creativity and difference. Censorship becomes an overarching strategy for sustaining the status quo, while simultaneously it frequently exhibits the inverse of its intended effect.[3] Censorship does not solely render an object or idea ob-scene, but a collusive *and* conspicuous inhabiting of one's consciousness through enforced neutrality. Judith Butler theorizes censorship as

> a way of *producing* speech, constraining in advance what will and will not become acceptable speech. …In the conventional view, censorship appears to follow the utterance of offensive speech: speech has already become offensive, and then some recourse to a regulatory agency is made. But in the view that suggests that censorship *produces* speech, that temporal relation is inverted. Censorship precedes the texts…and is in some sense responsible for its production (Butler 1997: 128).

In our "post-idea"[4] age, the fantasy of neutrality signals the termination of free will.[5] There can be no neutral political position, no neutral piece of art, there is not even a neutral/natural physical orientation for the human body.[6] Neutrality, a search for purity,[7] is born of patriarchal inscriptions on our cells and psyches. Grosz declares, "[t]here is no position outside [patriarchy's] orbit, not in our culture, but there are possibilities of transformation, historical change" (1994: 343). Neutrality is too often mistaken for balance. Rather, balance offers

---

3 The first incident of censorship of my photography provoked extensive public response. Before there had only been silence. Following the incident, numerous articles were written about my work, from both a critical standpoint of the university politics and psychoanalyzing the intentions of myself as the artist. The initial silence of art department professors was overwhelmed by the public outcry. I was interviewed and invited to give lectures on my photographic work in several campus departments. These public discussions were followed by another exhibition and an interactive performance.

4 If ideas cannot be instantly monetized they are rendered powerless. Consumer-oriented big ideas "may change the way we live, [but] they rarely transform the way we think. They "are material, not ideational". See Neil Gabler, "The Elusive Big Idea" in *The New York Times* Sunday, August 14, 2011: 1, 3.

5 "Neither-Norism", one of Barthes rhetorics of supremacy, demonstrates "'neutrality' or 'objectivity' in behavior". Binary-thinking is a reductive framework in which the citizen-subject "only has to endorse what already is" (Barthes 108)…"This apparent neutrality, 'objectivity,' and levelheadedness creates an inflexibility of being that supports the order of the dominant rather than that of some other moral, or political, order" (Sandoval 122.3).

6 In her *Hard Core: Power, Pleasure, and "The Frenzy of the Invisible"*, Linda Williams theorizes the ways in which "the mechanics of body movement…[underlay] the very invention of cinema" (36) and more specifically, the invention of pornography.

7 "So sanitary ideology tends insidiously to break society at the level of the bodily quality of individuals; it relieves them of their specificity" (Virilio 99).

a mapping for this "transformation, historical change". Balance is a dialogue/call-and-response of falling and catching one-self in the in-between.

When we peer into the socially constructed enfoldments of ethnicity, sexuality, and aesthetics, we witness the mechanics of collusive numbing. Observing closely, we can invoke both Arendt's precision of language and her commitment to vulnerability. She subverts the status quo by emphasizing the distinction between authority, power, and violence. Arendt deconstructs society's superstructures in order to examine how they proliferate through Oedipal assumptions that are both unwittingly and consciously reproduced: "The family man [is] the greatest criminal of the century" (Arendt cited in May 60).[8] Precision does not require reduction; specificity can expand ideas. Precise thinking demands a playful engagement with possibilities that reveal the unexpected. The status quo is violated when this kind of ambiguity enters the public domain rendering the norm vulnerable. Vulnerability cannot easily be regulated, thus it defies the neutrality of the status quo and is forbidden in the public sphere: "One way a hegemonic understanding of politics is achieved is through circumscribing what will and will not be admissible as part of the public sphere itself...The constraints are not only on content...but on what 'can' be heard, read, seen, felt, and known. ...Our capacity to feel and to apprehend hangs in the balance" (Butler 2004: xx-xxi).

The private within the public arena is synonymous with subversive activities and deviant behavior. The threatening condition of vulnerability exposes one's very humanity to the dangerous, unpredictable territory that such agency invokes. Consistently, the public/collective manifests itself as that which must be contained, easily assimilated, and reproduced at and as the lowest common denominator in order to maintain a neutralized status quo. The private/the individual transgresses civilization's prescribed, legislated boundaries. Reactionary assimilationist hegemony neutralizes difference and expurgates vulnerability rendering it palatable for the public. This civilizing neutralization defines the foundation of imperialist psychological tourism[9]–the roots of contemporary US-style democracy[10]–Wall Street government. In his introduction to Bataille's *On Nietzsche,* Sylvère Lotringer decries the "complicity and denial [that] are constitutive of morality whose concern for utility is merely there to suture the

---

8 In the context of totalitarianism, Arendt was addressing her accusation of the family man in the context of the Nazi regime—those who seek an enemy from whom they "protect" their family, regardless of the social or ethical implications.

9 As an extension of US imperialism, I am referring to imperialist psychological tourism as the ways in which citizen-subjects internalize the violence of the everyday–a violence that breeds convenience culture. Imperialist psychological tourism perpetuates our inherited culture of projected shame manifested in institutionalized suppression and self-censorship. Rather than making clear decisions rooted in our intuitive, creative, and interconnected thought-processes based on the "common-good", we have internalized shame, thus restricting the emancipatory possibilities of our bodies and minds.

10 "...Nietzsche's early readers took him as an antidote to Americanism" (A. Star 11).

wound" (xii). Foucault's "civilization" is this wound-the outgrowth of *scientia sexualis*: the "sexual science that gives form to the 'truths' that are confessed" (Williams 48)-"confession" as institutional and internalized coercion. In her *Blind Date: Sex and Philosophy*, Anne Dufourmantelle cites Foucault:

> Rather than the uniform concern to hide sex, rather than a general prudishness of language, what distinguishes these last three centuries is the variety, the wide dispersion of devices that were invented for speaking about it, for having it spoken about, for inducing it to speak for itself, for listening, recording, transcribing, and redistributing what is said about it: around sex, a whole network of varying, specific, and coercive transpositions into discourse (31).

The Other, the immigrant within, is positioned as perpetual outsider, internalizing the illusion that difference is deviant and obscene, and that such vulnerability must be categorized and contained by institutionalized authority. In cultural production, as in reception, vulnerability becomes a vital intervention in public-private discourse. We are allowed to experience and express vulnerability only in private. The private is construed and constructed as deficient and pathological, requiring unquestioned taxonomies of regulation and normalization. The tyranny of the normative neutralizes difference and must be recognized as the banality of evil[11] in its violence of everyday representation. Daily violence can be identified by the representations in which difference is neutralized/equalized. Abigail Solomon-Godeau reminds us that, "The most insidious and instrumental forms of domination, subjection, and objectification are produced by mainstream images of women rather then by juridically criminal or obscene ones" (237).

Insidiously, this sanctity of normalcy constitutes a hegemony of representation that colonizes our relationships with our bodies. It silently breeds distrust of our innate corporeal humanity. Institutionalized constructions of vulnerability bind the psychological to the physical: everyday of our lives we learn that to be accepted we must suspect and contain our bodily functions. Paul Virilio exposes our entrenched body-horror (self as other) as socially constructed:

The entire olfactory domain has been devalorised...a natural odor henceforth signifying a vile-smelling exhalation, culminating at its extreme point in the hygienic wind of so-called 'deodorant 'products, by which the advertising system demonstrates man's revulsion for his neighbor's odor (99). We judge this other

11 In her *Eichmann in Jerusalem: A Report on the Banality of Evil*, Arendt unravels the implications of thought-phobia that elides differing perspectives–consuming and disposing of democratic potential.

within as excess.[12] We must feel fear, shame,[13] guilt.[14] Our compliance is imperative. Paradoxically, our body-the "alluvions, sedimentations, coagulations, foldings, and recoilings that compose an organism" (Deleuze and Guattari 1980: 159)-become the stranger within. We become the spectacle of our own invisibility–an alienated, mythified, commodified site of colonization, reminiscent of Kristeva's reference to that which is "foreign not only to others but to him or herself, harboring not an essence but a 'pulverized origin'". (Suleiman 230*)*.

As the photographer and subject in my visual work, I consciously inhabit this uncanny-a deterritorialization-*l'informe* of vulnerability.[15] I choreograph my photographs and exhibit them with the intention of encouraging people to witness and question the violence that saturates our daily realities. We may not even realize that the invisible, habitual comfort zone exists because it is perniciously ingrained in our psyches. Louis Althusser's philosophy of how both the ideological state apparatus and the repressive state apparatus function to "make continued state force less noticeable, especially to those who 'fit in'" (Straayer 307) demonstrates the collusive nature of this invisibility. Below I discuss various manifestations of the insidiousness of US democracy, characterized by Bill Maher as a "system of open bribery", ranging from the invisibility of whiteness to the machinations of

---

12 Judgment as in Kafka's version of fear; excess as in what is publicly (collective coercion) interpreted as waste. Congruently, Gayle Rubin calls mainstream feminism a "system of sexual judgment" (282). I am exploring sex radical feminism as a manifestation of "literature"– a lived co-implication of *l'informe*: "Kafka sees "literature" as a way of "unjudging," and thus deconstructing, the "judged" version of the real towards its originary "unjudged" (undecidability)" (Ulfers Nietzsche seminar, EGS 2009).

13 The sex-shame-morality triad infiltrates common law: "Shame raises the question of transgressions and taboos. Sexuality, to the extent that it signified excess, the non-humanized, brought back into view, in the characteristics of animals, that which escapes all sociality. Animality has thus become, par excellence, that which casts us out of bounds, outside the civilized sphere, the human compact, the *polis*. Sex was not originally interpreted as an evil, then, but as one of the appetites through which our always latent inhumanity comes to be engulfed...As sex is appetite par excellence, its very root has to be extirpated, namely desire, lust, lasciviousness: in short, the body itself becomes guilty. Guilty of an excess that is always potentially revelatory of possible evil. In this legacy we convey the value of a body always capable of treason, a body on which we cannot rely. A body of shame. Shame exceeds the psychological distortion that it seems to establish naturally between self and self. It comes from a place much more remote than childhood; it comes from our radical doubt about the body, which may betray us at any moment, may tilt us once again towards the inhumanity that is–that is said to be our common origin. Sex is there to remind us that we are inhuman, that any measure taken with respect to desire is a secondary measure susceptible to being forgotten, suspended, eradicated, annihilated" (Dufourmentelle 29-30).

14 See Gerald Heard's discussion of how socially imposed pain represents an obstacle to expanding consciousness and sexual energy driving the evolution of the mind in his *Pain, Sex, and Time: A New Outlook on Evolution and the Future of Man.*

15 Precisely because it is slippery, messy, uncontainable, vulnerability, in its deterritorialized *essence*, is of *l'informe.*

mass consumerism. Too often, anything outside of the zone of the familiar is seen as socially inappropriate, and therefore deviant. We use the lowest common denominator of intellectual engagement as a justification for how we make our decisions for what can and what must not be allowed in the public realm.

In his article on pedagogy and Deleuze and Guattari, Charles Garoian cites educator Elliot Eisner's (1979) term *null curriculum:*

> what schools do not teach may be as important as what they do teach" (83). What Eisner is suggesting is that teaching students to conform to prevailing cultural representations in schools, which reflects the *hidden curriculum* of academic, institutional, and corporate desire, implies that students' differential knowledge and experiences acquired outside of school are insignificant (9).

Another "democratic" irony is that the same reactionary forces that require the art and entertainment industries to be regulated to protect children (labeled as the most vulnerable in society)[16] refuse regulation for health care[17] and environmental protection-ranging from lead in paint, toxins in air and water, fuel consumption to agribusiness and school lunches-let alone a refusal to regulate the NRA. Children's deaths from gun-related accidents continue to climb, as does research proving the dangers of cell phone use in early childhood development.

> It is not a matter of a simple entry of the excluded into an established ontology, but an insurrection at the level of ontology, a critical opening up of the questions, What is real? Whose lives are real? How might reality be remade? Those who are unreal have, in a sense, already suffered the violence of de-realization. ...Violence renews itself in the face of the apparent inexhaustibility of its object (Butler 2004: 33).

Such imperialist digital utopianism demonstrates misplaced priorities–creating more problems than it solves. This proliferation of technology serves to obliterate difference. Democratization of the other fuels our voracious global economy's addiction to convenience through consumption. In contrast to the chiasmic methodologies of Jacotot, The Ignorant Schoolmaster, the myth of Progress attempts to apprehend and conform our consciousness and our bodies into self-maximizing capitalist teleologies:

> Reason is, indeed, far more cunning than the liberal conscience will care to acknowledge. It sets 'the passions to work in its service'; it keeps Itself 'in the background, untouched and unharmed', while it 'sends forth the particular interests of passion to fight and wear themselves out in its stead'. No, the universality–the sovereign, tyrannical universality–of Reason remains

16 "...perversion is a recent concept, as is the protection of children" (*BD* 29).

17 While conducting research on pharmaceutical companies pandering to children diagnosed with Attention Deficient Disorder, I came across a statistic stating that it is not uncommon for children to be prescribed up to five medications.

> unscathed. ...Reason in its universalizing mission has been parasitic upon a much less lofty, much more mundane, palpable material and singularly invidious force, namely the urge of capital. ...Reason has travelled the world piggyback, carried across oceans and continents by colonial powers eager to find new grounds for trade, extraction and the productive expansion of capital. ...By now, of course, the historical identity between Reason and capital has taken on the form of an epistemic privilege, namely, 'development' as dictated by the advances of modern science and technology. ... [M]any of the problems faced by socialist countries today show to what extent the identity between Reason and capital, in its contemporary form of the unchallenged prerogative of 'modern' technology, still remains a reality (Chatterjee 168, 169, 170).

Reason as Progress is ob-scene–protected 'in the background'–as the divisive tactics of development politics have taken on a life of their own. Mutually parasitic equalizing "reciprocal contamination" (Ronell: 2009 xvii) maintains the force of Reason–ranging from US style democracy to "appropriate technology". Infinite incidents demonstrate back-door monoculturization of minds, bodies, and environments.[18]

2. Self-Censorship: Toxic Mimicry, Internalized Fascism, and Phallic Norms

First, you must give people a much larger degree of freedom in order to let them act as they want in the economic field. At the same time you must exert more and more control over them in their private, moral behavior.

Foucault interview with Thomas Zummer

Civilization markets freedom as an abstraction to be consumed (FOX News,[19] CNN, the art market, the culture industry at large, venture philanthropy, humanitarian imperialism, the corporatization of the Green Movement). As sacrificial lambs, citizen-subjects internalize these abstractions and unquestioned

18 While working with the Quijos-Quechua in Ecuador in 1991 on an ethno-botany program, I witnessed multiple culturally inappropriate projects that were implemented by "aid" organizations. Two examples of this corporation-determinate dependency include the absurdity of replacing thatched roofs with aluminum. Since the women cook on open fire in their homes, the roofs no longer absorbed the smoke. The rates of lung cancer, asthma, etc. soared. They then had to seek medical assistance from the urban areas. The story of extreme oppression begins there. Another example of insidious colonial control is when a major seed distributor planted soybeans along the sides of the most traveled roads. Villagers picked and used the soybeans, but couldn't produce the plant on their own and ended up having to buy it in quantity from the transnational agribusiness who had originally planted the soybeans.

19 Fox News viewers are less informed than people who don't watch or read any news. Fox News viewers are more likely to believe false information about politics. "Fox News Viewers Know Less Than People Who Don't Watch Any News: Study", 11/21/11, http://www.huffingtonpost.com.

fears of the other as abject.[20] Industrialized economies have become extraordinarily effective systems of self-censorship. Although "moral" fascism[21] still saturates and fractures our contemporary world, I am less concerned with overt moral crusades that have dictated our behavior and cultural norms over past centuries, and am much more wary of the insidious explicit and implicit ways in which we have internalized phallic norms and fear of our own bodies. In his introduction to Deleuze and Guattari's *A Thousand Plateaus,* Foucault identifies this vertiginous condition as the "fascism within". Analogously, Kathy Acker alerts us to this manifestation of fascism: "As long as we continue to regard the body, that which is subject to change, chance, and death, as disgusting and inimical, so long shall we continue to regard our own selves as dangerous others". Virginie Despuentes, the writer/director of the film *Baise Moi,* which was banned in her home country of France, states, "We are all familiar with the syndrome of the hostage who identifies with his captor. That is exactly how we have ended up policing each other, judging each other through the eyes of those who keep us under lock and key" (117). In the following paragraphs, I chart how ethnicity, sexuality, and aesthetics play out a tripartite problematic of internalized oppression demonstrated through the Stockholm Syndrome.[22]

1996. San Francisco. I was a docent at The Jewish Museum's exhibit titled, "Too Jewish?". I found myself confronted by this seemingly comprehensive traveling exhibition whose purpose was to expose stereotypes of Jewish identity. However, only Jews of Eastern European descent (Ashkenazi / "white Jews") were included to the exclusion of Sephardi, Mizrahi or any other non-Ashkenazi artists. What are the implications of such an omission? Both Jewish Museums in New York City and in San Francisco disregarded the viability of including any artists from global populations of non-white Jews (many of whom live and work in NYC and SF). The exhibition curators stated their mission automatically disqualified so-called "ethnic" Jews. The artists chosen focused on bawdy slapstick humor and self-deprecation–apparently not recognized as cultural characteristics for Jews of Spanish, Egyptian, Persian, Filipino, Ghanian, etc. descent—whose work was characterized as "poetic". What the curators failed to recognize in their conceptually uninformed exhibition was that, for example, *converso* Jews (forced converts to Catholicism) played the role of court jesters during the Inquisition–demonstrating the double-face of humor:

20 In the US, people fear others because they don't know they come from; elsewhere, others are feared because people do know where they come from.

21 In my research on Sephardic histories, I probe "moral fascism" in the context of *limpieza de sangre,* the Inquisitional laws of *purity of blood.*

22 The Stockholm Syndrome, in addition to identifying with and defending captors, is a paradoxical psychological phenomenon which displays a radically effective technique to subvert any attempts at self-definition or resistance to normalizing tendencies.

The *converso* perspective erupted through humor. The court jester, or *truhan*, became a feature of the Court in the fifteenth century. The jesters were largely or wholly *conversos*. This may have been due to the Jewish cultural acceptance of humor. It also reflected the *converso's* marginal status–it was easier for Old Christians to laugh at these former Jews and, conversely as outsiders, *conversos* looked more skeptically and satirically upon Castilian society (Gorsky 61).

Like Hip-Hop culture's cross-culturally disenfranchised youth,[23] Anton de Montoro, fifteenth century Castilian *converso* poet, "flaunted his Jewish heritage by dramatizing the plight of fellow converts, victims of...violent persecution". He used exaggerated humor to protest abuse: "We want to give you tributes, be your slaves and serve you, we are impoverished, cuckolded, faggots, deceived, open to any humiliation only to survive...What death can you impose on me that I have not already suffered?" (Ibid. 60-61). Whether we hear the voices from the fifteenth or twenty-first centuries, the message is the same:

> It amazes me how we as black people now enslave each other by determining what blackness is through a type of language (ebonics), dress, demeanor, money-makin', violence, and by skin color. We now use the chains that massa' used on us to kill our own individuality. In black culture, the term 'keepin' it Real' embodies a lifestyle that this particular black male has been incarcerated, shot, makes money illegally, is violent, liven' the thug life like Tupac, Biggie, Fifty Cent...This is the ultimate internalization of 'the man' (Kent Craig, *Digital Underground*).

The destructive elements of Hip-Hop culture have become the ambition of much of black youth, as well as white youth *wanna-bes* who take on these characteristics as models for success, fame, and fortune. Similarly, in his *Letters to Milena*, Kafka divulges his turmoil about having to contend with the most precise and penetrating forms of degradation that come from within. He anguishes over this internal crisis–the worst of all punishments.[24] As mentioned above, Foucault shares the terror of this self-imposed embattlement: "And not only historical fascism, the fascism of Hitler and Mussolini [...] but also the fascism in us all, in our heads and in our everyday behavior, the fascism...causes us to love power, to desire the very thing that dominates and exploit us" (Foucault's introduction to *Anti Oedipus* xii).

---

23 Director Joshua Atesh Litle's feature-length film, *The Furious Force of Rhymes* (2010), United States / France is an example of individuals exhibiting their collective struggles through Hip-Hop: "Back in the day when Blacks weren't allowed to learn to read or write, Hip-Hop's manipulation of language proved the man wrong—a clear display that Blacks are intelligent, even though we may not be educated. Not only as a public voice, but also as an economic opportunity through the music industry, the ability to manipulate words in this way speaks about the oppressive situation of minorities" (Kent Craig, *Digital Underground).*

24 See Kafka's, *Letters to Milena.* ed. Willi Haas; trans. Tania and James Stern. 1953. New York: Random House, 1999.

Black-on-black gang violence and riots destroying working-class communities resulting in prison encampments primarily populated by black male youth are two examples of the disenfranchised strategically positioned to self-destruct. During WWII, similar divisive tactics were used in concentration camps when a few prisoners were chosen as guards–asserting albeit restricted power over fellow prisoners in exchange for limited "privileges".[25] This calculated practice of divide and conquer turns prisoner against prisoner through suspicion and distrust–a variation of the Stockholm Syndrome in which the prisoner with privileges depends on his captors' favors for survival.[26] Those afflicted with this syndrome, which erodes individual and collective will to power,[27] gradually function as though they are isolated units, not integral within an interconnected entity.

Centuries of persecution and pariah-status in most if not all host-nations have led many Jewish peoples, like other diasporic populations, to become infected by forms of alienation and marginalization. In her discussion of statelessness, Arendt wrote about the "ecstasy of sovereignty" (May 29)–those in exile whose civil rights are negated compared ironically, to a "real citizen". Civil rights in the context of statelessness are a denied privilege. This exile also manifests as being in exile from oneself.[28] When the "real citizen", for example, the Italian (but not the Italian-Jew who is identified as stateless) commits a crime, the Italian, as a citizen criminal, would have more rights than the stateless undocumented alien: "He is no longer the scum of the earth but important enough to be informed of all the details of the law under which he will be tried" (Arendt cited in May 40-41). Such

25 Sonderkommandos were Jews who were forced to dispose of the bodies of Jews in the crematoriums. See the 2001 film, *The Grey Zone.*

26 Not surprisingly, the patient diagnosed with cancer quickly learns to fear, distrust, despise his body, identifying with the disease as self, and unable to recognize the self as independent from that which destroys life. His will to power is annihilated.

27 Ulfers examines two distinctions of Nietzsche's will to power: a cosmological variation, not a will to overpower or subordinate, but to manifest and imbue in potentiality to actualize itself. Like the First Law of Thermodynamics in which matter is neither created nor destroyed, but transformed, nature is a monster of energy reflecting the "real"—philosophy and art in and as continual exchange. The flow of energy is at the core of Nietzsche's eternal recurrence. The second distinction is the concept of will to power considered in this context: will to truth, equality, and knowledge in which the human instrument is used for survival, not political power. The latter distinction has historically been perverted by fascist ideologies, including in the work of Leni Riefenstahl.

28 Butler avows: "To be ecstatic means literally, to be outside oneself, and thus can have several meanings: to be transported beyond oneself by a passion, but also to be beside oneself with rage or grief. I think that if I can still address a 'we,' or include myself within its terms, I am speaking to those of us who are living in certain ways beside ourselves, whether in sexual passion, or emotional grief, or political rage" (Butler 2004: 24). I discuss another extension of this version of ec-static in the context of Nietzsche's *disidentification* in "Embodying the Unknown: Birth in the 21st Century".

psychological infiltration inseminates the cycle of internalized anti-Semitism[29] and its concomitant fantasy that anti-Semitism no longer pervades as our society's norm. This refusal to acknowledge the obvious serves to maintain the fascism within–a collusion with the invisibility of whiteness and with the dominating forces of academic, institutional, and corporate coercion. Because our roles of corporatized citizenship are so intricately intertwined with this coercion, we find ourselves within a neoliberal boomerang ethic of unaccountability. Uncanny "'intellectual uncertainty'...calls into question judgment; the *position* from which distinctions are drawn" (Weber 2000: 20). Lack of consciousness, the opposite of Soren Kierkegaard's call for awareness,[30] illuminates anxiety as the "dizziness of reason." Judgment and lack of consciousness are seamlessly bound:

> Why, Levinas asks, so much concern for the manslaughterer? He answers: because we are all manslaughterers. The manslaughterer is the one who is half-guilty, since he has killed, and half-innocent, since he did not mean to kill. We all participate in structures of oppression–this makes us guilty–but we participate for the most part unwittingly–this makes us innocent. Were we fully awake, he says, there would be no manslaughter. ... [As such] liberal cities are organized as cities of refuge [that]...allow or encourage their citizens to stand in exile from truth (Eisenstadt).

Our conscious and unconscious[31] participation in such institutionalized violence marks one of the most defining characteristics of being a post-human citizen in a global economy: "The body is the inscribed surface of events (traced by language and dissolved by ideas), the locus of a disassociated Self (adopting the illusion of a substantial unity), and a volume in perpetual disintegration" (Foucault cited in Butler 1999: 165). Our bodies perform this reactivity in ethnic, sexualized, and aesthetic contexts.

---

29 Hitler and Torquemada, The Grand Inquisitor zealot who conducted the *auto da fés*, are amongst the most demonic historical figures whose Jewish origins are the very identity they then seek to destroy. Turning themselves, their ancestry, into the most grotesque manifestation of the uncanny, they hyperbolize toxic mimicry.

30 For detailed analyses of waking as societal consciousness, see *Kierkegaard and Levinas: The Subjunctive Mood* and "The problem of the promise: Derrida on Levinas on the cities of refuge".

31 The litany of our collusion with corporate and imperial forms of domination is almost infinite. For example, our phone taxes pay for "death squads" throughout Central America, every time we look something up on Google we contribute to global warming, every time we refuse to look someone in the eye or when we sit in a chair unconsciously we undermine our bodies' homeostatic capacities. The most benign actions affect (in the Spinozan sense) our socio-political environments, equally if not more than, our obviously privileged positions. My point is not to belabor our unrecognized accountability, but to reinforce an acknowledgment of the complex impacts of our sexual, ethical, aesthetic, and political affiliations—in short, Derrida's *pharmakon* of interrelatedness.

1989. Tunis. As a Jewish eighteen-year old girl traveling in a Muslim country by myself, I never felt threatened because of my gender. On the other hand, being Jewish left me utterly vulnerable. As a Jew, I am familiar with my bodily presence provoking curious disgust and distrust. Because of this familiarity, I am fascinated by the ways in which sexuality provokes a corresponding repulsion[32] and seduction.[33] My body has had to unperform its ethnic insinuations. But, it refuses to submit to comparable sexual de-cisions–my body refuses to unperform its sexual insinuations.[34] My insinuating body is compelled to think through its contradictory, incomplete biological and cultural constructions. Dufourmentelle's thought-body is central to my investigation of how to reconceptualize (thus re-appropriate) vulnerability as agency:

> ...so much effort has been expended to fight it, to make it guilt-ridden, to bury it in shame to deny the freedom that bears it and that also constitutes its power of revolt; so that the enigma of desire can be reduced to the expression of a mechanical need. Because for a long time sex has aroused hatred. And we have yet to conceptualize the threats they both pose to the human community, threats that make sex and philosophy the objects of so many rules and taboos, so much violence. Hatred of thought and hatred of the desiring body have many lands, many exiles, and many foliations in common. The taboo on thinking and the taboo on loving may lie at the foundation of the social

32 The more primitive civilizations do not separate linguistically the taboo caused by awe of sanctity from that inspired by fear of defilement. The same term evokes all the supernatural powers from which one ought to stay far removed, whatever the motive. 'Blessed or accursed', 'miraculous or incomprehensible' impartiality is expressed using the same term for both. ... One desires to approach and possess it at the very moment in which one is keeping a proper distance from it (Caillois 36).

33 "*Human* existence commanded an abhorrence of all sexuality; this abhorrence itself commanded the attractive value of eroticism....for *humanity* would cease to exist the day it became something other than what it is, entirely made up of violent contrasts...obscenity itself is nothing but that natural animality, the horror of which establishes our humanity" (Bataille 1991: 18, 149).

34 Since I began to shoot photographs as an attempt to unwrite the world around me, I have identified my sexuality through the lens of socialized masculinity–my sexuality has a mind of its own: "Men have been seen to embody the idea of rationality. [Yet,] one could argue that the male sexual organ is the only part of the male body that is not controlled by the will but instead governed by a complicated interaction between blood, nerves and muscles. Men cannot control the raising or lowering of the penis by force of will. ... Our culture, to a great extent, has made a taboo of the erect male member. ... That physicians, biologists and cultural fictions have caused men to turn this upside down, associating the experience of pleasure with the penis, and referring to their penises as their brains, has created the basis for misunderstandings, self-deceit, a lessening of the real brain's capacity of pleasure, and the potential for sexual abuse. Sex becomes not just a weapon but a weapon that controls itself" (Žižek, NYU lecture October 15, 2009). Men have two types of erections: psychogenic erection from sexual/arousing thoughts and reflex erection from physical contact, including random stimulation like rubbing on pants.

> body, in an obscure way, because the freedom that thinking and loving arouse emboldens people to act against oppression, against the dictatorship of stupidity, against cowardly behavior, false appearances, and self-evident truths (12).

Habitually dichotomous constitutive conditions of patriarchy vilify the potentialities of embodying the physio-psychological. Pre-determined agendas obliterate the Now, the Moment, the equivocality of creative intelligence. Contra, instinct and vulnerability converge at the Moment of the psyche-somatic integrity of becoming-animal: "nothing...is older, stronger, more inexorable and unconquerable than this instinct-because this instinct constitutes the essence of our species, our herd...." (Nietzsche, *The Gay Science*, § 1, pp. 73-74). Because the animal only "knows" how to live in the Moment, the ever-extending, discontinuous Now, it evokes an absence of judgmental, classifying consciousness: "animals coincide with the instant of their presence" (Dufourmentelle 65). The poet Rene Char wrote, "Each act is virgin, even the repeated one". The utter presence (which becomes the formlessness of absence)[35] of being fully alive is the crux of John Cage's statement, "we have to go back to zero before reaching the next term" (92).

Deleuze associates this becoming-animal with Kafka's *écriture*-existence "that simultaneously opens the way to a 'thinking otherwise than being' (Levinas), a thinking that is not oriented to any 'Same' that is inherent in the very notion of Being and being, but to the 'other' as infinite interpretability [Nietzsche's phrase]" (Ulfers). "Of course one cannot even figure out one's own riddle; this is precisely the meaning of 'fear'" (Kafka *Letters to Milena* 237). Fear of one's self[36] charges representational social systems of women's bodies, disorder, and intellectual unfamiliar territory. Both men and women are engaged in a reifying, everted system of self-containment: "If humanity lives in fear, it will gradually, and almost without being aware of what it is doing, abdicate its capacity to think, to imagine, to dream. And thus also to love" (Dufourmentelle 83). Fear fuels the radical potency of divide-and-conquer strategies, maintaining the sanctity of normalcy. Questioning gender positions in relation to authority, power, and agency, Grosz asks: "[C]ould men's refusal to acknowledge the effects and flows that move through various parts of the body and from the inside out, have to do with men's attempt to distance themselves from the very kind of corporeality-uncontrollable, irrational-they have attributed to women?" (Grosz 1994:200).

35 "The affirmation of life...as play, is, as Derrida put it in his reading of Nietzsche, an affirmation that determines the absence of a center of Being ('presence') 'otherwise than as loss of the center.' This interpretation is one in which 'play must be conceived before the alternative of presence and absence,' that is, the alternative of Being and Becoming" (NAF 11).

36 In my article, "Aesthetic Obscuratism: The Ineffable, The Incomplete, *L'Informe*", I explore the constitution of male aggression toward their "internal" female.

Probing public response to the intimacies of my photographic images, I witness the infinite complexities of how difference is institutionally regulated and how normalcy is made so pervasive as to become invisible. In contrast, Jacques Rancière's concept of *being together apart* reflects a chiasmic space of the sensual–a third space "for at the same moment that it holds the two together as related, it also holds them apart" (Ulfers NYU Kafka seminar 2009). Ulfers elaborates:

> [T]he tragic, rather than constituting the "negating" side to an opposed 'affirming,' embodies, through the conception of opposites as interpenetrating, what Nietzsche calls an irreducible 'contradiction.' 'Contradiction,' for Nietzsche, does not mean the violation of binary logic, but an'intricate relation' between opposites, such as bliss and pain, that simultaneously unites them and holds them apart (NAF 5).

Congruent with Rancière's *together apart* and Nietzsche's tragedy, Lyotard's *compossibility* invoke these multiple potentialites which align political and libidinal economies. By exploring plural, contradictory pleasures, my photographic images don't simply counteract socialized notions of the body, but actively transform the possibilities of (inter)action and reflection. Bataille's non-hierarchical allegory generates a remapping of the liminal:

> Bataille is not simply privileging a new object (excrement, flies, ruptured eyes, the rotten sun, etc.) over the old one (the head, the king, spirit, mind, vision, the sun of reason, etc.). If, as Angus Fletcher has pointed out in *Allegory,* the medieval allegorical imagination posits a fundamental congruence between *hierarchy* in the body and the guaranteed, stable *meaning* of allegory (in the body, the highest element is the head; in society, the king; and in the universe, God), then we must conclude that a theory that simply substituted one hierarchy for another (a hierarchy that favors the *high* replaced by one that favors the *low*) would only inaugurate a new metaphysics and a new stabilized allegorical system of meaning. Filth would replace God. …[R]ather, what Bataille works out is a kind of headless allegory. ...The fall of one system… is not replaced with the elevation on another; the fall in Bataille's allegory is a kind of incessant or repetitious process. Thus filth does not "replace" God; there is no new system of values, no new hierarchy (1985: xiii-xiv).

Within the rhizomatic detours of internalized fascistic tendencies–habituated norms–the boundaries between collusion and agency become even more unstable and circuitous. Whether sex-workers,[37] who straddle the private-public corporeal construction of desire, or myself as photographer, who consciously deploys a radical perversity of subject-object interplay in order to illuminate the how of what we do not know, I believe it is possible to do what Ulfers claims is not

37 The conscious choice to decriminalize prostitution rolls into a denaturalization of the surburban (coerced) body. See Beatriz Preciado's "Pharmaco-pornographic Capitalism Postporn politics and the Decolonization of sexual representations".

possible: "To write at all, to think at all, is of necessity to do so–one cannot stand at both ends of the microscope at the same time" (NAF 23). How can the image-maker, writer, poet, philosopher[38] and their corresponding viewers/readers consciously resist this enfoldment of metaphysical[39] collusion in order "to stand at both ends of the microscope at the same time" (Ibid.)?

> For both representation as produced by the agent or manager or mediator of the reading–artist or photographer–and the reactions of the onlooker or reader of the image must be re-exposed in the light of a certain recent criticism putting into question the whole binary system of subject and object. This is a revision overdue and all the more problematic in Surrealism, which already wanted to overcome the split between seer and seen, visionary and view: thus, a problematics of the problematic, and how it is received (Mary Ann Caws, "Ladies Shot and Painted: Female Embodiment in Surrealist Art" 263).

There is a perverse apparent lack of self-awareness on the part of very well-known artists like the Brothers' Quay whose work appears to confront status-quo ethics (or lack thereof), but in fact directly participates in and profits from an "enforced stultification" (Rancière 1991: 16).[40] The art-world is a paragon of such mediocrity.[41] Museums are/have become institutions for the prostitution of anti-intellectualism. Intellectual labor and aesthetic labor is consistently reducible to market value. Art in the US is consistently reproduced as entertainment value,

---

38 Although, I disagree with Ulfers' privileging music over visual art and language, I will concur enough not to include musicians in this list. Ulfers privileges music as a sheer becoming. According to Ulfers' critique of metaphysics, music, unlike the visual and written arts, is non-assimilatable–exempt from the tyranny of conceptual language–in which the creative urge is not to be confused with etiology. Nietzsche writes: "*Die Musik ist eine Sprache, die einer unendichen Verdeutlichung fähig ist.*" "Music is a language that is capable of infinite interpretability".

39 Schirmacher's critique of metaphysics is that it clings to an illusory certainty and truth, a linear quest for progress rooted in binary logic and conceptual thought (EGS seminar 2008). Similarly, Ulfers identifies the "corner" of metaphysics as "the reign of a dualistic perspective that insists on *one* interpretation of the world: the interpretation, the ultimate truth, of the supremacy of Being and its variants functioning as perfection, goal, meaning, and judge over the world of Becoming, the world that is, apart from its interdiction, eternally in process" (NAF 10).

40 The Brothers Quay have made a few commercials for Monsanto's weed killer product. Monsanto is one of the world's leading polluters. They intend to absorb the world's entire food supply into a GMO maelstrom–converting 100 percent of the seeds that exist today to become genetically engineered and patented. That the Brothers Quay unabashedly supported this bio-industrial monolith that dictates the US FDA's (de)regulation procedure, indicates the severity to which many artists will go to be recognized in the absence of ethical thought and action.

41 One example is of this enforced dumbing-down is from The Palmer Art Museum (which was designed by the renowned post modern architect, Charles Moore) at Penn State University. The administrators of the museum are reluctant to exhibit the paintings of naked people in their collection because representations of the naked body have offended some visitors—ironically, even the paintings of Philip Pearlstein.

not education in the broadest, most relational sense of the word. An example of art-as-education can be found in Derrida's exploration of art-making as a way in which we can begin to see–seeing which offers a process of becoming-cognizant. This in-sight is not about seeing as a mind projection (which puts the ob-scene to rout), but a psyche-somatic reception, i.e. vulnerability that incites thought, exposure, listening, and action.

In contrast to becoming-vulnerable through cognition, everything in our consumer-culture indicates that unconsciously and consciously, we are desperate to be placated. Thought is feared because it is unstable; thought does not soothe. It makes us "tremble with uncertainty" (Cixous). We recoil from imbalance. Whether we are reacting to our addiction to certainty or our addiction to convenience culture,[42] we crush the vulnerability of doubt with a resounding univocality. My pedagogical and artistic commitments are rooted in actively engaging the hazardous intersections between the ineffable and language. This is one reason that, as a visual artist, I have tremendously high expectations for the scholarly component of artists working in an academic setting. Over the past years, I have been greatly disappointed by the quality of public discussion engendered (or not) by artists who are invited to speak about their work in academic environments–including Claire Denis, Annie Liebowitz, Alison Shotz, Janine Antoni, Suzan Frecon, and Pierre Huyghe. If artists are locating themselves within a pedagogical context, they must not assume that their work "speaks for itself."

I am addressing this quarantine of thinking in the context of institutionalized anti-intellectualism because the contemporary art world has become another instrument of consumption/entertainment. Institutionalized anti-intellectualism reifies the systemic habits of internalized racism and internalized anti-Semitism–relentlessly struggling to be normal, neutral i.e. to be white and accessible. In the context of normalized ethnicity, the fantasy of sameness renders whiteness invisible:

> ...ethnically neutral institution[s] like the Museum of Modern Art... Ethnically neutral? That's just code-term for white, the no-color, the everything-color. For whiteness is as much- or as little-a racial category as blackness, though it is rarely acknowledged as such wherever it is the dominant, default ethnicity...in our laws, our behavior, our institutions, our sensibilities, our dreams (Cotter 32).

42 The new books, *Plastic: A Toxic Love Story* and *Plastic-Free–How I Kicked the Plastic Habit and How You Can Too* and the feature-length documentary film: *Addicted to Plastic: The Rise and Demise of a Modern Miracle* both address the rhizomatic concrescence of our cultural plastic-habit. It would behoove political activists fighting the oil empire to incorporate a critique of plastic and convenience-culture into their argument. For example, while attending Antonia Juhasz's (my friend who I have known since we were three-years old) lecture on her new book *The Tyranny of Oil: The World's Most Powerful Industry–and What We Must Do to Stop It,* I was the only person in the audience who brought up our insidiously integral practice of plastic consumption as a critical element in maintaining the grip of the fuel industry.

The functionality of the invisibility of whiteness reflects my history of censorship and the public reception of my photographs. Both are rooted in an institutionalized extraction of the unknown–defined, judged, de-cided a priori. When "the public" is confronted with a divergence from their expectations, they panic.[43] The politics of inclusion,[44] the ostensible neutral, permeates each contradictory longitudinal intertwining of hierarchical relations–Euclidean geometry reigns. Whether extending into transnational fascism or the precarious intricacies of racial, ethnic, and gender "passing", the fantasy of selfsameness pervades our collective consciousness. It drives our desire to belong while simultaneously undermining the potential for a vital community rooted in difference–a difference that deters the universalization of dialectical approaches. In her discussion of the Matrix, Bracha Ettinger tells us "about that encounter between difference which tries neither to master, nor assimilate, nor reject, nor alienate. It is the symbol of the coexistence in one space of two bodies, two subjectivities whose encounter at this moment is not an either/or" (213). The Matrix fluctuates as a chiasmic unity.
www.carajudea.com

43 When Nijinski first performed Stravinsky's Rites of Spring ballet in Prague, 1907, the audience became enraged and stormed the stage. In addition to the music that they found shocking in its orgiastic repetitiveness, were the turquoise and orange costumes. Not only did the color combinations provoke outrage, but also the way the costumes exposed Nijinski's body incited the audience to violence.

44 The politics of inclusion form the foundation of what is proselytized as equality.

Rice, Shelley, ed. *Inverted Odysseys: Claude Cahun, Maya Deren, Cindy Sherman.* Cambridge: MIT Press, 1998.

Ronell, Avital. *Finitude in Philosophy, Literature and Art,* The European Graduate School, August, 2009.

__________________. *Antigone and Hegel,* NYU Lectures, October, 2009.

Royle, Nicholas. *The Uncanny.* New York: Routledge, 2003.

Rubin, Gayle. "Thinking Sex: Notes for a Radical Theory of the Politics of Sexuality" in *Pleasure and Danger: Exploring Female Sexuality.* Carole Vance, ed. Boston: Routledge & Kegan Paul, 1984.

Sachs, Wolfgang, ed. *The Development Dictionary: A Guide to Knowledge and Power.* London: Zed, 1991.

Sandoval, Chela. *Methodology of the Oppressed.* Minneapolis: University of Minnesota Press, 2000.

Saltman, Kenneth. *The Edison Schools: Corporate Schooling and the Assault on Public Education.* New York: Routledge, 2005.

Schirmacher, Wolfgang. "From the Phenomenon to the Event of Technology" in *Philosophy and Technology".* F. Rapp. Rede, ed. Boston Studies in Philosophy of Science 80, 1983.

Shell, Patrick. *Kieregaard and Levinas: The Subjunctive Mood.* Burlington: Ashgate Publishing Ltd., 2010.

Singer, Penny. "P.S. 30's Helping Hands: College Mentors", *The New York Times,* May 24, 1992: 31.

Solomon-Godeau, Abigail. *Photography at the Dock: Essays on Photographic History, Institutions, and Practices.* Minnesota: University of Minnesota Press, 1991.

Smith, Jeffrey. *Seeds of Deception: Exposing Industry and Government Lies About The Safety of the Genetically-Engineered Foods You are Eating, Pathways Magazine,* issue 30/ Summer 2011, 22-23.

Star, Alexander. "The Overman: How Friedrich Nietzsche inspired and provoked his American readers", in *The New York Times Book Review,* Sunday, January 15, 2012.

Stewart, Susan. *On Longing: Narratives of the Miniture, the Gigantic, the Souvenir, the Collection.* Baltimore: John Hopkins University Press, 1984.

Straayer, Chris. *Deviant Eyes, Deviant Bodies: Sexual Re-Orientation in Film and Video,* New York: Columbia University Press, 1996.

Suleiman, Susan Rubin. *Risking Who One is: Encounters with Contemporary Art and Literature.* Boston: Harvard College, 1994.

Sussman, Ann Douglas and John R. M. D, *The Unofficial Guide to Having a Baby,* New York: Hungry Minds, Inc. 1999.

Stafford, Barbara. *Body Criticism: Imagining the Unseen in Enlightenment Art and Medicine.* Cambridge: MIT Press, 1993.

Terry, Beth. *Plastic-Free–How I Kicked the Plastic Habit and How You Can Too.* New York: Skyhorse Publishing Company, 2012.

Thompson, Chris. *Felt: Fluxus, Joseph Beuys, and The Dalai Lama.* Minneapolis: University of Minnesota, 2011.

Ulfers, Fred and Mark Daniel Cohen. "The Embracing of an Undecided Fate".

______________________________. "Zarathustra, the Moment, and Eternal Recurrence of the Same: Nietzsche's Ontology of Time".

______________________________. "Nietzsche and the Future of Art," in *Hyperion.*

Ulfers, Fred. *Nietzsche in Contemporary Thought.* seminar, The European Graduate School. June, 2008.

van Gelder, Sarah, David Korten, and Steve Piersanti. "10 Ways the Occupy Movement Changes Everything", *Huffington Post,* 11/11/11.

Virilio, Paul. "Sanitary Ideology," Zummer, Thomas and Robert Reynolds, eds. *Crash: Nostalgia for the Absence of Cyberspace.* Thread Waxing Space, New York: 1994, 98-101.

Weber, Samuel. *Legend of Freud.* Stanford University Press: Stanford, 2000.

Williams, Linda. *Hard Core: Power, Pleasure, and "The Frenzy of the Visible".* Berkeley and Los Angeles: University of California Press, 1989.

Young-Breuhl, Elisabeth. *Why Arendt Matters,* New Haven: Yale University Press, 2006.

Žižek, Slavoj. *The Metastases of Enjoyment: Six Essays on Woman and Causality.* London and New York: Verso, 1994.

__________. NYU Lectures in Avital Ronell's *Antigone and Hegel.* class, October, 2009.

Zummer, Thomas and Robert Reynolds, eds. *Crash: Nostalgia for the Absence of Cyberspace.* New York: Thread Waxing Space, 1994.

_______________. 'Project and Dis/embodiment: Genealogies of the Virtual" in *Into the Light: The Projected Image in American Art, 1964-1977,* ed. Chrissie Iles, New York: Whitney Museum of Art/Abrams, 2001.

Chapter 4

What Account can Philosophy give of Culture?

Thomas Storck

1. Introduction

The philosophy of culture suffers from a double difficulty. In the first place there have been varying meanings attached to the word *culture*, and secondly, there has been even greater disagreement over what the philosophy of culture is or ought to be. With regard to the first difficulty, what exactly we mean by culture, at least in recent decades philosophers concerned with culture usually understand it as do anthropologists, as something like "a common way of life - a particular adjustment of man to his natural surroundings and his economic needs," and which is "based on a social tradition...embodied in its institutions, its literature and its art."[1] This concept is relatively new as part of mankind's intellectual heritage. It developed in the nineteenth century in Germany and England, and has become standard in anthropology and sociology.[2] It is generally held that in the English-speaking world this usage of the word was introduced by Edward Burnett Tylor in his *Primitive Culture* (1871). Tylor wrote "Culture, or civilization,...is that complex

1 Christopher Dawson, *Dynamics of World History*, (La Salle, Ill. : Sherwood Sugden, 1978), 4 and 104. This definition ignores the question of a spiritual or ideological unity which shapes a culture. See section 4 for a discussion of this.

2 In recent years, however, there has been considerable dispute among anthropologists about the meaning and even the utility of the concept of culture. See, for example, William H. Sewell, Jr., "The Concept(s) of Culture" in Victoria E. Bonnell and Lynn Hunt, editors, *Beyond the Cultural Turn: New Directions in the Study of Society and Culture* (Berkeley : University of California, 1999), 35-61.

whole which includes knowledge, belief, art, law, morals, custom, and any other capabilities and habits acquired by man as a member of society."[3]

A culture as "a common way of life" is more than "a particular adjustment of man to his natural surroundings and his economic needs," however. The definition quoted above from Christopher Dawson is incomplete, as he himself indicated in many other places. He wrote, for example, "In the last resort every civilization is built on a religious foundation: it is the expression in social institutions and cultural activity of a faith or a vision of reality which gives the civilization its spiritual unity."[4] Pope John Paul II expressed this same idea in a striking passage in his encyclical *Centesimus Annus* (no. 24),

> At the heart of every culture lies the attitude a person takes to the greatest mystery: the mystery of God. Different cultures are basically different ways of facing the question of the meaning of personal existence.[5]

This truth is shown in the fact that different peoples have adapted to the same environment in different ways. For example, Spanish architecture of the American Southwest attempted to build in harmony with the arid and semi-arid climate, while Anglo-Americans often imported styles of building and expectations for living that may have worked well in New England or parts of the Midwest, but which were ill-adapted to the Southwest.

The presence of such a unifying ideal in a culture does not mean, though, that there must be only one such ideal at the heart of a particular culture, for it is possible for ideas and inspirations received from different sources, even opposed to one another, to coexist uneasily and create cultures which are marked by contradictory tendencies. Also it should be recognized that the continuing influence on a culture of some spiritual ideal does not mean that that ideal is

---

3 Tylor is said to have been the "first man to introduce this clear scientific meaning" of the term culture. Etienne Vermeersch, "An Analysis of the Concept of Culture," in Bernardo Bernardi, editor, *The Concept and Dynamics of Culture* (The Hague : Mouton, c. 1977), 10. In their review of the various meanings of culture, Kroeber and Kluckhohn trace the anthropological usage to the German writer Gustav Klemm's *Allgemeine Culturgeschichte der Menschheit* (1843-1852). They write: "It is difficult to be sure that Klemm's concept of culture was ever fully the same as that of modern anthropologists. On the other hand, it would be hard to believe that he is never to be so construed. Most likely he was in an in-between stage, sometimes using the term with its connotations of 1780, sometimes with those of 1920 - and perhaps never fully conscious of its range, and, so far as we know, never formally defining it." A. L. Kroeber and Clyde Kluckhohn, *Culture, a Critical Review of Concepts and Definitions* (New York : Vintage, 1952, 1963 printing), 14, 46.

4 Christopher Dawson, *Understanding Europe* (Garden City, N.Y. : Image, 1960), 211.

5 This central spiritual element in a culture can also be described in terms of values. "Die Wertesind das entscheidende Element einerKultur.... Der von Wertengebildete Kern der Kulturbestimmtentsprechend die sozialeEntwicklung in mindestensdemselben Masse wie die natürlichen Gegebenheiten und die materiellenTechniken." Constantin von Barloewen, *Werte in der Kulturphilosophie Nord- und Lateinamerikas* (Frankfurt am M.: Athenäum, 1989), 12.

necessarily active as an actual belief. The cultural effect of such ideals may persist even if the explicit ideal has been forgotten.

> A nation once Calvinist in Creed may have ceased for the most part (as Scotland has) to believe in Predestination or to trouble about Conversion and the Reprobate sense; but it will continue for generations, and probably until a new set of doctrines shall be taught it, to think (therefore, to act) in the Calvinist manner. It will incline to the Calvinist attitude toward wealth and the acquirement thereof. It will take for granted an inexorable process of cause and effect. It will concentrate upon the responsibility of the individual to himself, the isolation of soul, and a consequent cultivation of what it will call 'Character.'[6]

Any culture, therefore, will exist as a dialectic between the environment, the fundamental ideals or values which the particular social group holds, and, as we will explore below, human nature.

Although philosophical interest in culture largely reflects the development of the concept in anthropology, there has been little agreement over exactly what shape this philosophical interestshould take. As the contemporary Danish philosopher Steen Brock said, "Denn, was heisst Kulturphilosophie? Es gibt wohl keine allgemein akzeptierte Definition von dies!"[7] Although this conclusion, that there is no generally accepted definition of the philosophy of culture, parallels the lack of agreement among philosophers on many other matters, nevertheless it is probably the case that there is less consensus even on what questions the philosophy of culture should address than is the case in most other areas of philosophy. But there are certain questions which seem to be primary in any philosophical discussion of culture, and they mostly concern the relations between culture and nature, especially human nature. It is with these questions that this paper will mainly concern itself.

2. Culture and Nature

The relationship between culture and nature raises the most interesting as well as the most perplexing questions in the philosophy of culture. Often nature and culture are seen as opposed to each other, or at least as separate realms. "'Culture' means practically everything which is not 'from nature': the whole human world with its customs, artifacts, knowledge, material products, ideas and values."[8] Yet here is a paradox. All the specified items, "customs, artifacts, knowledge, material products, ideas and values," in fact flow more or less directly from human nature

6 Hilaire Belloc, "The Two Cultures of the West," in *Essays of a Catholic* (Rockford, Ill.: TAN, [1931] 1992), 240.

7 *Kulturphilosophie: Bohr, Cassirer, Wittgenstein, Cavell, MacIntyre, Winch, Taylor [und] Haraway: SechsVorlesungen am Humboldt Universitätzu Berlin, August 2006*, [8]. Accessed from http://pure.au.dk/portal/files/41412787/kulturphilosophie.pdf, (February 15, 2015).

8 TõnuViik, "What about the Philosophy of Culture?" *ActaPhilosophicaFennica* 65 (2000), 247.

in the sense that man naturally creates these things and in fact needs them in some form to fulfill what seem to be the demands and capacities natural to him. Yet obviously the particular "customs, artifacts, knowledge, material products" and so forth which humanity creates are artificial, even if they are demanded by human nature.[9] Thus culture is natural at the same time as every particular culture is artificial and contingent.

This natural human requirement for culture is shown most clearly in language. It is obviously natural for human beings to speak, but any particular language is a construct and an aspect of a culture. The explanation for this paradox lies in human nature. Our abstract capacity to speak needs to be made concrete or specific in order to be actual. But as concrete each language is necessarily something constructed and contingent, something cultural. Thus culture is natural as something necessary for expressing the abstract capabilities of human nature. But no single particular cultural product can be said to be natural as such. We cannot say that any one language is natural, since each is a human artifice. We can say, however, that language is natural to humanity and that in general each of mankind's cultural products reflects at the same time human nature's needs and its ability to create some means to satisfy those needs, even if there are many possible ways to meet any particular need.

Of course when I say that any particular culture is constructed, I do not mean that all or most cultural components are consciously created. The origins of most elements of culture are unknown to us, e.g., the origins of a language or of any of the widely varying types of family structure or of music or painting. Nor is there any way to discover how or why one original cultural choice was made rather than another. By the time historians or anthropologists are able to examine any culture, its basic structures are already in place, and all subsequent developments, though sometimes shaped by conscious human choice, nevertheless take place within a framework whose outlines and boundaries already exist.

Since a culture of some kind is a consequence of natural human needs and capacities, a human being without culture of any sort - at least without a specifically *human* culture - is actually living in an unnatural condition. The anthropologist Ruth Benedict wrote of Carolus Linnaeus' encounters in the eighteenth century with children who had been abandoned by their parents and raised perhaps among beasts. He

> classified them as a distinct species, *Homo ferus*, and supposed that they were a kind of gnome that man seldom ran across. He could not conceive that

9 Although, it is sometimes asserted today that human nature itself is something constructed, this hardly seems possible if we understand nature in its original and modest sense (following Aristotle) of how a particular type of thing acts according to its inherent nature or qualities, following the scholastic maxim, *agere sequitur esse*, action follows being. As we will see, due to the indeterminate quality of human nature, the *agere* of human beings can vary immensely and yet still follow from the *esse* of human nature.

> these half-witted brutes were born human, these creatures with no interest in what went on about them, rocking themselves rhythmically back and forth like some wild animal in a zoo, with organs of speech and hearing that could hardly be trained to do service, who withstood freezing weather in rags and plucked potatoes out of boiling water without discomfort. There is no doubt, of course, that they were children abandoned in infancy, and what they had all of them lacked was association with their kind, through which alone man's faculties are sharpened and given form.[10]

While these unfortunates were undoubtedly human as members of the species *homo sapiens*, most or all of their specifically human capabilities had never been developed, even though those capabilities were certainly possessed by them, at least originally.[11] As Jacques Maritain said, "The labour of reason and the virtues is natural in the sense that it is in conformity with the essential inclinations of human nature.... It is not natural in the sense that it is supplied ready made by nature...."[12] Maritain's mention of "reason and the virtues" brings up the further point that one of culture's functions is or should be educative. As the feral children needed to learn from a human community in order for their specifically human attributes to become manifest, so the culture of any particular community can help or hinder the development of our human capacities, and in particular those that pertain to "reason and the virtues." If we can rightly designate man as a *rational* animal, then it would seem that those things which concern our specifically rational nature are among the most important aspects of culture, since they are what distinguish us as a species from other types of animals.

Culture, then, and some particular culture, is necessary if we are to live according to the fullness of our nature as rational animals. But any particular culture is not only a means for making concrete and determinate some of the many indeterminate capabilities of human nature; it in turn, mediates how we interact with nature, even with our own human nature and with the natures of the many other things that exist in the world. Even those aspects of human life that partake in such a high degree of our bodily constitution and instincts as eating or reproduction are hardly unaffected by culture. To take a simple example, foods that are consumed avidly in some places are not eaten at all in other places, or are even regarded with revulsion, and perhaps would not be touched except to avoid starvation. This shows the interdependence and close connection of even our bodily needs with the cultural superstructure which is likewise a demand of human nature.

---

10 *Patterns of Culture* (Boston: Houghton Mifflin, c. 1934, 1961), 12-13.

11 Most probably these human capacities were dormant because the relevant physical organ had atrophied due to lack of use. Nor can one deny the possibility of damage caused by poor diet, exposure to cold, disease, etc.

12 "Religion and Culture" in *Essays in Order* (New York: Macmillan, 1931), 3.

Although there are probably no human activities which are not affected by culture, does it follow from this that each and every culture does an equally adequate job of expressing these fundamental needs or capacities of human nature? Or, in other words, do some cultures cultivate human nature better than others? To continue with our example of eating: If among the various purposes of eating the fundamental purpose always remains human nourishment, we might ask if in some cultures eating is no longer primarily about nourishment but about consumption of edibles which have a symbolic value but whose ability to actually nourish the human body is limited or which are even detrimental to human health. Contemporary North America, especially the United States, is one such example, where highly processed edibles with little nutritional content are widely consumed, resulting in a population with a large number of people obese or ill, and at the same time lacking in important nutriments. The necessarily cultural activity of eating has become divorced from its most basic requirement. The cultural filter which forms how human persons interact with their food does not simply shape this activity in some particular way - something which is necessary and occurs everywhere - but in this instance shapes it in such a way that it is now opposed to its natural function. Culture has here become the enemy of nature, rather than culture facilitating nature in the task of the bodily nourishment of human beings.

Certainly philosophers, anthropologists and historians, studying various cultures in the present and the past, must be careful not to pronounce too hastily that a certain cultural custom is opposed to human nature, or to assert that any particular culture is superior in general or with regard to one or more of its features. But we would be unfaithful to the philosophical task were we to refuse ever to make such judgments on the plea that all cultures are equal in every respect. If there is such a thing as human nature, then the possibility exists that its indeterminations, while being made determinate by a particular culture, can also be deformed or impeded.

Any particular culture's understanding of God and the world is embodied not only in customs and institutions, but usually in explicit beliefs and ideas. Although in many instances it is possible for an individual to consciously reject overt cognitive norms which his culture maintains and attempts to impose - in European culture this has been common for centuries - there are other and more subtle norms which one can escape from only with difficulty. Thus it is not unusual to see people who ostensibly adhere to a particular religion at the same time manifest on a deeper and perhaps less conscious level beliefs and behaviors which are in conflict with those of the religion whose tenets they claim to accept. Thus many have pointed out that Catholics in the United States very often accept unconsciously and uncritically certain notions derived either from the Enlightenment principles upon which that country was founded or from the Protestant culture which has long shaped its social order. Such Catholics usually do not realize how or to what an extent their actual operating principles of thought and conduct contradict those which historically have derived from Catholic beliefs.

This raises the question of whether and to what extent a person in any particular culture can escape the ways of interacting with reality that his particular culture imposes. Some have argued that we are in a sense imprisoned by our cultures. Ruth Benedict stated this view thus:

> No man ever looks at the world with pristine eyes. He sees it edited by a definite set of customs and institutions and ways of thinking. Even in his philosophical probings he cannot go behind these stereotypes; his very concepts of the true and the false will still have reference to his particular traditional customs.... From the moment of his birth the customs into which he is born shape his experience and behavior. By the time he can talk, he is the little creature of his culture, and by the time he is grown and able to take part in its activities, its habits are his habits, its beliefs his beliefs, its impossibilities his impossibilities. Every child that is born into his group will share them with him, and no child born into one on the opposite side of the globe can ever achieve the thousandth part.[13]

But surely the author herself demonstrated that this is too extreme a statement of this view, for she, as well as many others, has been able to look with some degree of detachment on her own culture as well as gain some understanding of other cultures. Alfred Kroeber stated the difficulty is less drastic terms:

> The degree to which every individual is molded by his culture is enormous.... The formal or deliberate part of the process we call education: education through schools, in religion, and in manners, and morals primarily at home. These agencies convey the mores and some of the folkways. But perhaps a larger fraction of the cultural tradition is acquired by each individual at his own initiative.... In this class are his speech, bodily postures and gestures, mental and social attitudes, which he imitates from his elders or from near-age mates, and a thousand and one activities...which a child "learns," often without any formal instruction, because he has seen others do these things and wants to do them too.[14]

Experience makes it obvious that many people do manage to see the world at least partly outside of the "set of customs and institutions and ways of thinking" inculcated by their cultures. In principle, there is no cultural construct which cannot be transcended or rejected. The difficulty is in recognizing that one has such a custom or mode of thinking or acting in the first place. For many of the "mental and social attitudes" acquired as a child are not easily identified, and in

13 Ruth Benedict, *Patterns of Culture*, 2-3.

14 *Anthropology: Culture Patterns and Processes* (New York: Harcourt, Brace & World, 1963), 96.

some cases, even when identified, are not easy to overcome. But in principle it would seem that it is always possible to do so.

Human nature, the shared possession of all human beings, will not change. But unless determined and formed by a particular culture, human nature cannot realize itself - or will be reduced to Linnaeus' *Homo ferus*. Therefore our first question, the question of the relations between nature and culture, can be resolved by saying that culture is both natural and artificial. Our specifically human powers and needs almost always require some culture to make them actual, even though the resulting cultural form is constructed and to a great extent arbitrary. Moreover, although any particular culture can give expression to human nature's abilities and needs, there is no necessary equality between cultures in how well they do this. As we saw in the case of food, although there can be and are many different cultural choices, all of which give more or less equal expression to mankind's needs, there can also exist cultural norms which work against what is natural to humanity and to that extent fail in culture's task of making the needs and demands of human nature concrete and thus able to be fulfilled.

Although any one culture is necessarily particular, we must now discuss the question of whether there can be anything that is transcultural.

3. Are Some Things Transcultural?

Human life is profoundly shaped by culture, or rather in the concrete, by any one particular culture. Although one can say that there is no truly human existence that is not a cultural existence, does it follow from this that nothing exists which we can rightly regard as transcultural, that is, as in some manner transcending any particular cultural expression? We have already examined the question of whether it is possible for a culture, instead of serving as a more or less adequate means of realizing some demand or capacity of human nature, to frustrate to a greater or lesser extent that natural demand or capacity. In fact, we may call the fundamental demands of human nature transcultural, even though they can never be realized without being embodied in some particular cultural expression. In this section we are concerned with something different, however, with the question of the existence of ideas or concepts which can be termed transcultural. This concerns not only philosophical concepts which claim universality, but also religious concepts claiming universality and based on a revelation, real or otherwise.

The opinion is not uncommon that the existence of cultures does in fact mean that there are "no universal truths." Viik describes the prevailing view as follows:

> "Culture" means practically everything which is not "from nature": the whole human world with its customs, artifacts, knowledge, material products, ideas and values. As such, culture is considered to be the most important determinant of human life. From this perspective human being seems to be essentially *In-der-Kultur-Sein* instead of Heidegger's *In-der-Welt-Sein*. It

> means that all human thoughts and actions are constituted by culture and the world of culture serves as a horizon for any possible activity. Consequently philosophy has no universal truths at its disposal and is nothing but an expression of the "spirit of an age."[15]

Let us consider whether this viewpoint can be sustained.

Despite the diversity of cultures, we cannot escape the fact that things simply *are*, and thus are the same for all of humanity. Although culture can affect how we view even ordinary things around us, this must not be understood to mean that reality itself is constructed. Philosophy has long claimed the ability to discover and express truths about reality, including metaphysical truths. Such truths claim a universality founded in the nature of things, such as (at the simplest) the principles of non-contradiction or of identity. But since such truths must be stated in words, and words not only are in a particular language but imply some kind of intellectual heritage, how or to what extent is the wording of such statements bound to a particular culture? And on the other hand, to what extent can something be expressed in different words and in the context of a different intellectual tradition and still signify the same truth?

In the first place, therefore, our question concerns language, language as a medium for expression of concepts or propositions, a point of difficulty long ago recognized with regard to translation. As the ancient Greek translator of the Old Testament book of Sirach (Ecclesiasticus) wrote, "For what was originally expressed in Hebrew does not have exactly the same sense when translated into another language" (Sirach, prologue). Languages divide up reality in somewhat different ways, the denotations, and still more the connotations of words in different tongues differ, and a language may even lack a word for a particular concept. Hilaire Belloc sketched some of these difficulties in his Oxford lecture on translation.

> The reason there are no such things as exact equivalents between two terms in two different languages lies in two characters of the Word. First each word, however simply used, is used with multiplicity of meaning. Secondly, the history of a word, its use in the prose and verse of the language to which it belongs, its sound-value in that language, its connection in the mind of the cultured reader of that language with its use in certain masterpieces and remembered phrases, and in general all the atmosphere of its being, make it one thing in one language from what it is in another even where the use being made of it is similar.[16]

15 Viik, "What about the Philosophy of Culture?", 247.

16 "On Translation" (1931) in *Belloc, a Biographical Anthology*, edited by Herbert Van Thal (New York: Alfred A. Knopf, 1970), 291-92.

St. Thomas Aquinas gives a concrete instance of this association of meanings beyond their merely verbal denotation in the following discussion of Greek and Latin theological terminology.

> It is said among the Greeks...that the Father and the Son and the Holy Spirit are three hypostases; among the Latins however, it is incorrect [*non rectesonat*], if anyone says that they are three substances, although hypostasis means the same among the Greeks as substance among Latins according to the literal meaning. For among Latins substance usually is taken for essence, which both we and the Greeks confess to be one in the Deity. On account of which, as the Greeks say three hypostases, we say three persons.... Whence it pertains to the duty of a good translator that...he preserve the meaning, [but] that he change the mode of speaking according to the properties of the language into which he translates. (*Contra ErroresGraecorum*, part 1, prologue)

We have here a question of varying customary meanings attached to technical terms, so that although hypostasis - from *hyphistasthai*, to stand under - literally means the same as substance, on account of the Latin usage of substance as equivalent to essence, an obvious difficulty and source of error would arise were hypostasis translated into Latin as substance [*substantia*]. If linguistic confusion could arise in the case of two cultural worlds that shared much common history and had similar intellectual climates, both professing the same religious faith, how much more so when we consider two cultural worlds unknown to each other, each perhaps with long and sophisticated intellectual traditions of its own.

This last point brings up the further and more complex question of the culturally-conditioned nature of every language. Can the concepts expressed in one language simply be transferred into another, even allowing for such translation difficulties as we just looked at?

And in light of the necessary origin of any statement from within a particular culture, can we reasonably maintain its universality and thus its applicability to all humanity? Does such a statement necessarily carry with it its own cultural outlook, and does this vitiate its claim to universality? One approach to this question is the following.

> [N]o assertion of universality takes place apart from a cultural norm, and, given the array of contesting norms that constitute the international field, no assertion can be made without at once requiring a cultural translation. Without translation, the very concept of universality cannot cross the linguistic borders it claims, in principle, to be able to cross. Or we might put it another way: without translation, the only way the assertion of universality can cross a border is through a colonial and expansionist logic.[17]

17 Judith Butler, "Restaging the Universal: Hegemony and the Limits of Formalism" in Judith Butler, et al., *Contingency, Hegemony, Universality: Contemporary Dialogues on the Left* (London: Verso, 2000), 35.

But let us look more closely at the dilemma asserted or implied here, which, it seems to me, needs to be clarified.

It would appear that Butler is not raising the question of whether a concept such as universality can be *understood* in another culture, but whether the acceptance of a concept that originated in a different culture necessarily represents "a colonial and expansionist logic." Does the existence of various cultures with their own intellectual traditions require that concepts themselves be altered to reflect the ideas native to those different cultures? Surely, however, the idea of universality is true or false, and if true, is applicable anywhere, even if not previously recognized everywhere, or even if in need of explanation in order to be understood. Although certain ideas have originated in particular places, and no doubt reflect in some manner the cultures of those places, this does not mean that in principle the expression of such ideas is so shaped by a particular culture as to be an improper imposition on the rest of humanity.

It seems, then, that the objections which we have considered do not constitute a definitive barrier to understanding or to the dissemination of truths across languages or cultures. Despite any theoretical difficulties raised by the existence of culturally different worlds, in practice humanity has been able to understand other modes of thinking and speaking, at least after sufficient study and effort. Naturally we should avoid any hasty claim that we have grasped the meaning of unfamiliar terms and systems of thought, but it does not follow that with patience we cannot achieve a sufficient understanding. Truths can be expressed not only in various languages, but any truths can be appropriated by other cultures.

A point, moreover, usually overlooked by those who assert in any absolute manner that "philosophy has no universal truths at its disposal," is that this difficulty likewise arises in the case of cultures separated by time as well as place, and while we acknowledge the difficulties of comprehending earlier cultures, we do not usually despair of doing so. Rather we work to improve our understanding and to discard preconceived ideas and prevent the simple transfer of modern notions to the past. And we rightly assume some success, even if not perfect.

Whether or not we can rightly make use of ideas that originate in one culture outside that particular culture arises most pointedly in connection with the claim that philosophy as traditionally developed in Western culture does in fact possess a universality unique in the world. Is it correct to say, as Jacques Maritain did, "It was in Greece alone that philosophy achieved her autonomy and was explicitly distinguished from religion"?[18] Is this claim true, or is it ipso facto an example of

18 Jacques Maritain, *An Introduction to Philosophy* (London: Sheed and Ward, 1947), 33. Cf. Edmund Husserl's remarks on this point in his famous 1935 Vienna Lecture, which are substantially in agreement with Maritain. This lecture is reproduced in Husserl, *The Crisis of European Sciences and Transcendental Phenomenology* (Evanston: Northwestern University, 1970), and his remarks appear at 279-80.

"a colonial and expansionist logic"? And what does this imply about the adoption of European philosophy in other cultures?

If philosophy as understood in the Greek tradition does uniquely offer the fundamental intellectual tools to understand reality, then it could hardly constitute "a colonial and expansionist logic" if that philosophy is received in other cultures. If it changes aspects of the intellectual life of those cultures, then it does so by way of modifying them in the interest of a better perception and understanding of reality. If the philosophical use of reason as that developed in Greece has been able to discover many truths about God, man and the world, the mere fact that such exercise of reason developed originally in one place hardly seems to constitute an objection that it is culturally bound in any limiting sense - at least any important limiting sense. Whether in fact what Maritain said is true, whether the proper autonomy of philosophy developed only in the Greek tradition, is beyond the scope of this paper to consider.[19] But if what Maritain claims is correct, and the Greek philosophical tradition does constitute a unique method of investigating and attaining those truths which are proper to philosophical inquiry, then it seems to me to enjoy a rightful claim to a status as something fundamentally transcultural, despite the fact that it originated within one particular culture and undoubtedly bears certain marks of that cultural origin.[20]

At the same time as it is widely asserted that Western philosophy is merely one cultural expression among many, with no special status to be accorded it, there is one kind of knowledge which is widely seen as transcultural, although that also originated in the Western world. This is the domain of the natural sciences. Science is cultivated in all parts of the world, scientists collaborate with one another regardless of their homelands, and education in physics, chemistry, biology and so on is essentially the same everywhere. As a result, it is regarded as an impersonal technique both for ascertaining the truth about reality and for controlling it in the interests of human welfare. But there is much to be said against this view and in favor of the opinion that the natural sciences, though obviously powerful tools for manipulating matter, are in large part a reflection of cultural trends that arose in the modern West.

The viewpoint that the natural sciences are not a straightforward means for the discovery of truth about reality is often associated with the work of Thomas

19 On this see, for example, Carine Defoort, "Is there Such a Thing as Chinese Philosophy? Arguments of an Implicit Debate," *Philosophy East and West* 51, no. 3 [2001]: 393-413 or Min OuYang, "There is No Need for *ZhongguoZhexue* to be Philosophy," *Asian Philosophy, An International Journal of the Philosophical Traditions of the East* 21, no. 3 [2012]: 199-223.

20 Of course, in the West today there are many competing ways of doing philosophy, not all of which can communicate well with each other or which even recognize each other as being properly philosophy, even though all of them share a common past that can trace its origins back to the ancient Greeks.

Kuhn and his 1962 book, *The Structure of Scientific Revolutions*,[21] although this thesis is by no means unique to him. His view, in brief, is that the vast field of nature cannot be investigated in an orderly fashion without some prior theory or "paradigm" which claims at least to be able to sketch how nature, or some aspect thereof, is constituted. "And since nature is too complex and varied to be explored at random, that map [paradigm] is as essential as observation and experiment to science's continuing development."[22] Confronted with the varied and vast amount of material provided by the natural world, scientists must obviously choose among many possible experiments and observations, and they do not usually make such choices at random.

> Science does not deal in all possible laboratory manipulations. Instead, it selects those relevant to the juxtaposition of a paradigm with the immediate experience that that paradigm has partially determined. As a result, scientists with different paradigms engage in different concrete laboratory manipulations.[23]

Other twentieth-century philosophers and historians have said things very similar. For example, the literary scholar and intellectual historian, C. S. Lewis, in one of his last books, *The Discarded Image*, spoke of the scientific enterprise in ways quite close to Kuhn.

> It would therefore be subtly misleading to say 'The medievals thought the universe to be like that, but we know it to be like this'. Part of what we now know is that we cannot, in the old sense, 'know what the universe is like' and that no model we can build will be, in that old sense, 'like' it.

And he concludes significantly a few pages later: "We can no longer dismiss the change of Models as a simple progress from error to truth. No Model is a catalogue of ultimate realities, and none is a mere fantasy."[24]

In fact, the acceptance of scientific theories has not been free from the cultural trends which influence other areas of thought. It is generally accepted, for example, that the initial acceptance of Copernican astronomy was not because of its superior scientific status or because of rigorous observational data.

> First of all, there were no known celestial phenomena which were not accounted for by the Ptolemaic method with as great accuracy as could be

21 Chicago: University of Chicago, 1st ed. 1962, 2nd. ed., 1970. All references are to the 2nd edition.

22 *Ibid.*, 109.

23 *Ibid.*, 126.

24 *The Discarded Image* (Cambridge University Press, 1964, 1971 printing), 216-218, 222. Lewis' entire approach is very similar to Kuhn's, for example in his discussion of paradigm change (he does not use that term) on 219-222 and Lewis's very Kuhnian statement that "nature gives most of her evidence in answer to the questions we ask her" (223).

> expected without more modern instruments. Predictions of astronomical events were made which varied no more from the actual occurrence than did predictions made by a Copernican.[25]

Jacob Klein posits that the reason that people "insisted that the Copernican system was truth without sufficient evidence" lay in certain Renaissance intellectual fashions, for example, in an interest in the ancient Greek cult of the sun.

> Now, for the first time in a long period, the sun has recovered its former position of dignity, which we observe in Plato, in the neo-Platonic tradition, and in a certain cult called the Mithras cult.... Now this tradition [of the sun cult]...was perfectly well known to Copernicus and his followers. Copernicus himself mentions in the tenth chapter of the first book that the sun is the lamp of a very beautiful temple, lantern of the world, mind of the world, mentor of the world. He quotes Hermes Trismegistus...as having called the sun the visible God.[26]

From this we can see that the idea that scientists do their work with no reference to the surrounding intellectual atmosphere, isolated in a pure pursuit of truth, is hardly the case. Like other investigators, they are influenced by their own cultures and the intellectual trends of their environment, and they reflect those trends in their work.

One obvious objection that can be raised to the viewpoints expressed by Kuhn or Lewis, an objection that is often considered as a decisive refutation of their views, is that science *works*. The technological application of science proves that it gives a more or less accurate account of the universe, no doubt in need of correction at many points, but in the main corresponding to what really exists. But perhaps surprisingly, this need not be the case. For example, what is called celestial navigation, navigation on the earth's surface by means of the apparent position of stars and other heavenly bodies, still used today, is based not on the heliocentric astronomy of Copernicus and his successors, but on the framework of spheres and planetary motion characteristic of the geocentric model of Ptolemy. Geocentric astronomy can produce usable results, even though it was long ago rejected as a true description of the natural world.

> The navigator is concerned less with the actual motions of celestial bodies than with their apparent motions as viewed from the Earth. The heavens are pictured as a hollow celestial sphere of infinite radius, with the Earth as its center and the various celestial bodies on its inner surface.[27]

---

25 E. A. Burtt, *The Metaphysical Foundations of Modern Science* (Garden City, N.Y.: Doubleday, rev. ed. 1932), 36.

26 "The Copernican Revolution" in *Lectures and Essays*, edited by Robert B. Williamson and Elliott Zuckerman. (Annapolis : St. John's College, c. 1985), 109-110.

27 Alton B. Moody, "Celestial navigation" in *McGraw-Hill Encyclopedia of Science and Technology*, Vol. 3 (New York : McGraw-Hill, 8th ed., 1997), 361-2.

If one wishes to consider Copernicus' theory as true, then one must admit that a false theory can produce usable results. On the other hand, if one looks at both Ptolemy and Copernicus as working according to paradigms, neither of which perfectly coincides with the real world, then that argues for the view of science associated with both Kuhn and Lewis.

If these arguments are correct, then it is wrong to look at the natural sciences as so many disciplines pursuing the truth about nature abstracted from cultural models and the general intellectual climate. The questions that are asked by scientists are potentially infinite, and, at least since the sixteenth century, their intellectual project has been closely linked with the modern Western desire to dominate nature. The fact that this conception of science has come to be accepted throughout the world speaks only to its technological effectiveness.

> The world has been made one, first by European trade, conquest and colonization, and later by Western science and technology. And behind the railway, the motor lorry and the airplane, there has spread a wave of secular ideas which had their origins in Europe....[28]

If for no other reason than military technology, all nations that can afford to do so have imported and used the science and technology that originated in the Western world. But although obviously such science *works*, it does not follow that its claimed description or model of reality accurately corresponds to the real world.

It may seem odd that I have defended the ability of philosophy to speak truths across cultural boundaries, while at the same time calling into doubt the truth claims uttered by modern science. But the two cases are not the same. Philosophers certainly can err, but philosophy in principle seeks to know what is knowable about God, man and the world by means of the use of reason. No doubt, as I noted above, philosophers have been influenced by the general cultural trends of the societies in which they lived. But philosophies can live within widely different cultures, such as the tradition flowing from Aristotle which has lived in the ancient Greek *polis*, the Hellenistic empires, medieval Europe and even in the modern world. The questions it asks are fundamental questions about reality, and philosophers of all ages and places are free to offer their comments and critiques of its doctrines, and it has matured under their criticisms.

Modern science, on the other hand, has as its primary focus to control, not to understand. Though certainly the techniques which it has discovered are real, and although in certain areas it can point to truths of nature that is has uncovered, its investigations are always undertaken according to a paradigm (Kuhn) or model (Lewis). This question becomes important within a discussion of culture because the natural sciences are uncritically taken to embody transcultural knowledge and

28 Christopher Dawson, *Christianity in East & West* (La Salle, Ill.: Sherwood Sugden, c. 1959) 104-5.

to be perhaps the only or best example of such knowledge. Thus if we recognize that its status as a neutral discoverer of truths about the world around us can be called in question, we will be less ready to regard it as the best example of humanity's ability to know reality across cultural boundaries.

4. Conclusion

Philosophical concern with culture parallels philosophical concern with humanity and all its institutions. Just as political philosophy seeks to understand man as a political creature and what necessarily follows from that understanding, so the philosophy of culture attempts to understand humanity as necessarily living in culture. The cultural structures which humanity has built are fascinating in their complexity and differences and the concept of culture serves as a means of unifying interest in the religious and intellectual, the social, and the material aspects of mankind's life. If philosophy is to remain vital and assist humanity in its quest to understand both ourselves and the rest of reality, then it must turn its attention to all the facets of human life. Culture is surely one of the most important of these. If the philosophy of culture becomes more recognized as a part of philosophy, even though we can hardly expect a general agreement about all points, perhaps we will no longer have to say, "Denn, was heisstKulturphilosophie? Esgibtwohlkeineallgemeinakzeptierte Definition von dies!"

Bibliography

Barloewen, C. von (1989). *Werte in der Kulturphilosophie Nord- und Lateinamerikas*, Athenäum, Frankfurt am M.

Belloc, H. (1970). "On Translation" in H. Van Thal (ed.), *Belloc, a Biographical Anthology*, Alfred A Knopf, New York, 285-307.

Belloc, H. (1992) "The Two Cultures of the West," in *Essays of a Catholic*, TAN, Rockford, Ill., 237-245.

Benedict, R. (1934). *Patterns of Culture*, Houghton Mifflin, Boston.

Brock, S. (2006).*Kulturphilosophie: Bohr, Cassirer, Wittgenstein, Cavell, MacIntyre, Winch, Taylor [und] Haraway: Sechs Vorlesungen am Humboldt Universitätzu Berlin, August 2006*. Available at http:// pure.au.dk/portal/files/41412787/kulturphilosophie.pdf

Burtt, E. (1932). *The Metaphysical Foundations of Modern Science*, Doubleday, Garden City, N.Y.

Butler, J. (2000). "Restaging the Universal: Hegemony and the Limits of Formalism" in J. Butler et al., *Contingency, Hegemony, Universality: Contemporary Dialogues on the Left*, Verso, London, 11-43.

Chapter 5

The Nature of Political Philosophy

James V. Schall

"Then we're not legislating impossibilities or indulging in mere wishful thinking, since the law we established is in accord with nature. It is rather the way things are at present that seems to be against nature."

– Plato, *Republic*, 456c

I.

In this universe, members of the human race are the "mortals." That is, they are unique beings in the sense that they will die. But all living, corporeal beings, not just men, die. What is the difference? The difference is that men know that they will die. Understanding what a human being is, then, includes this awareness of its finitude in this world. The "when" one dies is not certain, the "that" is. Whether the fact of death might have been otherwise, whether a world lacking in death could exist, is an abiding topic of human speculation.

But even though science sometimes claims that we can lengthen human life to hundreds of years, a grasping for inner-worldly immortality, it is difficult to see how such a lengthy life would be anything but agonizing. Death in this light of on-going existence in this world seems a blessing. This realization of some wisdom in death is why the second form of immortality, that of the soul or spirit, came into play. Immortality may be intimated by a conscious experience of knowing unchangeable being and principle. But it is also brought in view because of the general awareness that the injustice of individual human lives is not always punished and virtue not always rewarded in this life, no matter how long it lasts. Our lives, in other words, have something to do, not with how long we live, but with how we live while we are in this world for whatever length, wherever or whenever human beings live.

What human beings are plays itself out against the background of the particular death of each person who comes to be in the universe. Any society at any time, be it tribal or political, is filled with members who are being conceived and born, growing up, reaching maturity, then old age, and death. The membership of any lasting society is transitory in this sense. Though polities themselves also pass away in time, usually they last well beyond the life span of given individuals who compose them. Members of any polity are here for a time, then pass on. This motal condition allows for both newness and tradition, for replacement and continuity.

Most people who have ever lived on this planet do not live out the famous "four score and ten" (90) years said to be allotted to some of the more vigorous. But few of those who live so long are able actively to participate in what might be called the "ordinary" affairs of mankind, that is, the economic efforts to keep alive and prosper, the efforts to identify what is good and what is evil, and the efforts to attend to things of nobility and beauty. The classical comments of Socrates in book one of the *Republic* and of Cicero in his essay "On Old Age," were designed to address the issue of the importance of age and wisdom to a human community from which the individual citizens would sooner or later depart.[1]

Philosophy is said to be itself a "preparation" for death. Politics, however, are held to be what we do before death, that is, what we do during the period from our conception and birth through our education, public life, old age, and death. Politics concerns the life of the mortal being while he is "mortal", while he lives, flourishes, and declines. The connection between how we live and how we die is not arbitrary. The oft-repeated notion that "we die as we lived" is designed to stress this relationship. The notion of asking for "forgiveness" for aberrant personal acts implies an effort to reconnect how we did live to how we ought to have lived. One of the original purposes of having a political order in the first place was to establish a rule of law and justice whereby disorder could be punished and order restored. No political order in history has achieved more than limited success in this endeavor. This fact leaves the question of justice open to something beyond politics.

Man, though he belongs to the mortals, is not merely a "mortal." He is also seen to have something about him that is "divine" or "immortal." Politics has something to do with this "immortality". The human dignity of each person is related to the fact that something about him exists that is more than political or finite. The word "immortality" itself has two related meanings. The polity was set up so that the passing words and deeds of men who lived in them would not be lost to the generations that followed them. This is why we have monuments, poems, and written words. To know what we are, we need to know what we have

1 Plato, *The Republic*, 328a-331d; Cicero, "On Old Age," *Selected Works* (Harmondsworth: Penguin 1971), 211-50.

been and done. We need to know the record of great men and terrible tyrants, as well as the deeds and words of ordinary people.

Thus, we have an "inner-worldly" immortality that consists of our remembering those who have lived before us, who have shown by their lives and deeds what is great and what is heinous. Polities, consequently, are "founded" so that what we have done or what we ought to have done are not forgotten. Polities are constituted with "authority" to decide on what ways of action and word are to be followed and why. This "founding" is not arbitrary but has many elements that can vary. There are often many good ways of doing many differing things.

Likewise, there are many ways to put into effect what is wrong or evil. The freedom that human beings possess is a freedom that follows on their intelligence, not a freedom that lacks any direction or order. Freedom means that we can do evil, but that we need not. Freedom does not make the difference between good and evil but recognizes it and seeks to act accordingly. Man is free to choose evil, but not without choosing it under the aspect of its being good. This is why the controversies of reason about what is true and good are unavoidable. A free polity is one that is open to such discussions as fundamental to its public order.

II.

When we inquire about the "nature" of something, we want to know and understand *what it is*. This endeavor to know what something, besides ourselves, is assumes that something exists in the universe that is worth knowing. We ourselves are legitimate members of this same universe. We can tell the difference between what is real and what is imagined. Once we know something is real, we can imagine something that is not real. Not to be able to tell the difference between what is real and what is imagined is a sign or madness or derangement.

We also observe that not everything is exactly the same, though all things do have some things about them that are rightly common. Nothing is so different that we have no way of identifying it. If each thing is simply unique and diverse, nothing can be said about it. All efforts to speak about it become artificial constructs with no relation to what is being identified. It is not an accident that a polity is defined as a place where speech is to be grounded in a reality that can be verified as true. We can know what is "out there" and affirm its reality. The only way a polity can be held accountable for the acts of its leaders and citizens is if there is a standard in which all acts and words can be grounded.

Political entitles are not direct produces of nature like vegetation or animals. They are not "substances". But they are "natural" once we have human beings who can act together to achieve something, in this case a common life. In this sense, politics are a reality but not a *substance*, not another "being" with a "life" independent of the citizens who compose it. Rather a polity describes rational beings insofar as they related to one another to form an association in which many goods can best be achieved, particularly the development of a virtuous life of the citizenry. To say that man is "political" by nature means that he will invariably put this organization into existence once he comes to a point where he needs to act in common to achieve goods that are worthwhile but impossible to achieve solely by himself.

In this sense, the polity is not set up as opposed to men's achieving what they can by themselves but as completing what they can achieve in a more complete form in union with others. Since man's life is finite and temporal insofar as he is mortal and political, the polity is a late-arrival. Many things are necessary before it can fully develop, just as when it is finally organized, it is by its own nature open to something that is not properly itself. This is one reason why the academy, while a proper institution of any common good, it not itself simply another agency of rule. The academy is, or should be, a sphere in which not only politics but what is beyond politics can be freely and reasonably addressed. The good of any polity requires that it grant a space for what is not just political. Otherwise, it will not understand the limited sphere in which politics is to be itself.

By adding the word "political" to the word "philosophy", we do not intend to change the nature of either politics or of philosophy. We can say that "politics" is a legitimate object of philosophical inquiry. Likewise, we can say that the politician needs to know what intelligence and mind are about lest he misunderstand the nature and good of the citizens who are to be ruled and guided to the many ends to which they are open. The temptation to tyranny is, at its most dangerous, the subsumption of philosophy into a politics which allows no purpose but itself.

Politics are concerned with human action and interaction insofar as men are organized together by custom and law to attain a common good. Private goods are perfectly valid and should be protected and encouraged. The common good is not a sum of private goods. The "nature" of each human being is such that he needs a polity to be what he ought to be. That good is not just any "good" or "desirable" thing. The common good is what is good for what it is to be a human being in all its variety and breadth. The common good means that there are goods that cannot be attained by oneself alone or even by small groupings, which are themselves necessary to any common good. Neither politics nor philosophy means anything if there is no mind to think them. The fact of beings with minds existing in the universe is not the result of human agency. It is a given. Thinking is not caused by politics. Politics is the result of thinking.

All things that flow from this givenness of human reality are themselves implicit in the original power to know. Among these powers that flow from reason is the use of the mind to relate human beings one to another in a coherent social unit in which beings with reason could participate because they could know. The origin of politics is not, as such, force. Force, though not intrinsically irrational in its use, always appears as the result of a failure to use reason with an effort to correct its improper use. To say that man is a "political being" means that he is a being capable of causing associations based on reason in order to achieve his further purposes. Most of the things most needed in life are only achieved with the ordered cooperation of others. This cooperation presumes intelligence and freedom, with a limit based on truth.

In other words, *what it is to be man* is not itself subject to the function of politics. It is assumed by it. If man were not already a rational being, politics could not make him so. Any politics that rests solely on force cannot transform itself into reason. But a reasonable being can understand why force is sometimes needed in every political order. In order to know the whole of "things political", we need to know not just the good or best regimes, but also the worst and those in-between. The total comprehension of "things political" includes understanding the reasons for disordered regimes. Aristotle even explains, for our understanding, how to be a "good" tyrant, as if to say, that the complete knowledge of what is good includes what is not good.[2]

Philosophy seeks the knowledge of the whole. Its proper object is *all that is*. Aristotle tells us that politics is the highest of the practical sciences but not the highest science.[3] The highest science is metaphysics or ontology, including the causes of being. Its object is being as such, *what* is. It we deny the force or existence of metaphysics, we automatically make politics into a pseudo-metaphysics that claims to be able to account for all things by its own practical methods. Politics is the highest "practical" science, not the highest science as such. Practical knowledge presupposes an end that is given to it, one not constructed or made by man. Politics deals with the means to attain a given end already contained in *what man is*. When politics claims to define ends and not means, it has absorbed metaphysics into itself.

When it is said that Machiavelli is the founder of "modern" political philosophy, it means that the "prudence" that guides particular human action to its highest good is replaced by the "art" whereby the politician artist directs the polity to an end defined by nothing but the ruler, whether he be prince or democrat. In this sense, modern politics is defined by the loss of a natural end that limits the politician to *what* is. This limitation is the charter of any possibility of a critique in the name of reason of any existing regime.[4] From Machiavelli's premise, carried forward by Hobbes, the good state is not that one in conformity with human nature. Rather it is one that corresponds to what the prince or democrat wants. In other words, the politician is not limited by anything but his own will. Such a view, as Aquinas had pointed out, goes back to the principle of Roman Law that "Whatever the prince wills, is the law."[5] This recurrent position in the history of

---

2 Aristotle, *Politics*, 1313a33-17b26.

3 Aristotle, *Ethics*, 1141a20-22.

4 See James V. Schall, *At the Limits of Political Philosophy* (Washington: The Catholic University of America Press, 1996).

5 Thomas Aquinas, "Treatise on Law", *Summa Theologiae*, I-II, 90, 1, obj. 3, ad 3.

political philosophy is the origin of a voluntarism that has no reference to being as a check on its scope of power.

III.

Political philosophy begins with the trials of Socrates and Christ, that is, with the presence before the laws of an existing state of the philosopher or prophet for being what he claimed to be. Both Socrates and Christ obeyed the laws of the polity under which they were tried.[6] Their trials were not "illegal" in any technical sense. The Athenian jury and the Roman governor did not violate any procedural laws in the course of either trial. But, as readers of accounts of these trials throughout subsequent history have recognized, there was obviously something wrong with both legal scenes. Was the problem in the laws themselves, which were generally considered the best laws of their time, or in the souls of those who executed authority?

Both Socrates and Christ died obeying the laws of the states in which they were executed. Paradoxically, the only way for them to leave the question open with regard to their innocence or guilt was to die willingly. Socrates lives, as he tells us in the *Crito*, according to the laws of Athens. He did not want to destroy its laws by refusing to obey them at his death. His death that brings us back to the relation of mortality to immortality, as he tells us in his *Apology*.[7] Socrates dies in peace obeying the laws because he knows his death is itself a judgment of those who wrongly tried and executed him. Christ died before a Roman governor who was not sufficiently concerned with truth to find out what was happening before him.

Neither Socrates nor Christ wrote a book entitled: "What Is Political Philosophy?"[8] Yet, we know about them because accounts of their trials were written by Plato and Xenophon, by Matthew, Mark, Luke, and John. Some there are, no doubt, who go away from these public trials and executions to conclude that both Socrates and Christ should have been sentenced. They were guilty of upsetting the settled political order of the polities in which they lived. The authorities were merely looking for public peace. "It is better that one man die than the whole nation perish" (John 11:50). Such a principle deftly bypasses the question of justice which is what a city was set up to uphold. A polity has a "right" to defend itself against those who undermine the existing public order. The language of "rights" based on the will of the prince is consistent with itself

6 See James V. Schall, *The Politics of Heaven and Hell* (Lanham, Md.: University Press of America, 1984), 21-38; Schall, *At the Limits of Political Philosophy*, Ibid, 104-22.

7 Plato, *Crito, 49a-54d;* Apology, 38c-42a.

8 See Leo Strauss, "What Is Political Philosophy?" *What Is Political Philosophy and Other Essays* (Glencoe, Il.: The Free Press, 1959), 5-55; Charles N. R. McCoy, *The Structure of Political Thought* (New York: McGraw-Hill, 1963); Robert Sokolowski, "The Human Person and Political Life," *Christian Faith & Human Understanding* (Washington: The Catholic University of America P:ress, 2005), 179-198.

but not with the truth. It is this latter principle that mostly measures political entities today. Obedience to the laws means accepting whatever the ruler "wills".

Others, knowing of the same trials, are thus less happy with their results. They are aware of a possible conflict between philosophy and polity. When, as a young man, Plato witnessed the fate of his mentor and friend Socrates, he could not but ask himself: "Must it always happen this way?" "Will something like these trials eventually exist in and undermine every polity?" "Or, is there a place where philosophy and politics can exist in harmony?" It is in this sense that the origin of political philosophy arose from the soul of the young Plato. He asked the questions that demanded reasonable answers, not just solutions of power.

Plato clearly concluded that only in argument, only in speech, could the conflict be resolved. And Christ taught, in effect, that only in the transcendent order could the practical conflicts ever be resolved. All existing political orders would be less than perfect. Indeed, the implication was that the most dangerous political order was in fact the one that did claim to be perfect in this world. More philosophers and prophets have been killed by regimes claiming perfection in this world than by the pragmatists like Pilate who was just trying to avoid problems. This conclusion meant, in practice, that all existing regimes would be more or less imperfect. This conclusion did not mean that some regimes were not better than others.

The description of regimes in terms of better or worse was one of the functions of Aristotle's *Politics*. He distinguished between good regimes that ruled according to law and bad regimes that ruled according to the end of the ruling man or body. What this classification meant, in effect, was that certain basic issues that every person had to cope with were, in principle, "beyond politics". But it also meant that existing regimes could be the context in which a repetition of the fate of Socrates and Christ was repeated in other times and in other forms. Most regimes, even the worst, have in fact attempted to avoid being in the position of making martyrs of its philosophers and religious leaders. When they have been killed, it was usually on the same justification that Socrates and Christ were killed, namely, as threats to the state and its laws.

Modern democratic theory, in its own way, tried to avoid this confrontation by reducing to insignificance the import of metaphysics and revelation. But most modern democratic regimes came to base themselves on the principle that nothing was higher than the positive laws of the state. If something was "legal", it was therefore moral. Any disagreement would be considered a "private" matter. The classic problem of tyranny did not exempt democracies from its scope. Indeed, democratic tyrannies can prove to be even more dangerous than the classic ones described by either Plato or Hobbes. Whether a king, a dictator, a parliament, or a democracy be the body that enforces the principle that the positive laws of the state are the only laws, it will still be classified as a tyranny in the broader understanding of that term. It means that the will of the ruler is the law.

IV.

What much modern democratic theory and Islam have in common is a form of philosophic voluntarism. In principle, both are rooted in the pseudo-metaphysics that stems from denying that there is such a thing as a human nature that is itself not subject to political manipulation. Put more broadly, we have systems of voluntarism, whether rooted in the will of the prince or the will of Allah, that deny the stable nature of any existing thing, particularly of any human thing. Man is infinitely malleable. He can be the opposite of what he is without inconsistency, or so it is claimed. There is no standard or reason that measures actions other than of that authority that can will the opposite of what it willed before.

In the initial passage cited from Plato, he remarks on the possibility that the *things that are* at present are contrary to nature. What is he saying here? He implies that nature can remain normative or ruling for human beings in a polity even if the actual polities that they create and live in are in fact contrary to the human nature that ought to be. This means that a criterion whereby to judge disordered regimes was the major reason Plato wanted everyone to have a "city in speech" that was capable of retaining an order of good even if it did not exist in political reality. Without a city in speech or mind, we are limited to the existing laws when it comes to evaluating their justice. The figures of Socrates and Christ in political philosophy abidingly stand as judgments on existing regimes.

Plato noted that the best regime was not just "wishful thinking". Indeed, existing regimes are more in the nature of "wishful thinking" insofar as they deviate from the good and insist on calling themselves the best practical regimes about which nothing better can be imagined. This is Machiavelli's regime that contains not what men ought to do but what they "do" do. In other words, it is a regime that refuses any criticism of its laws based on a higher law in which the sins and errors of actual regimes are requited, as Plato argued they would be in the last book of the *Republic*. In this sense, Plato's "city in speech" is not a utopia, a wishful thinking designed to be embodied in this world, but a permanent criterion by which the dangers of utopia in this world are recognized and existing regimes are not exempt from standards they do not formulate or observe.

Theoretic voluntarism was invented or argued from both political and theological sources. It meant that reason did not direct will but was subject to it, in its service. No "objective" truth or reality existed to correct what is willed. In the West, the line from Scotus, Occam, Marsilius of Padua, to Hobbes resulted in a concept of the good of the state as dependent on the will of the Leviathan. Eventually, this Leviathan could have monarchic, legislative, or democratic forms. The Roman Law principle, "whatever the prince wills, is the law", as we saw, had already envisioned this principle. It exempts the prince from any reference to a transcendent criterion that would limit his rule. The absolute supremacy of the English parliament was based on the same notion. In Islam, voluntarism arose because of contradictions in the Qur'an that needed to be justified.

If Allah could command both *jihad* and peace, both violence and non-violence, it was necessary to explain why this view was at all justifiable. If God or the Leviathan were pure will, and if reality itself had within it no order or natural law, then all that men could do would be to submit to the will of the god or ruler. Submission to the law, whatever it was, became the only "virtue' required. Men did not have to ask; indeed they could not ask, whether the law of the state and the law of the god were in conflict with reason. Any grounds for asking such a question had been eliminated by the premises of voluntarism.

The well-being of men in polities depends, ultimately, on the thought on which their polities are built. But the thought behind polities is itself a result of thought about *what is*. It is not merely thought about politics alone. To understand politics, we always need to know more than politics. Aristotle had noticed in the last book of his *Politics* that what happens in a good regime is a passage from politics to leisure. The term "leisure" (*skole*) did not mean relaxation or laziness. It meant the intense activity and curiosity about all things that comes when material needs are met.

Mere physical well-being produces a life, as Glaucon said in the second book of the *Republic*, fit only for "pigs".[9] He did not mean that physical well-being was bad, but that it was just the foundation, the presupposition for considering what human life really meant. The key question became: "What do we do when all else is done?" We seek in peace, free from ordinary needs, to know the truth of things.[10] In this sense, the polity exists that sufficient virtue might be present to transcend immediate needs and disorders of soul to arrive at a free and true understanding of *what is*.

When we have a good regime, what is it we "do"? In other words, are politics sufficient for man? In a famous passage in the *Politics*, Aristotle brought up the question of the "wickedness" that is found in every existing regime as rooted in human beings.[11] Such "wickedness" seems endemic to human nature as it actually exists. It is Machiavelli's justification for saying that politics do not deal with what men "ought" to do, but with what they do "do".[12] But if this *what men "do" do* becomes our criterion of rule, we necessarily end up justifying some evil in the name of what men "do" do instead of striving to correct it on the basis of a justice we know of from the city in speech or reason.

Aristotle suggested that, if the reason for this "wickedness" was that men were hungry, they could be given property to supply their needs by themselves. If it was because of pleasure, they could be taught virtue. But if this "wickedness" was just because men wanted power to do what they wanted, there was no solution

9 Plato, *The Republic*, 372d.

10 See Joseph Pieper, *Leisure: The Basis of Culture* (San Francisco: Ignatius Press, 2009); James V. Schall, *On the Unseriousness of Human Affairs* (Wilmington: ISI Books, 2001.

11 Aristotle, *Politics*, 1263b20.

12 Machiavelli, *The Prince* (Harmondsworth: Penguin 1999), Chapter 15.

but philosophy.[13] Why philosophy? Philosophy was the only discipline that could actually confront the adequacy of the reasons given for one's supposed self-rule over all of nature. Augustine was later to treat of this issue under the notion of pride.

But there was one problem with this approach. It was a problem that every politician who was a good man but not a philosopher had to face. And a mistake here could be fatal for himself and his polity. This is the problem of the sophists, of the philosophers whose souls are corrupt or whose minds are themselves not ordered to any true good. This is, as it were, the Socratic political problem, the problem of Athens, the city of philosophy, the best existing city. It did not recognize the philosopher when he appeared before them. The citizens did not want to "examine their lives", as Socrates had often tried to incite them to do.[14]

If present societies are "against nature", as Plato suggested that they might well be, we will not likely find any society according to nature among the existing cities. This conclusion takes us back to the philosophers who are like the captain of the ship in book six of the *Republic*. The sailor/citizens thought him mad. They were not able to recognize him because their own souls were in disorder. Their state ships lurched randomly all over the range of evil and good.

Thus, in conclusion, we return to our original inquiry about "the nature of political philosophy". We must recognize that political philosophy is a discipline of thought. It recognizes not just that some regimes are better than others because we can know what is good, but also that some philosophical systems are truer than others. The politician knows how sophists, undisciplined or unwise academia, can undermine his polity. Philosophers know of Callicles, in the *Gorgias*, the handsome and intelligent politician who contemns any inquiry into any thought that might question his rule. He will not accept that mind can judge power. But the sophist will not admit that mind can judge mind either. The great battles of politic are first fought out in the minds of the dons and the thinkers seeking to explain *what is*.

In the end, political philosophy is a testimony that the final regime, the final happiness that we seek, is not political. The citizens and philosophers who recognize this truth are, nevertheless, all born into some actual polity, the kind of polity that did or could kill Socrates the philosopher or Christ the man-God. The premises that justify these killings are all based on a voluntarism that accepts the principle that whatever the prince or the democracy wills is the law. Yet, philosophy does not solve all its own problems, however open to reality it is. And this is the final theme that politics leaves with the philosopher who is concerned with *what is*.

Philosophy is open and true, when its practitioners rise out of a good polity, in leisure. Must they also be open to a revelation that addresses not only

13 Aristotle, *Politics*, 1267a2-15.

14 Plato, *The Apology*, 38a.

the "wickedness" of human nature, but also the realization that some answers to philosophic questions come to it from outside philosophy, though not in contradiction to it? Both the political order and the philosophical order reach a point of incompleteness when they are in fact being good politicians and good philosophers. The nature of political philosophy, as well as that of philosophy, is to remain open to the whole, to what cannot be supplied by itself. This is why, in their depths both politics and philosophy are gift oriented. Politics is both an end, a highest practical good, and a means to something beyond itself, to philosophy and truth. Political philosophy, at its best, recognizes its crucial contribution to the fulfilment of human nature by understanding what politics are, it leaves man free to understand himself as oriented beyond death to something greater than, but not contradictory to, politics.

Bibliography

Aristotle, *Basic Works*. New York: Random House, 1941.

Cicero, *Selected Works*. Harmondsworth: Penguin, 1971.

Machiavelli, *The Prince*. Harmondsworth: Penguin, 1999.

McCoy, Charles N. R., *The Structure of Political Thought*. New York: McGraw-Hill, 1963.

Pieper, Josef, *Leisure: The Basis of Culture*. San Francisco: Ignatius Press, 2009.

Plato, *Complete Works*. Indianapolis: Hackett, 1997.

Schall, James V., *At the Limits of Political Philosophy*. Washington: The Catholic University of America Press, 1996.

________, *The Politics of Heaven & Hell*. Lanham, Md.: University Press of America, 1984.

________, *On the Unseriousness of Human Affairs*. Wilmington: ISI Books, 2001.

________, *Reason, Revelation, and the Foundations of Political Philosophy*. Baton Rouge: Louisiana State University Press, 1987.

Sokolowski, Robert, *Christian Faith & Human Understanding*. Washington: The Catholic University of America Press, 2006.

Strauss, Leo. *What Is Political Philosophy and Other Essays*. Glencoe, Il.: The Free Press, 1959.

Chapter 6

Philosophy and Jurisprudence
Some Parallels and Challenges

Kevin Otieno Mwandha

1. Introduction

It seems that philosophy and jurisprudence belong to opposed and irreconcilable schools of thought. Philosophy is a speculative and abstract science. Jurisprudence is a practical science. A thing is practical when it has an immediate usefulness and concrete application to the reality within a given place and time. The contrary is abstract, theory, philosophy or story. Anything abstract is unconditionally subjected to a jungle of opinions destined towards nonrepresentational and ideological thoughts. Unfortunately, even in the institutions of learning, there is a tendency to lean towards the practical and to repel the abstract. No wonder the faculties of jurisprudence tend to have more students compared to the faculties of philosophy. From this point of view, philosophy is condemned without hearing by its fact of abstraction whereas jurisprudence is glorified by its fact of being practical.

Such judgement may seem unjustified taking into account the fact that both philosophers and jurists are restless rational beings. A philosopher - lover of wisdom - is restless not until he/she arrives at truth. A jurist - lover of justice - is restless not until he/she arrives at that which is objectively just. So, where is the converging point between a philosopher and a jurist? If a philosopher can wisely arrive at truth with moral certainty and that truth is nothing less or more, but what is just, then he/she is not only a philosopher but also, to some extent, a jurist. Similarly, if a jurist is able to acquire and embrace a logical, wise and realistic philosophical argument to an extent of acquiring moral certainty about a particular truth, and if that truth is nothing else but justice, then he/she is not only a jurist but also, a philosopher to some extent. A philosopher can be a jurist and vice versa. However, philosophy and jurisprudence are not one and same thing. There are parallels and differences in each discipline.

Taking into account the existing parallels and differences, one of the lacuna of this article relies on the fact that, however much general thoughts are shared between some philosophies and jurisprudence, not every school of thought agrees or disagrees with these general converging or diverging elements. This, however, should not lead to subjectivism or to inclination of a particular school of thought without consideration of the others. It is, therefore, reasonable and just to treat each thing according to its nature taking into consideration all the necessary existing tools. There is need to strike a balance with objectivity in such a manner that what is sound is recognised for its soundness and what is weak is equally recognised for its weakness.

2. Contributions of Some Philosophies in Jurisprudence

Philosophy is important in jurisprudence. It may bring to light some abstract notions, which in a sense can be useful in developing a case without prejudice to the art of a jurist, which supersedes a mechanical application of abstract concepts without a realistic correspondence. It is tragic considering philosophy as a mere abstraction without any touch with the realities of the world. Such a position may lead to a remark that whatever has no touch with the realities of the world is un-useful and has no meaning and therefore not worth existing. For example, metaphysics is considered as the most "abstract" and the least "practical" part of philosophy. In practical sense, nothing has more utility or is so helpful for being fully actualised in life as the wisdom that comes from metaphysics.[1] Jurisprudence is incomplete without the so-called abstract sciences. Mathematics, considered a speculative science, governs the whole institution of *temporis supputatione* in jurisprudence. There is no contradiction, therefore, to say that speculative science – even if it contains little or nothing practical, as some would allege – plays a role in knowing and practicing the law, a practical science. In reality, nothing is as useful as un-useful thing.

Abstraction and practical supplement each other. A mere knowledge of what is just is nothing less than a mere utopia until granted practically and concretely in modest and prosaic terms. In this sense, jurisprudence does not remain enclosed in the yoke of abstracts, but transcends mere ideology, because justice is concretely practical. Philosophy is central to jurisprudence. The latter is incomplete without the former. In fact. The art of legislation is based on abstraction. A law is worth its name (law) when human understanding is capable of grasping and abstracting the common qualities in certain groups of beings, individual facts

1 Javier Hervada, *What is Law? The Modern Response to Juridical Realism,* Monrèal: Wilson and Lafleur 2009, 8.

or acts, reducing them to representative form and making a juridical judgement about them that is proportionate to each person's rights and duties.[2] One needs a grounded philosophy in order to understand jurisprudence. There is necessity of philosophical courses in any structural formation and study of jurisprudence because of the deep affinities that exist between law and philosophy.

Law is a discursive discipline. Lawyers and judges are searches of truth. They live in the domain of reasons and meanings. They only give judgements or opinions when they have acquired a sufficient moral certainty. The jurist, as the wise person, knows whether the intended justice is a mere political utopia or something much more within reach to all peoples in equal measure. However, if law is a discursive discipline, the same is true of philosophy, which is a discursive discipline *par* excellence. Both disciplines are concerned with rational and logical thought and not just endless speculations and mere utopias. Philosophy and jurisprudence are arts. Every art corresponds to a need. Every art comes into being in order to satisfy a general or particular need.

Jurisprudence and philosophy require a dialectical skill. It may seem contradictory, but in the real sense, philosophical inquiry into law brings to light and makes explicit what is often implicit. Philosophical inquiry illuminates jurisprudential inquiry in terms of legal interpretations and reasoning. Law is political (art of legislation). Jurists ought to understand the politics of law. This is much more different from a mere political philosophy, or rather, an analysis of the conceptual apparatus behind a law. In fact, even if a positive law may originate from a logical political philosophy - without prejudice to the contributions of political philosophy in the study of jurisprudence – law is not about political justice. Law is a part of the art of politics, which is responsible for constructing society according to justice, freedom and solidarity. It is therefore the responsibility of the jurist as opposed to the political philosopher not only to know justice but also to manifest the same justice in action and in real situations for a just social order by allotting respective rights to a rightful titular. Therefore, there is a greater gap between knowing justice and doing justice.

To understand the politics of law and to do justice, in this sense, means to study with realism the rationale of law. A person can know and understand the rationality of a particular law even if he or she is not a jurist. However, a jurist (judge) is entrusted with the responsibility of knowing not only the rationality of law, but also granting realistic justice. For example, Aristotle is not only a philosopher but also a jurist to some extent. His works on *Nicomachea Ethics* are, until today, relied upon by jurists because they lay down common principle on juridical prudence, *epicheia* and equity. Another example is Saint Thomas Aquinas, considered as one of the leading philosopher and theologian of the

---

2 Cf. Javier Hervada, *Introduction to the study of canon law,* Montréal: Wilson and Lafleur 2007, 81.

scholastic period, yet his treatise on law is more applicable to juridical realism rather than philosophy or theology.

Irrespective of the diversities in individual philosophers, their contributions to the development of law as a science is eminent. This does not imply that all existent philosophical schools of thought should be embraced in jurisprudence. In fact, a philosophical school of thought such as methodological scepticism, without prejudice to its insistence on the search for truth, may cause some unresolved challenges in jurisprudence.

2.1 Methodological Skepticism and Jurisprudence

Cartesians or the followers of Rene Descartes's philosophy through their methodological skepticism argue that rational beings should doubt everything because nothing is certain in reality. Jurists on the other hand assert the existence of doubt and agree that positive laws can at times be objectively doubtful. Jurists do not propagate the methodological Cartesian school of thought. They give a practical solution. For example, if a law is objectively doubtful and no resolution can be arrived at, even after consulting all possible sources, then a doubtful law does not bind in that particular case.[3]

Both philosophers and jurists tend to agree that doubt is a fact of existence for the human mind that enjoys the sufficiency of reason. The mind inevitably copes with doubt through the pursuit of understanding. While trying to move from doubt to understanding, the individual is ordinarily unsettled until he arrives at a reliable truth. The path leading to the truth, when strewn with rubble, may distract the mind from considering the realities of some facts to an extent that the knowledge seeker may become stuck along the way.

The one seeking knowledge is stuck, not because he lacks the desire to proceed searching for truth, but because the doubting mind cannot follow a clear path to acquire the reliable truth necessary for its security. Until a person arrives at the reliable truth with moral certainty, justice requires that there should be no obligation to abide by what is unclear in meaning or what is contradictory and ambiguously comprehensible.

When in doubt, the mind finds itself in a state of *aporia* or *dubitalia.* It faces a vexing problem or difficulty that causes anxiety while in search of truth. The perplexed mind faces contradictory propositions. The affirmation of one would imply the negation of the other, and vice versa. At no one point can both propositions be simultaneously true and false. The mind, at this moment, is in a state of wonder and investigation with a certain form of involuntary ignorance because it acknowledges the imperfection in arriving at objective knowledge of things as they are in reality. However, it continues to interrogate itself about the true proposition in order to eliminate doubt and attain moral certitude. In the

3 Kevin Mwandha, *Doubt of law: Juridical and Moral Implications,* Romae: Pontificia Universitas Sanctae Crucis 2004, 1-2.

process of interrogating the rationality of law, a jurist may arrive at moral certainty in law and in fact necessary to grant justice to the titular. In the contrary, a jurist may remain in doubt, which may rubble the path towards justice.

When the mind is in a state of awareness of doubt, it can prefer multiple choices. It can decide to suspend the judgement, choose the part that appears probable, or the so-called "close to the truth or to the reality", or choose the falsified proposition with the conviction that it might give birth to a maximum utility. To whichever choice the mind is inclined, there is a tendency to construct an opinion. Such opinions are ordinarily complicated with fear of error because the choice of any one opinion contains moral-juridical implications. In order to avoid such complications, jurists concur that when a law is objectively doubtful and no resolution can be arrived at with moral certainty, even after consulting all possible sources, then having taking into consideration the rights of the third parties and the effects of law, a doubtful law should not bind in that particular case.

Methodological scepticism can be considered as a philosophical opinion of Rene Descartes and his followers and they are justly entitled to it. However, jurisprudence holds that, an opinion lacks weight unless it serves to convert the ignorance of a community to wisdom or unless it enriches the wisdom of the people. Without prejudice to the freedom of expression, some abstract philosophies such as skepticism only indicate the audacity of people to solve the problems incorrectly without arriving at the moral certainty, hence considering even the realities of the world and natural rights disputable and relative or subjective. Some things are not subjects to points of view or subjectivism. One example is justice. Justice would not exist if there were only relative values (subjective opinions). Justice pertains to objective reality and therefore it requires a well-founded moral certainty.

Every legal argument involves both an abstract rule and its application in a concrete setting. In fact, if a jurist were not situated in a tradition, a culture, a historical time and place, he or she would be incapable of *applying* any legal rule. The lack of such situatedness and understanding of the culture and values of one's society would not merely be an impediment to decision-making, it would render it impossible and lead to a naive legal formalism, subjectivism and voluntarism. Law is a teleological enterprise even if positivists do not share this position. It constitutes judicial rationality so much so that it cannot be discussed in a vacuum or in endless methodological doubt without its concreteness in justice. Justice is an existential fact. It identifies and allocates concrete rights (material or immaterial) to rightful titular.

2.2 Existentialism and Jurisprudence

A philosophical school of thought based on existentialism is concerned with identifying the most authentic and fulfilling way of life possible for individuals. It focuses on the uniqueness of each human individual as distinguished from abstract universal human qualities.[4] To some extent, it leads to subjectivism. In fact, it claims that subjectivity is what makes up each person's unique existence. In this regard, objectivity cannot reveal the whole truth about the individual person. Existence involves being a certain kind of individual, an individual who strives, considers alternatives, chooses, decides and above all commits himself.[5]

There is no doubt that the philosophy of existentialism, by the very fact of negating the reality of objectivity, leans towards subjective rights. In other words, there are no natural rights or objective rights. Jurisprudence instead acknowledges the existence and the uniqueness of individual persons. It acknowledges that persons have some inalienable rights or acquired rights. To this extent, jurisprudence prefers to use the term individual rights rather than subjective rights. Individual rights may belong to persons through some acquired rights such as privileges.

Individual rights are not equivalent subjective rights (the so-called rights per personal egoistic means and end). They are geared towards the common good or an objective usufruct for the common good of the community. Law are not personal. They are promulgated to a community, which has capacity to receive them. The philosophy of subjective rights which emanates from the recognition of the individual existential uniqueness also finds some support from the utilitarian school of thought.

2.3 Utilitarianism and Jurisprudence

Utilitarianism is built on the principle that an act is good if it is useful in achieving pleasure and diminishing pain for the greatest numbers of people involved in that act. Everyone desires pleasure and happiness and therefore always act to produce the greatest happiness and reduce pain. The greatest happiness involves the maximization of pleasure and the minimization of pain. The need for happiness and self-satisfaction makes people, for example, give special weight to their own projects and children at the expense of other children and projects in greater need. The inclination towards what is apparently gives maximum pleasure sums up better the theory of Utilitarianism.[6]

From their perspective, law should concentrate on acts that minimise pain and increase pleasure. Ordinarily, utilitarian may not propagate for the promulgation of laws until convinced that such laws will grant highest pleasure. However, the fundamental principle of law is not based on human pleasure but on human justice. Laws are at the service of justice. Justice is not a pleasure but a virtue of granting to persons what they rightly deserve irrespective of their emotional status.

---

4 Cf. William McBride, "Existentialism" in *The Cambridge Dictionary of Philosophy*, 2nd ed. Robert Audi ed. Cambridge: Cambridge University Press 1999, 730.

5 Cf. Samuel Enoch Stumpf, *History of Philosophy, from Socrates to Sarte,* New York: McGraw Hill 1988, 476-83.

6 Cf. Michael Proudfoot and A. R. Lacey, "Utilitarianism," *The Routledge Dictionary of Philosophy* 4th ed. New York: Routledge 2010, 433-4.

Justice is not geared towards minimising pain and increasing pleasure. Justice do not favour individuals. It grants to them their respective rights. It is not based on democracy or what pleases the majority. It is based on rightful things and acts.

A law that does not have a moral good is fruitless. In fact, laws ought to be promulgated only when they are imbued with the moral good. Moral obligation is rooted in the natural law. What the moral law forbids an individual to do, cannot be imposed on a group of human beings by positive human law because «non omne quod licet honestum est».[7] A juridical act that has no moral value is not even juridical in the first place. Every juridical obligation presupposes moral obligation. In this sense, pragmatism as a philosophical school of thought may play, to some extent, an important role in jurisprudence as far as the distinction of meaningful and meaningless laws are concerned.

2.4 Pragmatism and Jurisprudence

Pragmatism as a philosophy stresses the relation of theory to praxis and takes the continuity of experience and nature as revealed through the outcome of directed action as the starting point for reflection.[8] Pragmatism distinguishes between meaningful and meaningless actions. A meaningful concept is determined by manner in which it can modify purposive action.[9] The fundamental question is, what is the purpose of this particular action? Human actions should lead to the individual holistic growth and development of the societal common good.

Jurisprudence holds that laws are the service of the society and not vice versa. Sabbath was made for man and not man for Sabbath. It is the role of the courts of law or tribunals to distinguish meaningful and meaningless laws, just or unjust laws. A legislator may promulgate a law by virtue of his/her office. However, the jurist (judge) also called *ius dicere* has the responsibility to determine if a law is just or unjust. A jurist is a pragmatic philosopher per excellence because he/she is charged with the responsibility of determining the theory and praxis, the meaningful and meaningless, justice and injustice. He/she determines the existing objective truth in law and in fact so as to arrive at a plausible moral certainty in truth because «veritas est basis, fundamentum seu mater iustitiae».[10]

In the search for the truth, a jurist goes beyond being a mere functionary of legislation, and strives towards the search for justice in favor of the society.[11] It is

---

7 Cf. Franciscus Foramiti, *Corpus Iuris Civilis,* Venetiis 1836, *Digesta,* 50.17.144 [Paulus].

8 Cf. Charlene Haddock Seigfried, "Pragmatism," *Cambridge Dictionary of Philosophy*, 2nd ed. Robert Audi ed. Cambridge: Cambridge University Press 1999, 411-15.

9 Cf. James Tiles, "Pragmatism," *Edinburgh Dictionary of Continental Philosophy,* John Protevi, ed. Edinburgh: Edinburgh University Press 2006, 470-1.

10 Augustinus [Agostinho] Barbosa, *De Axiomatibus Iuris usufrequentioribus,* Axioma 224, Veritas, n. 5, in Aa. Vv, *Tractatus varii,* Lyons 1678, 136; cf. Thomae Aquinatis, *Summa theologiae,* (=S. Th.), Venetiis 1586-, I, q. 21, a.2.

11 Cf. Javier Hervada, *What is Law?* 100.

not the responsibility of the jurist to establish the law (to promulgate the law). In this process, a jurist should seek the sense of the piece of legislation and not only abide by the prescription of the legislation. When necessary, a jurist should go beyond the mere prescriptions of norms for the sake of justice. This is not a simple task. In fact, two schools of thought based of positivism and realism influence jurists in decision making to an extent there is a risk of having two opposed juridical schools of thought.

2.5 Positivism and Realism

Is there a conformity of thought among the jurists? Ronald Dworkin puts it, "jurists disagree about what legal rights are in much the same way as philosophers who argue about justice disagree about what justice is."[12] At the offset, it may appear that this statement is exaggerated. However, without prejudice to the fact that jurists have a common and a greater responsibility in granting justice to rightful persons, there is no doubt there are diversities of thoughts among them. Worthy of mentioning are positivistic jurists and realistic jurists with their respective influence from philosophical positivism and realism. Philosophical positivism asserts that every reliable knowledge should come from scientifically approved sources. Philosophical realism instead holds that science alone is not sufficient to explain all the realities of the world. There are some knowledge that are natural and do not need scientific approval to assert their existence in reality. These schools of thought influence jurisprudence to some extent.

Influenced by the scientific approved knowledge, juridical positivism asserts that the only reliable law is whatever the sovereign promulgates. According to them, a law is a dominion of the power of the master. For example, a legal philosopher John Austin concisely puts it, "law is the command of a sovereign." Law is worth its name if it comes from a recognized authority and enforced by that authority. It is whatever pleases the master or the ruler. The subjects, irrespective of the effects of the law, are bound to follow the orders or the will of the legislator. The judge is therefore to apply the text of law as it is promulgated by the legislator.

Classical juridical realism calls a realistic and analytic jurisprudence. It is concerned with providing necessary and sufficient conditions for the existence of law that distinguish law from non-law. It tracks the linguistic usage and establishes an evaluative test for the concept-word, hence stipulating meanings and determining what is important or essential. It is also concerned with logical analysis of whether what is intended as positive law has any reference to morals or law of nature or if there is no relationship whatsoever. This is one of the challenges of the positivistic jurists who assert that law is anything willed by the sovereign.

Juridical realism embraces analytical jurisprudence and assert that a positive law that does not derive its force or authority from natural law is not a law and cannot legally bind because there can be no legally valid standards that conflict

12 Ronald Dworkin, *Taking Rights Seriously*, Cambridge: Harvard University Press 1978, 351.

with the natural law. There are diversity of thoughts about this position. In fact, juridical positivism contradicts realism. They argue that "naturalism" belongs to another school of thought, and is not concerned in analyzing prudentially what law is.[13] Juridical positivism argues that what is more important to the juridical realism or is the moral obligation of a law rather than the execution of law as promulgated by the legislator. Positivists assert that there are no necessary moral constraints on the content of law. What is more important for the validity of a law is its promulgation procedure.

Positivists insist that law should be expressed in general terms, publicly promulgated, prospective in effect, expressed in understandable terms and consistent with one another. A law should be perpetual (some form of stability) and not changed so frequently that the subject cannot rely on them. Consequently, a law must be applied in a manner consistent with their wording.[14] Whereas legal positivism applauds this position, classical juridical realism adds that irrespective of all the qualities aforementioned, the role of a law is to help bring social order and the common good to the society taking into account the juridical and moral obligation of each law.

The diverging opinion here is that positivists and normativists are not interested in the moral effect of law. Their main point of departure and arrival is the will of the legislature. Whatever the legislature wills is law. The will of the legislature – voluntarism - expressed through promulgation is what they call legal validity of law. It does not matter whether such will is just or unjust. Legal validity is weighed on the balance of social facts and conventions and is therefore totally opposed or separate from natural facts and moral obligation.

Juridical realism declare null and void laws that do not cater for the common good and the social order in the society. They maintain that the art of the jurist is to give an analytic juridical and moral justification of a given a law in light of juridical and moral effects or obligations of a law.[15] The correct legal principle is the one that makes the law the moral best it can be. A legal law that has no moral obligation is neither legal nor law. It might be some human desire to say the least.

The aim of bringing to table the common principles and diversities between juridical positivism and juridical realism is not simply to show that positivism provides a poor account of legal system, but to show that positivism provides a poor conception of the concept of a legal right and justice.[16] Another possible argument against the philosophy of juridical positivism is that a society is not simply an aggregation of persons, it is born from the very nature of persons as

---

13 John Finnis, *Natural Law and Natural Rights*, Oxford: Clarendon Press 1980, 23-24.

14 Lon Fuller, *The Morality of Law*, New Haven, CT: Yale University Press 1964, 1-8.

15 Ronald Dworkin, *Taking Rights Seriously*, 40-44; Ronald Dworkin, "Natural Law Revisited," *University of Florida Law Review* 1982, vol. 34, no. 2, 171.

16 Ronald Dworkin, *Taking Rights Seriously*, 352.

social and relational beings. In fact, juridical obligation has its meaning only when there are relational beings.

To this extent, a law is promulgated to a society or a community (composed or relational beings), which has capacity to receive law. A law is not promulgated to an individual except in a very grave case. If laws are promulgated to a society, and since a society is not something that is merely kept together physically if not held by the invisible bonds of common thought, it implies that a common morality is part of the bondage of a society so much so that a shared morality is essential to the existence of a society. Therefore, any positive law must take into consideration the moral bondage that exists in a society.[17] To this extent, one of the fundamental functions of law is to preserve the shared morality as a means of preserving society itself and grant juridical obligations to the respective parties.

If juridical realism go by the philosophical arguments of positivists, then there cannot be a moral obligation to obey the law. Jurists have a common goal of validly granting justice to the right titular, however, the positivist account of legal validity is hard to reconcile with in terms of justice. Positivists claim that law as such, no matter what its content, deserves our respect and general obligation. Even if law is bad and unjust law, persons have obligation to obey it simply because it is an expression of the will of the legislature. Such philosophy tends to argue that a law should be obeyed even if its existence has nothing to do with its fundamental principle – the moral content. Juridical realism holds that judicial decision is guided far more frequently by political (art of legislation) and moral intuitions about the facts of the case instead of mere application of legal rules or legal formalism.

Juridical realism is not stuck to the sole will of the legislator as the only source of law. Not everything promulgated by the legislator is worth the name law. A law is worth when it is capable of producing juridical and moral effects. They hold that the nature of a manifest law is pro-missive as in a covenant, provisive as in a counsel and imperative as in a command. A jurist must be able, with a sense of realism, to grasp the weight of justice inherent in a particular case. In other words, the task of the jurist should not be reduced to a mere logical philosophical positivistic operation, but to a prudent decision on the specific case without prejudice to *epicheia* and equity. This is one of the reasons why there is need to evaluate jurisprudence from the perspective of classical juridical realism.

Juridical realism holds that positivistic philosophies and jurisprudence may easily weaken the concept of classical natural concept of justice. If a particular philosophy or school of thought does not acquaint itself with what things really are in their nature before forming a philosophical opinion about them, then such opinion may lead to a fair of absurdities. This does not imply that realism totally negates the some positivistic positions. In fact, Saint Thomas Aquinas gives a classical definition of a positive law as «rationis ordinatio ad bonum commune, ab

17 Patrick Devlin, *The Enforcement of Morals*, Oxford: Oxford University Press 1965, 10.

eo qui curam communitatis habet, promulgata».[18] A law is not just a philosophy but also an order of reason that creates order in the society. In other words, a law is reasonable social order destined to common good of the community capable of receiving it.

Most of the classical doctrines take into account this notion of law even if some tend to incline towards the authority or the power of the legislator. For example, some positivistic-realistic jurists define law as «recta agendarum ratio, a publica Potestate communitati denuntiata, cum voluntate eam perpetuo obligandi ad aliquid agendum, vel omittendum».[19] Some associate law with a norm, a precept, a rule. Others associate it with the traditional latin word *ius*, which in actual sense refers to a right, rather than law in terms of *lex*. Alphonsus Maria of Liguori distinguishes law from a precept and notes that «lex et praeceptum, prout hic indistincte accipitur, est recta agendorum aut omittendorum ratio. Interim, cum a superior, non communitati, sed alicui tantum aut aliquibus in particulari aliquid praecipitur, non appellatur lex, sed praeceptum tantum».[20]

In these definitions and other similar ones, law is seen not solely as a command of the legislator or a mere exhortation but as a right order of reason pronounced by a competent public legislative authority to the community which has the capacity to receive the law. A manifest and just law should have the power and perpetual obligation permitting an act or prohibiting an act for the social order in the community. The objective purpose of law is the social order. The *ratio* is the idea that the operator (in this case the legislator) has about the operation. Without prejudice to human reason and wisdom, law does not necessarily refer to the intellectual capacity or the academic prowess of the legislator.

Law is generated by a rational being and it requires that it should be rational. However, the rationality of law is not an intellectual capacity of the legislator, which of course is also necessary, but a just, manifest and stable order of reason rooted in the nature of things - human nature and social reality - for the common good and order of the society. Rationality of a law implies that it should be capable of producing the desired effects taking into account the juridical and moral obligations of each case or each effect.

Justice demands that the office of the legislator should be guided by *ratio ordinis* while promulgating laws because the political art or prudence of ordering or regulating social life by promulgating laws belongs to the legislative organ or authority. The *ratio ordinis* in law is called for because of the great harm, which might be endangered by the law itself. Since law is enacted with a view of assuring

18 S. Th., I-II, q. 90, a.4.

19 Anacletus Reiffenstuel, Jus *canonum universum,* Romae 1831, vol. I, Lib. I, tit. 2, §2, n. 23; cf. Lucius Ferraris, *Bibliotheca canonica iuridica,* Romae 1839, ad verbum *lex,* Vol. V, no. 11.

20 Alphonsus Maria De Liguori, *Theologia moralis,* Mechliniae: P. J. Hanicq, 1803, Lib. I, tract. II, cap. I, n. 90; cf. Franciscus Suárez, *Tractatus de legibus ac Deo legislatore in decem libros distributus,* Neapolis: Ex Typis Fibrenianis, 1872, I.6.9.

the welfare of all, everything must be done to render ineffectual the possibility of harm, which might conceivably arise out of dubious legislation.[21]

Social contract philosophies tend to believe that since a society is nothing less than an aggregation of persons, rational individuals tend to voluntarily consent explicitly or tacitly to the will of the legislator in an exchange to the protection of the rights. However, it has been said explicitly that law is something much beyond a mere will of the legislator. The statute of law - *aliqua ratio iuris* - is to create order in the society and regulate human relations according to justice because only between persons is there a juridical relation and duty of obligation.[22] Law is a social reality that grants order in the society. It is the rationale or measure of social life legislated in accordance with its nature and presided over by the principle of justice. It can be considered sufficient when its properties can respond to its formal, final and ultimate sufficient cause. The formal cause of law is based on its order of reason, which acts as its practical reason. The final cause of law is the common good that is truly just (based on equity) and equally common to all. The formal and final cause of law would not be sufficient in themselves unless there is both an efficient and ultimate efficient cause. This should bring some unity among classical jurists who stress more on the formal and final cause of law on one hand and the positivistic jurists who stress on the efficient and ultimate efficient cause of law on the other hand. This unity should lead to a moderate classical juridical realism school of thought.

3. Conclusion

Philosophical positivism seems to have influenced juridical positivism to an extent that positivism seems to be the dominant perspective of law today. There is no doubt that positivism allied to voluntarism and intellectualism erodes the concept of law as to mean, that which is willed by the governor irrespective of the common good and the social order. It risks having so many invalid laws. In order to avoid the tragedy of philosophical positivism and its influence in jurisprudence, it is necessary to develop a moderate classical juridical realism. A construction of a classical juridical realism is not just for the sake of traditional or customary nostalgia of realism as a school of thought *per se* but for the sole motive of renewing and concretizing juridical science. Justice is not obtained by strict observance of the text of the norm or to think that whatever is promulgated is law without taking into consideration its rationality and common good. At the same time, a law is instituted by promulgation. The office and power of a legislator cannot be underestimated. Classical jurists would not have anything to call a positive law unless a competent authority promulgates it.

Jurists concur that jurisprudence is not subject to personal opinions or philosophies drawn from subjective point of view. Similarly, it does not seek for

21 Cf. S. Th., I-II, q. 95, a.3.

22 Cf. Javier Hervada, *Introduction to the study of canon law*, 43.

the agreement of everyone because majority does make a right. If everyone were in agreement about law, law would be nothing else but a democratic conformity based on the consent of the majority rule. Natural law would not exist because it is based neither on majority opinions - democratic votes – nor on positivism. This is the sole reason why positive law is not based on the majority opinion but above all on *ratio ordinis,* common good, social order and the promulgating authority.

Both jurist and philosopher must ever desire that justice should be the shield and defender of every society in such a manner persons may dwell in peace and unity. A just thing is a right thing. It is that which belongs to the titular by right. Ulpian describes the art of justice as *constans et perpetua voluntas ius suum cuique tribuendi.*[23] A philosophy that negates the freedom of expression of opinions and the entitlement of such opinions by their titular – as long as they contain some wisdom, the object of philosophy - may not be a just philosophy. Similarly, a rushed or a delayed justice without any form of wise reflection on the true objective state of events and acts is not justice in the first case. In this manner, philosophers need justice just as jurists need wisdom. Both wisdom and justice are elements are of societal growth. Just as the fundamental goal of philosophy is that the society should be wise, so the fundamental goal of the science of law is that the society may be just, with that real and concrete justice that consists of respecting and giving each person the rights that are his or hers. Jurisprudence calls for a desire to understand the law, zeal to defend it, prudence to interpret it, equity to apply it. Equity in this context calls the jurist not only to bear in mind that the primary requirement of justice is the respect of persons, but also to look beyond the text of the law and strive for *epikeia.*[24]

An interpretation of a law is an important aspect in the ministry of a jurist. It is a legal hermeneutics that is authentically juridical and which continually rotates on the wheels of justice with the crucial questions of what is just in each single situation. It is a special kind of hermeneutics, which seeks to understand the core of the message of the law, the sense of the law through its symbols, and the significance of the law rather than its signifier. In this sense, a jurist goes beyond the signifier and embraces the significant in order to judge with justice - «dicere ius». With the help of philosophical logical and juridical hermeneutics, a jurist determines if the order established by the legislator through the laws is just or unjust, if the order is juridical in conformity with the rights or not, and if the order promotes the rights - *ius* - or causes injustice - *iniuria.*

---

23 *Digesta,* 1.1.10.

24 For some doctrines about *epikeia* and equity see Aristotle, *Nicomachea Ethics,* London: Oxford University Press 1954, V, 1136b 31-35, 1137a-1138b; S. Th., II-II, q. 120, a.2; Franciscus Suárez, *De legibus,* VI.7.6-14, VI.8.4-6; Alphonsus Maria De Liguori, *Theologia moralis,* Lib. I, tract. II, cap. IV, n. 201; Louis Bouyer, *L'Église de Dieu, Corps du Christ et temple de l'Esprit,* Paris 1970, 599; Pierre Andrieu-Guitrancourt, *Introduction sommaire à l'étude du droit en général et du droit canonique en particulier,* Paris 1963, 22.

A jurist is the law itself speaking - «magistratum legem esse loquentem».[25] They have a special commitment to know adequately and eloquently the ontological sense of the law so that they are not imprisoned by evolutive interpretations or phenomenological philosophies, which consist in hypothetical and deontological judgements. A jurist needs to cultivate more the virtue of prudence or *prudentia iuris.* It consists of juridical prudence which requires that the *ratio ordinis* fundamentally needed in the promulgation of laws must be ordered socially and justly according to the nature of the situation and the moment of time in such a manner that the choices made can be adapted to reality. The *prudentia iuris* should be comprised of experience, intuition, counsel, good judgement, timeliness and equity.[26]

The task of every legal system should be geared towards the service of the truth, which is the only solid foundation, which can support personal and social life. Any choice that goes against this principle endangers juridical and moral good. The criterion that inspires the deontology of the judge is the love for the truth. Therefore, the truth must be sought with a genuine desire to know it, despite all the inconveniences that may derive from such knowledge. The truth sets the conscience free from every form of compromise with interested falsehoods or egoistic pleasures. St. Thomas teaches that «quandoque iustitia veritas vocatur».[27] This implies that the jurist and all those who participate in various phases of the procedure towards the just judgement should search that truth which is justice, and of that justice which is truth. In the search of the truth and justice, philosophies and moral values play fundamental roles in constructing plausible juridical relations.

Bibliography

Aristotle, *Nicomachea. Ethics,* London: Oxford University Press 1954.

Barbosa, Augustinus. *De Axiomatibus Iuris usufrequentioribus,* AA. VV, *Tractatus VARII,* Lyons 1678.

Bouyer Louis, *L'Église. de Dieu, Corps du Christ et temple de l'Esprit,* Paris 1970.

Cicero Marcus Tullius, *De legibus,* Milano: C. Signorelli, 1935.

De Liguori Alphonsus, Maria. *Theologia moralis,* Mechliniae: P. J. Hanicq, 1803.

De Segusio, Henricus [Hostiensis]. *Summa aurea,* Lyon 1537 - Aalen 1962.

Devlin, Patrick. *The Enforcement of Morals,* Oxford: Oxford University Press 1965.

Dworkin, Ronald. "Natural Law Revisited," *University of Florida Law Review,* 1982, Vol. 34, no. 2, 165-188.

---

25 Marcus Tullius Cicero, De leg*ibus,* Milano: C. Signorelli, 1935, L. 3, n. I, 2.

26 Cf. Javier Hervada, *Introduction to the study of canon law,* 71. It is necessary to note that equity is not another kind or category of justice. It is not a dispensation from justice. It is justice in the concrete case. See for example, Henricus De Segusio [Hostiensis], *Summa aurea,* Lyon 1537 - Aalen 1962, Lib. V, *de dispensationibus,* fol. 289rb.

27 S. Th., II-II, q. 58, a.4.

Dworkin, Ronald. *Taking Rights Seriously*, Cambridge: Harvard University Press 1978.

Ferraris, Lucius. *Bibliotheca canonica iuridica,* Romae 1839.

Finnis, John. *Natural Law and Natural Rights*, Oxford: Clarendon Press 1980.

Foramiti, Franciscus. *Corpus iuris civilis,* Venetiis 1836.

Fuller, Lon. *The Morality of Law*, New Haven, CT: Yale University Press 1964.

Guitrancourt Pierre, Andrieu. *Introduction sommaire à l'étude du droit en général et du droit canonique en particulier*, Paris 1963.

Hervada, Javier. *Introduction to the Study of Canon Law,* Montréal: Wilson and Lafleur 2007.

Hervada, Javier. *What is Law? The Modern Response to Juridical Realism,* Montréal: Wilson and Lafleur 2009.

McBride, William. "Existentialism" *The Cambridge Dictionary of Philosophy*, 2nd ed. Robert Audi ed. Cambridge: Cambridge University Press 1999, 730-731.

Mwandha, Kevin. *Doubt of law: Juridical and Moral Implications,* Romae: Pontificia Universitas Sanctae Crucis 2004.

Proudfoot, Michael and Lacey, A. R. "Utilitarianism" *The Routledge Dictionary of Philosophy* 4th ed. New York: Routledge 2010, 433-4.

Reiffenstuel, Anacletus. *Jus canonum universum,* Romae 1831.

Seigfried Charlene, Haddock. "Pragmatism" *Cambridge Dictionary, of Philosophy*, 2nd ed. Robert Audi ed. Cambridge: Cambridge University Press 1999, 411-15.

Stumpf Samuel, Enoch. *History of Philosophy, from Socrates to Sarte,* New York: McGraw Hill 1988.

Suárez, Franciscus. *Tractatus de legibus ac Deo legislatore in decem libros distributus*, Neapolis: Ex Typis Fibrenianis, 1872.

Thomae, Aquinatis. *Summa theologiae,* Venetiis 1586-.

Tiles, James. "Pragmatism" *Edinburgh Dictionary of Continental Philosophy,* John Protevi, ed. Edinburgh: Edinburgh University Press 2006, 470-1.

Chapter 7

Challenges for a Christian Worldview

Benedikt Paul Göcke

1. What is a Worldview?

A worldview is a set of assumptions that, consciously or unconsciously, shapes the way in which each one of us understands what is going on in their life and in the world as a whole. A worldview captures theory and practice both by way of providing an interpretational story of the origin, fundamental nature, and purpose of the universe and by way of implying what has to be done from an ethical point of view in order to foster the purpose of the universe (cf. Göcke 2014). Life without a worldview is practically impossible for human beings. Whether we like it or not, each one of us has a worldview that explicitly or implicitly shapes the way in which we understand and perceive what is going on in the world. As Vidal (2012: 312) says, "most people adopt and follow a worldview without much thinking. Their worldview remains implicit. They intuitively have a representation of the world [...], know what is good and what is bad [...], and have experience about how to act in the world [...]. And this is enough to get by. Every one of us is in need of a worldview, whether it is implicit or explicit."

Philosophers distinguish between the *ideal* and the *empirical* possession of a worldview. Ideally, a worldview should be a set of assumptions that is subject to several normative constraints of rationality. A worldview, if fully spelled out, should be (1) consistent, (2) coherent, (3) inclusive, and (4) true.

Consistency: A worldview is consistent if and only if there is no contradiction entailed by the different assumptions that constitute it. For instance, if it is part of one's worldview that no supernatural entities exist, then one must not hold at the same time that angels exist because the existence of angels contradicts the assumption that there are no supernatural entities.[1] Coherence: A worldview is coherent if and only if the assumptions constituting it are in mutual support. For instance, if it is part of one's worldview that a morally perfect and loving God exists, then this concept of God should have a direct impact on what one assumes to be the right thing to do. Inclusiveness: A worldview is inclusive if and only if the set of assumptions could integrate new insights, formerly unknown, in such a way that the consistency and coherence of the worldview is not rejected. If it is unable to do this, then the worldview will change or collapse. In other words, if based on the principles that are part of the worldview in question, a new phenomenon cannot be accounted for, then either one has to change the basic principles in such a way that the new phenomenon becomes accountable or else the worldview as such has to be rejected (cf. Quine 1951, Kuhn 1996). For instance, the discovery of quantum phenomena posed a serious challenge to Newtonian physics and its stance on the world. Since Newtonian physics was unable to deal with the phenomena adequately, the Newtonian worldview collapsed and was replaced by the worldview of quantum mechanics (cf. Polkinghorne 2002).Truth: It is difficult to spell out the idea of a true worldview because there are different interpretations of truth, and often a definition of truth is part of a particular worldview. If the truth of an assumption is nothing over and above its consistency and coherence with other assumptions one holds, then different worldviews can be referred to as true. However, if truth consists in the correspondence with the way things really are – and this is what I assume – then only one worldview can be true (they can all be false, though). Since one's worldview restricts and predetermines one's perceptions and judgements on certain phenomena to be met with in the world, it is hardly to be expected that in the near future humanity agree on a particular worldview. As Dretske once said, 'one man's modus ponens is another man's modus tollens.'

Although there are ideal constraints on the concept of a worldview, most if not all people fall short of possessing a worldview that corresponds to the conditions specified. The reason is that the ideal conditions of holding a worldview presuppose that human beings are ideal rational believers, whereas an ideal rational believer is a subject that knows what it knows and that knows what their knowledge implies.[2] Since we are hardly aware of what we know and of what is implied by our knowledge it is very likely that we would discover many contradictions in our actual system of belief, if we could spell it out fully. Furthermore, since our body of knowledge changes all the time, a worldview is best addressed as the horizon in which we move, and life, and have our being.

---

1 Cf. Mautner (1996: 416): "Supernatural beings exist above or beyond nature, where 'nature' is to be understood in a wide sense, to take in all of space and time and everything existing within that framework, i.e., the whole of the physical universe."

2 That is to say, for any propositions p an ideal rational believer knows whether she knows that p, and if p implies q, then she also knows that q is the case.

2. Core Features of a Christian Worldview

First of all, there is no such thing as *the* Christian worldview[3]; there are simply too many different denominations that refer to themselves as 'Christian' while at the same time the corresponding worldviews entail assumptions that are in conflict with presuppositions that are part of other Christian worldviews. For instance, according to some protestant Christian worldviews, there is no genuine human freedom because God's foreknowledge yet already fixed what is going to happen in this world and, consequently, who will be saved from a soteriological point of view. On others, though, there is genuine human freedom that allows us to be the ones that determine our own fate. Furthermore, according to some Christian worldviews like the Roman-Catholic one, reason itself is a valuable way to support the overall Christian case, whereas other Christian denominations suppose that reason is fallen and that the only way to deal with God is by faith alone (sola fides).

However, although the different Christian denominations vary in the precise formulation of their overall worldview, two things are clear. First, each Christian denomination is an all-encompassing worldview because each one attempts to provide "a complete understanding for the subject's known world and [tries] to introduce ways of living that encompass every aspect of life, including one's religious and ethical perspective as well as social associations" (Carvalho 2006: 114). Second, although they differ as fully spelled out worldviews, there are certain fundamental assumptions without which no Christian worldview could be classified as Christian and which consequently all Christian denominations share with one another. In what follows, I mention four of them.

First, the existence of God belongs to the core assumptions of any Christian worldview. If God does not exist, then there is no point in being a Christian. It is, though, not only the bare existence of *a* God that is relevant for Christian worldviews: God is characterised in the Bible as the loving creator and sustainer of the world who has a providential plan for the universe, and most importantly, for us human beings. God is loving, caring, powerful, knowing, wise, and wants His people to be saved. In order to achieve His providential plans, God is able to act in the world (cf. Göcke 2014a and Göcke 2015).

Second, God became human in Jesus of Nazareth, who was crucified and resurrected from the dead. Jesus brought salvation to the world and reconciled it with God. He is the central figure in Christianity. If Jesus Christ did not exit, then there is no point in being a Christian, even if God exists. As McGrath (1991: 289) says, "Christians regard Christ as authoritative because, in the end, they recognize him to be none other than God Himself, coming among us as one of

3 For academic reasoning: Unfortunately, Christians are not only attacked on an academic level these days. In many parts of the worlds Christians are persecuted and killed for their faith in Jesus Christ. It goes without mention that nobody should ever be persecuted, tortured, and killed for their faith alone, whatever their faith may be.

us. The authority of Christ rests in his being God incarnate. His teaching is lent dignity, weight and authority by his identity. And that identity can only be spelled out fully by the doctrine of the person of Christ. Christian principles thus rest on Christian doctrine."

Third, there is life after death and each one of us will be judged according to the moral value of the life one has led (cf. Hebrews 9.27). Although it is controversial whether life after death is best accounted for in terms of an immortal immaterial soul or in terms of bodily resurrection (cf. Murphy 2006), and although it is a matter of on-going theological dispute how precisely judgement day is supposed to work, and how drastic the judgement might be, the assumptions *that* there is a life after death and *that* something will happen that is related to our lives are essential parts of Christian faith.

Fourth, the plausibility of the idea that the way we lead our lives and build on us as persons with a particular character has an impact on our life after death presupposes that there are objective moral truths according to which we should direct our lives. Without the assumption that there are objective moral truths, the idea that our behaviour in this life matters for our life after death becomes entirely meaningless: how could we be judged in a fair divine trial from a moral point of view if there are no objective moral truths to begin with? According to Christian faith, the Decalogue (Exodus 20: 1-17 and Deuteronomy 5: 4-21) and the Golden Rule (Matthew 7: 12) express some of the most fundamental objective moral truths that impose normative constraints on how we should behave.

If any of the aforementioned assumptions of a Christian worldview can be shown to be false, then there is no point in being a Christian. There is no way a Christian worldview could be plausible while at the same time the denial of any of these assumptions is assumed to be true.

3. Arguments against the Plausibility of a Christian Worldview

Almost every core assumption of Christian worldviews is disputed these days.[4] In what follows, I briefly discuss some of the most prominent arguments against the plausibility of a Christian worldview before, in the next section, I show ways to deal with the arguments from a Christian point of view. Since there is an unmanageable amount of literature on each of the following topics, I will only

4 Cf. Zuckerman 2009. It seems that atheism is particularly viral in the Western civilisation that used to be heavily influenced by Christianity. As Zuckerman (2009: 60) says, "loss of belief in God has occurred over the course of the twentieth century in Canada, Australia, and various European countries, including Germany, the United Kingdom, the Netherlands, and Scandinavia. However, secularization is quite limited to specific advanced industrialized nations (with relatively low birth rates), and has not occurred throughout much of the rest of the world." Although, from an empirical point of view the numbers of atheists are growing, philosophical interest in God returned as a central piece of metaphysical speculation in the 1960s. As Smith (2001: 197) says, "God is not 'dead' in academia; he returned to life in the late 1960s and is now alive and well in his last academic stronghold, philosophy departments."

discuss the structure of the arguments and sketch how their premises typically are justified in the discussion.

3.1 The Existence of God

The first argument against the plausibility of a Christian worldview is directed against the assumption that God exists. The argument has the following structure:

(1) *If God does not exist, then a Christian worldview is untenable.*
(2) *God does not exist.*
(3) *Therefore: A Christian worldview is untenable.*

Since the argument is logically valid – if the premises are true, then the conclusion has to be true as well – we have to take a closer look at the putative truth of the premises. The first premise is de facto true: if God does not exist, then the Christian worldview is untenable because in this case one of its core assumptions is false.

According to the second premise, God does not exist.There are at least two different types of arguments against the existence of God (cf. Göcke 2013). The first kind of argument is directed at the internal consistency and coherence of the Christian concept of God.[5] It can be formulated as follows:

The Argument from Inconsistency:

(1) *The concept of God entails that God is x, y, z.*
(2) *Nothing can exist that is x, y, z.*
(3) *Therefore, nothing can correspond to the concept of God.*
(4) *Therefore, God cannot exist.*

Arguments of this typeproceed by way of specifying a concept of God that is shown to be inconsistent. For instance, in a first step one could argue that God is supposed to be an immaterial, eternal, immutable person. Based on this assumption one could in a second step argue that for conceptual reasons a person cannot be immaterial, eternal, and immutable. However, if this is the case, then God does not exist.[6]

5 Cf. Craig (2009:71): "During the previous generation the concept of God was often regarded as fertile ground for antitheistic arguments. The difficulty with theism, it was said, was not merely that there are no good arguments for the existence of God, but, more fundamentally, that the notion of God is incoherent."

6 Another example is based on the assumptions that God is a perfect being and that a perfect being cannot exist. However, if a perfect being cannot exist, then God does not exist. Cf. As Bishop (1998:174) says, "Can it be consistent to adhere to theism, and yet to reject the belief that *omniGod* exists, where *omniGod* means a unique omnipotent, omniscient, omnibenevolent, supernatural person who is creator and sustainer of all else that exists? On the assumptions prevailing within Philosophy of Religion, at least as practised by analytical

The second kind of argument proceeds by way of showing that the existence of God is inconsistent with what we know to be true about the universe:

The Argument from Consequences:

(1) *God exists if and only if God is x, y, z.*
(2) *If something is x, y, z, then v cannot be real (alternatively: v has to be real).*
(3) *V is real (alternatively: v is not real).*
(4) *Therefore, nothing is x, y, z.*
(5) *Therefore, God does not exist.*

Proponents of this kind of argument start by way of specifying a concept of God as well and argue that if God thus understood exists, then the universe should have, or should not have, some other feature. The next step of the argument usually points out that the universe in fact has, or lacks a certain feature to be expected if God exists. Based on this it is concluded that God does not exist. For instance, the logical problem of evil belongs to this category of arguments. It proceeds as follows: God is morally perfect, omnipotent, and omniscient. If there is a morally perfect, omnipotent, and omniscient God, then God is morally obliged to prevent gratuitous evil from existence. There is gratuitous evil in the world. Therefore, God is not morally perfect, omniscient and omnipotent, which is to say that God does not exist.[7]

3.2 The Resurrection of Jesus Christ

Whereas the existence of God as such is not an exclusive assumption of a Christian worldview but is shared with any monotheistic religion – particularly with the two other Abrahamic religions – the existence and divinity of Christ is a demarcating feature of Christianity. Because the divinity of Christ is essentially related to the alleged fact that God resurrected Christ from the dead, it follows that another way to argue against the plausibility of a Christian worldview consists in arguing that Christ was not raised from the dead. The corresponding argument has the following form:

(1) *If Jesus of Nazareth did not rise from the dead, then a Christian worldview is untenable.*
(2) *Jesus of Nazareth did not rise from the dead.*
(3) *Therefore: A Christian worldview is untenable.*

---

philosophers, the answer is clearly 'No'. Such philosophers typically presuppose that theism virtually by definition requires belief that omniGod exists."

7 Cf. Mackie (1955: 200): "In its simplest form the problem is this: God is omnipotent; God is wholly good; and yet evil exists. There seems to be some contradiction between these three propositions, so that if any two of them were true the third would be false. But at the same time, all three are essential parts of most theological positions: the *theologian*, it seems, at once *must* adhere and *cannot consistently* adhere to all three."

The first premise is true.The Bible is quite explicit about this: "If there is no resurrection of the dead, then Christ has not been raised; if Christ has not been raised, then our preaching is in vain and your faith is in vain. We are even found to be misrepresenting God, because we testified of God that He raised Christ, whom He did not raise if it is true that the dead are not raised. For if the dead are not raised, then Christ has not been raised. If Christ has not been raised, your faith is futile and you are still in your sins. Then those also who have fallen asleep in Christ have perished. If for this life only we have hoped in Christ, we are of all men most to be pitied" (1 Corinthians 15, 12-19). Paul explicitly states with logical rigour that without the resurrection of Christ, Christian faith is in vain and those who follow Christ are to be pitied.

Again the crucial premise is the second one. There are at least two kinds of arguments in its favour. The first type of argument is a historical argument. According to it, Jesus did not raise from the dead for the simple reason that Jesus of Nazareth never existed.

The Argument from History:

(1) *If Jesus of Nazareth did not exist, then Jesus Christ did not raise from the dead.*
(2) *Jesus of Nazareth did not exist.*
(3) *Therefore, Jesus Christ did not rise from the dead.*

The first premise is analytically true. If there was no such person as Jesus of Nazareth, then there was no such person that was crucified and could have been raised from the dead. What is said to speak in favour of the second premise of this argument is the following: there are insufficient valid historical sources confirming the existence of Jesus of Nazareth. Based on this assumption the conclusion is drawn that, therefore, we should either withhold belief that Jesus of Nazareth existed or else should assume that the best explanation for the fact that there are insufficient valid sources is that Jesus of Nazareth never existed.[8]

A second type of argument for the conclusion that Jesus did not rise from the dead can be referred to as the argument from fiction. Arguments from fiction against the resurrection of Jesus Christ are based on the assumption that that even if Jesus did exist and was crucified, his resurrection nevertheless is not an actual fact. Instead, the resurrection of Jesus of Nazareth is a hoax made up by his disciples:

8 Cf. Doherty (2009: vii-viii) who argues that "no historical Jesus worthy of the name existed, that Christianity began with a belief in a spiritual, mythical figure, that the Gospels are essentially allegory and fiction, and that no single identifiable person lay at the root of the Galilean preaching tradition."

The Argument from Fiction:

> (1) *If it is a piece of fiction that Jesus raised from the dead, then Jesus did not raise from the dead.*
> (2) *It is a piece of fiction that Jesus raised from the dead.*
> (3) *Therefore: Jesus did not rise from the dead.*

The first premise is analytically true: if it is a piece of fiction that Jesus raised from the dead, if it was entirely made up by some of his disciples that he did, then it follows that Jesus never raised from the dead. Those arguing in this way often assume that resurrection is excluded as a possibility a priori. According to them, the best explanation of why people started to tell the story in a different way is framed in psychological terms: his disciples could not stand that Jesus did not rise from the dead, so, in order to make sense of Jesus and themselves after all, they made up the story of his resurrection.

3.3 Life after Death

Another argument against the plausibility of a Christian worldview is directed against the very possibility of life after death. Life after death is central to Christian faith because without life after death Christ's promise of an eternal life is empty and the idea that our live is judged according to its moral integrity is a pointless piece of fiction; at the end of the day, it does not really matter how we live and all the evil that occurred in the world will simply be forgotten without any possibility to make good any moral damage done. However, according to the following argument the chances that there is a life after death are slim indeed:

> (1) *If life after death is impossible, then a Christian worldview is untenable.*
> (2) *Life after death is possible if and only if eithereach individual is identical with an immaterial soul or bodily resurrection is plausible.*
> (3) *There is no immaterial soul.*
> (4) *Bodily resurrection is implausible.*
> (5) *Therefore: Life after death is impossible.*
> (6) *Therefore: A Christian worldview is untenable.*

The first premise is analytically true: if there is no way for us to have a life after death, then our hope as Christians is in vain and there is no point in being a Christian. In this case, it is false when shortly before his death Jesus says on the cross: "Truly, I say to you, today you will be with me in Paradise" (Luke 23.42).

The second premise of the argument is equally true: life after death is possible for me if and only if there is something that exists in the afterlife that is identical to me: I can have a life after death if and only if that which now is me myself exists in such a way that in the afterlife I know that it is me myself who once had a particular life in this universe. As Tapp (2010: 207) says, "a central object of Christian hope is that God will resurrect you on the Last Day. If it is really *you* who is subject to resurrection, then there must be quite a strong relation between you and somebody in heaven (I use 'heaven' as shorthand for the realm of the resurrected without any further connotations), a relation so strong that the existence of that heavenly person makes the statement 'you were/have been resurrected' true."[9]

Since, the two plausible options are that either we are identical to an immaterial soul or else are identical to our body, it follows that either our immaterial soul has to survive bodily death or else that our bodies have to be resurrected. The crucial premises of this argument, therefore, are the third and fourth one.

Typically, arguments in favour of the third premise have the following structure. They are at home in a naturalistic worldview according to which we are nothing over and above our material body:[10]

The Argument from Naturalism (I):

(1) *An immaterial soul exists if and only if its existence is consistent with scientific knowledge of the universe.*
(2) *The existence of an immaterial soul is not consistent with scientific knowledge of the universe.*
(3) *Therefore: There is no immaterial soul.*

The argument is based on the assumption that science is our primary means to obtain knowledge concerning the universe. However, according to science, it is said, the existence of an immaterial soul is refuted. When scientists describe the world, all they find is familiar physical stuff. If an immaterial soul existed and could influence what happens in this world by way of causing certain events to obtain, then this would contradict a scientific worldview since it contradicted the assumption that the universe is causally closed.[11]

---

9 Cf. Swinburne (2001: 420): "There are two philosophical questions about personal identity. The first is: what are the logically necessary and sufficient conditions for a person P_2 at a time t_2 being the same person as a person P_1 at an earlier time t_1, or, loosely, what does it mean to say that P_2 is the same person as P_1? The second is: what evidence of observation and experience can we have that a person P_2 at t_2 is the same person as a person P_1 at t_1?"

10 Cf. Fales (2009: 118): "Naturalism and physicalism are metaphysical positions commonly associated with atheism. Both are stronger than atheism: they entail atheism, conceived (minimally) as the denial that there is an all-powerful, omniscient, perfectly good disembodied personal being who has created the physical universe. Naturalism and physicalism are, therefore, natural allies of atheism, and offer a philosophical framework within which atheism finds a natural home."

11 Although, there are different versions of causal closure discussed, the general idea is that the actual world is causally closed because every obtaining state of affairs S has a purely physical causal history that is responsible for S's obtaining. As Clayton (2008: 135) says, "a basic assumption of many modern physicists is that physical systems are closed to causal interventions from outside (the principle of the conservation of energy). According to Papineau (2002: 17),

Arguments against the plausibility of bodily resurrection proceed as follows:

The Argument from Implausibility:

(1) *Bodily resurrection is plausible if and only if life after death takes place in a physical universe like our own.*
(2) *Life after death does not take place in a physical universe like our own.*
(3) *Therefore: Bodily resurrection is implausible.*

The rationale behind this argument is as follows: if we are identical to our body, if the existence of our body at least is a necessary and sufficient condition for us to exist, then we can exist in a particular situation if and only if our body can exist in that situation. Since our body can exist only in a physical universe like the one we are living in right now it follows that life after death is possible if and only if life after death takes place in a physical universe like our own. However, since the assumption that life after death takes place in a physical universe like our own entails that life after death is like our life now – we would have to eat, grow, suffer – and since this assumption is not what people assume to be a plausible description of life after death, it follows that bodily resurrection is implausible. Therefore, based on the assumption that we neither possess an immaterial soul nor should reasonably expect a bodily resurrection it follows that another core assumption of the plausibility of a Christian worldview is refuted.

3.4 The Existence of Moral Truths

The idea that we will be judged according to the moral integrity of our life goes together with the idea of life after death.[12] It presupposes that the way we lead our lives makes a difference to our life after death. However, the way we lead our lives can only make a difference if there are objective moral truths according to which we can act and live.[13] We obtain the following argument against the plausibility of a Christian worldview:

---

the completeness of physics can be states as follows: "All physical effects are fully caused by purely physical prior histories." Cf. Papineau (2000) for a justification of the validity of the principle of causal closure. See Göcke (2008) and Lowe (2008) for a critical discussion of the plausibility of causal closure.

12 Cf. Copan (2004: 150): "We humans, who have been created in God's image, are endowed with moral capacities [...] so that, at a minimum, we may infer a personal Being to whom each of us is accountable (Romans 1:19-20; 2:14-15) and with whom we must be in right relationship."

13 Cf. Brink (2009: 149): "Our commitment to the objectivity of ethics is a deep one. Ethics is objective just in case there are fact or truths about what is good or bad and right or wring that obtain independently of the moral beliefs or attitudes of appraisers. A commitment to objectivity is part of a commitment to the normativity of ethics. Moral judgement express normative claims about what we should do and care about."

(1) *If there are no objective moral truths, then a Christian worldview is untenable.*
(2) *There are no objective moral truths.*
(3) *Therefore: A Christian worldview is untenable.*

The first premise is true. Without the assumption that there are objective moral truths, the Decalogue and the Golden Rule appear to be little more than suggestions how one might behave in this life, if one so wishes. Since this is not what Christians assume, they cannot let got of the idea that there are moral objective truths. The crucial premise of this argument is the second one. Arguments in its favour either have a relativistic or a naturalistic form.

The Argument from Relativity:

(1) *If there are objective moral truths, then every human person has to recognize the same moral values.*
(2) *Not every human person recognizes the same objective moral values.*
(3) *Therefore: There are no objective moral truths.*

The first premise is based on the idea that objective moral truths have to be accessible and recognizable as such by any human being that strives to get to know them, similar perhaps to mathematical truths that, as it were, are supposed to be accessible by anyone by way of rational insight. The second premise is based on the empirical observation that de facto not every human person or every human culture recognises the same objective moral values. However, if this is the case, then it follows that there are no objective moral truths.

The second argument against the existence of objective moral truths has the following structure:

The Argument from Naturalism (II):

(1) *If there are objective moral truths, then something exists that is not accountable for by scientific enquiry.*
(2) *There is nothing that is not accountable for by scientific inquiry.*
(3) *Therefore: There are no moral truths.*

The argument is similar to the argument against the existence of an immaterial soul. It is based on the assumption that if there were such things as objective moral truths, then scientific enquiry should be able to access them and to deal with them. Since, though, science is silent on the existence of objective moral truths, and since the existence of entities like objective moral values that influence, even in an indirect way, what happens in the universe rejects the assumption that science is complete, it follows that there are no objective moral truths. However, without the existence of objective moral truths also the fourth core assumption of a Christian worldview collapses.

4. Assessment of the Arguments against a Christian Worldview

We have seen the structure of the most popular arguments against the existence of God, the resurrection of Christ, life after death, and the existence of moral truth. In face of these arguments the plausibility of a Christian worldview seems entirely in vain. However, although the arguments presented are logically valid, I should like to start responding by way of reflecting once more on the logic and hermeneutics of a worldview before I briefly show general ways in which Christians could respond to the arguments directed against the plausibility of their worldview.

4.1 Meta-Assumptions and Circularity of a Worldview

Although, ideally, a worldview is a consistent, coherent, inclusive, and true set of assumptions that helps us getting along in the universe, and although empirically each one of us has a particular worldview that constitutes the horizon in which we live, move, and have our being, there is another feature concerning the logic of a worldview that so far we did not mention: there are fundamental assumptions of each worldview that, for lack of a better word, constitute the soil in which the particular worldview roots. We can refer to them as the meta-assumptions of each worldview. These meta-assumptions concern the fundamental metaphysical, hermeneutical, logical, and epistemological principles that direct and shape the rest of the worldview in question.

There are philosophically relevant features of these meta-assumptions: first, they constitute the realm of fundamental philosophical and theological discourse. Philosophers and theologians grapple with the plausibility of particular meta-assumptions. Second, questions concerning the plausibility of the meta-assumptions of a worldview are questions for which we have no method to answer them.[14] Unlike physics or chemistry, where we can deploy a particular scientifically accepted method in order to answer questions concerning physical or chemical problems, questions concerning the fundamental assumptions of each worldview cannot be dealt with in this way. There is no clear method on which we could rely in order to settle questions concerning, say, the existence of a mind-independent external world. Third, the adaption of one of those meta-assumptions as a constitutive feature of one's own worldview involves element structurally similar to what is known as faith within the boundaries of reason. That is to say, fundamental assumptions concerning the interpretation and understanding of the world as such do not impose themselves on us with inevitable logical force. We adopt them either unconsciously or by way of deciding to see the world

14 Cf. Priest (2007: 1): "Philosophy is the attempt to answer philosophical questions" and Priest (2007: 2): "A philosophical question is one we have no method for answering."

in a certain way, whereas our decisions must not contradict reason. However, since one's stance on the power and limits of reason is itself a fundamental meta-assumption of a worldview, the logic of a worldview is yet already always a circle of understanding.

4.2 The Existence of God

In respect to God, then, Christians can argue that the arguments presented against the existence of God presuppose either an inadequate understanding of "God" – one not shared by any Christian – or else that the apparent consequences that are supposed to contradict the existence of God in fact are problematic only if understood in a worldview that yet already deals with the corresponding phenomena in a way that presupposes that God does not exist, and thus begs the question against the Christian.[15]

Furthermore, the Christian can argue that there are certain fundamental assumptions that are shared by Christian and Non-Christian worldviews alike that support the claim that there is a supernatural cause of the existence of the world, and that this is what they refer to as "God". For instance, the principle of sufficient reason together with the metaphysical contingency of the universe seem to lead to the conclusion that there is a supernatural cause of the existence of the universe. In general, the Christian can refer to the traditional arguments for the existence of God, which start on widely agreed and plausible premises. As Craig (2004: 112) says, "insofar as we mean by a 'good argument' an argument which is formally and informally valid and consists of true premises which are more plausible than their negations, there do appear to be good arguments for God's existence, and there are on the contemporary scene many philosophers who think so."

4.3 The Resurrection of Jesus Christ

Although there is no sound philosophical argument for the resurrection of Jesus Christ the premises of which are shared by Christians and Non-Christians alike, the Christian can in a first step argue that given what we know about history, the existence of Jesus of Nazareth is as certain as one could wish for. As Ehrman (2012: 12) states: "Despite [an] enormous range of opinion, there are several points on which virtually all scholars of antiquity agree. Jesus was a Jewish man, known to be a preacher and teacher, who was crucified (a Roman form of execution) in Jerusalem during the reign of the Roman emperor Tiberius, when Pontius Pilate

15 Very often atheists argue against a straw man. For a particularly inadequate concept of God that shows lack of sufficient exegetical understanding cf. Dawkins (2007: 51): "The God of the Old Testament is arguably the most unpleasant character in all fiction: jealous and proud of it; a petty, unjust, unforgiving control-freak; a vindictive, bloodthirsty ethic cleanser; a misogynistic, homophobic, racist, infanticidal, genocidal, filicidal, pestilential, megalomaniacal, sado-masochistic, capriciously malevolent bully."

was the governor of Judea. [T]his is the view of nearly every trained scholar on the planet."

Based on the assumption that Jesus of Nazareth existed, the Christian can in a first step point out the implausibility of the assumption that his resurrection is a hoax made up by his disciples. Since, though, even if this is no guarantee that Jesus did rise from the dead, Christians can in a second step argue that based on their concept of God and based on their concept of nature the only case in which Jesus Christ could not have risen from the dead is when resurrection is a priori excluded as a genuine possibility. Since, though, the resurrection of Christ does not contradict the Christian concept of reason, God, or nature, Christians are free to endorse as a fundamental meta-assumption of their worldview that Jesus Christ did in fact rise from the dead. Assuming this, they do not contradict science or metaphysics as such.

4.4 Life after Death

In respect to life after death the Christian can point out that the only argument against the existence of an immaterial soul is formulated in a worldview that yet already supposes that science is our only means to obtain genuine knowledge of what exists. The Christian can in a first step argue that such a restricted naturalistic worldview itself is incoherent – science does not say that science is our only way to obtain knowledge of the world, so, those asserting this assert something that is not assumed to be true by science and therefore contradict themselves. Second, when it comes to bodily resurrection, the Christian can argue that it is either within the power of God to resurrect our physical body in a universe such that everything negative is excluded in that world, or else that God resurrects a spiritual body that individuates us in heaven.

4.5 The Existence of Objective Moral Truths

Although there is a huge discussion concerning the existence of objective moral truths, and although it is true that not everyone factually accepts the same moral values, the Christian can argue that, first of all, the naturalistic argument against the existence of objective moral truths is hardly convincing since, again, it is formulated in a framework based on assumptions not shared by the Christian and not entailed by science itself. Furthermore, the Christian can point out that the fact that not everyone factually accepts the same moral values does not entail logically that there are no objective moral truths. Third, the Christian can argue that any reasonable worldview entails the existence of moral values, and that the existence of moral values in a universe devoid of God is unintelligible. As Copan (2004:168) argues, "ontologically, then, objective moral values would not exist if God did not. But if they exist, then we have very good reason to think God exists."

4.6 Summary: The Christian Worldview

We have seen some of the most fundamental arguments against the plausibility of a Christian worldview and we have seen ways in which the Christian can, in principle, respond to the arguments. Overall, most of the arguments against the plausibility of a Christian worldview are based on premises the Christian is not forced to accept because they are fundamental assumptions of worldviews that yet already assume the implausibility of Christian faith. Based on plausible interpretations of reason, nature, and faith the Christian can show that none of the core assumptions of Christian faith contradicts metaphysics or science, and that based on Christian faith, an all-encompassing, plausible, coherent, and consistent worldview can be established. Perhaps we'll only know in heaven whether it is true.

Bibliography

Bishop, John. "Can there be Alternative Concepts of God?" In: *Nous*. Vol. 32. 1998, 174-188.

Brink, David O. "The Autonomy of Ethics." in Michael Martin (eds.): *The Cambridge Companion to Atheism*. Cambridge: Cambridge University Press. 2009, 149-165.

Carvalho IV, John J. "Overview of the Structure of a Scientific Worldview." In: *Zygon*. Vol. 41. 2006. 113-124.

Clayton, Philip. *Adventures in the Spirit. God, World, Divine Action*. Fortress Press, 2008.

Copan, Paul. "The Moral Argument." in Paul Copan, Paul K. Moser (eds.): *The Rationality of Theism*. London: Routledge. 2004, 149-174.

Craig, William Lane. "The Cosmological Argument." in Paul Copan, Paul K. Moser (eds.): *The Rationality of Theism*. London: Routledge. 2004, 112-131.

Craig, William Lane. "Theistic Critiques of Atheism." in Michael Martin (eds.): *The Cambridge Companion to Atheism*. Cambridge: Cambridge University Press. 2009, 69-85.

Dawkins, Richard. *The God Delusion*. Black Swan, 2007.

Doherty, Earl. *Jesus: Neither God nor Man*. Age of Reason Publications, 2009.

Ehrman, Bart. *Did Jesus Exist? The Historical Argument for Jesus of Nazareth*. Harper One, 2012.

Fales, Evan. "Naturalism and Physicalism." in Michael Martin (eds.): *The Cambridge Companion to Atheism*. Cambridge: Cambridge University Press. 2009, 118-134.

Göcke, Benedikt Paul. "Physicalism QuaerensIntellectum." in *The Philosophical Forum*. Vol. 39 (4). 2008, 463-468.

Göcke, Benedikt Paul. "An Analytic Theologian's Stance on the Existence of God." in *European Journal for Philosophy of Religion*. Vol. 5, 2013, 129-146.

Göcke, Benedikt Paul. *A Theory of the Absolute*. Basingstoke: Palgrave Macmillan, 2014.

Göcke, Benedikt Paul. "Did God do it? Metaphysical Models and Theological Hermeneutics." in *International Journal for Philosophy of Religion*. Online First, 2014a.

Göcke, Benedikt Paul. "The Many Problems of Special Divine Action." in *European Journal for the Philosophy of Religion*, 2015.

Kuhn, Thomas. *The Structure of Scientific Revolutions*. Chicago: The University of Chicago Press, 1996.

Lowe, E. J. *Personal Agency. The Metaphysics of Mind and Action.* Oxford: Oxford University, 2008.

Mackie, J. L. "Evil and Omnipotence." in *Mind.* Vol. 64. 1955, 200-212.

Mautner, Gareth (eds.). *A Dictionary of Philosophy.* Oxford: Blackwell, 1996.

McGrath, Alister E. "In what way can Jesus be a Moral Example for Christians?". in JETS. Vol. 34 (3). 1991, 289-298

Murphey, Nancey. *Bodies and Souls, or, Spirited Bodies?* Cambridge: Cambridge University Press, 2006.

Papineau, David. "The Rise of Physicalism." in M. Stone and J. Wolff (eds.). *The Proper Ambition of Science.* London: Routledge, 2000.

Papineau, David. *Thinking about Consciousness.* Oxford: Oxford University Press, 2002.

Polkinghorne, John. *Quantum Theory. A Very Short Introduction.* Oxford: Oxford University Press, 2002.

Priest, Stephen. *The British Empiricists.* London: Routledge, 2007.

Quine, W. V. "Two Dogmas of Empiricism." in *The Philosophical Review.* Vol. 60. 1951, 20-43.

Smith, Quentin. "The Metaphilosophy of Naturalism." in *Philo.* Vol 4. 2001, 195-215,

Swinburne, Richard. "Personal Identity: The Dualist Theory." in Michael J. Loux (eds.): *Metaphysics. Contemporary Readings.* Routledge. 2001, 420-447.

Tapp, Christian. "Joseph Ratzinger on Resurrection Identity." in Georg Gasser (eds.): *Personal Identity and Resurrection. How do we Survive Our Death?* Ashgate, 207-224, 2010.

Vidal, Clément. "Metaphilosophical Criteria for Worldview Comparison." in *Metaphilosophy.* Vol. 43. 2012, 306-347.

Zuckerman, Phil. "Atheism Contemporary Numbers and Patterns." in Michael Martin (eds.): *The Cambridge Companion to Atheism.* Cambridge: Cambridge University Press. 2009, 47-65.

Chapter 8

The Great Escape
Remarks on Anachoresis Then and Today

Jonna Golec

1. The Unclear Beginnings

The anachoresis movement was born in the 3rd century AD in the Eastern and African provinces of the late Roman Empire. Its basic establishment was to make its followers lead an ascetic life in remote, deserted places and total separation from the world outside. The term itself comes from Greek and it can be translated into *retirement* which in this case could be understood as *retirement from the earthly life*. Unlike the idea of *coenobium* instituting community-type of monasteries, the anachorite hermits or lavra hermitages laid emphasizes on self-experience of the divine powers by monks. It could take different forms from the total isolation to the partial one, like the stylites who were living on the top of high pillars inside the community, still having no or little contact with the people down. There were also *lavras* that consisted of multitudes of cells inhabited by the eremites and connected into a small, yet secluded community.

The first such full eremite was supposed to be either Paul of Thebes or Anthony, the life of the first one described in St Jerome's *Vita Pauli primi eremitae* and the latter by Athanasius of Alexandria's (ca. 296-373) *Vita Antonii*.[1] In this article I would be elaborating on the life of Anthony as an example of an eremitic life.

As for Paul of Thebes, his authenticity has been long disputed and the discussion is still going on, if he was a real person or just the character created

1 Athanasius, *Life of St Anthony*, 3.10-15.

by Jerome. Some scholars, like Kevin Roddy[2] write that creating the character of Paul could be the result of Jerome's reluctance towards what he saw as *a monastic life* in then Egypt; building the monasteries near the communities, accepting food donations and not being enough isolated from the society. We shall highlight the view of what was *the perfect life of an eremite* back in the Late Antiquity.

At the beginning of Jerome's work, Athanasius gives us historical frames of this story. The word *storm*[3] is used to describe the wave of persecutions undertaken by the Roman Emperor Decius (ca. 201-251) starting from 250 AD and the following ones from 257 AD undertaken by Valerian (ca. 200-264). Both were tragic and violent events contrasting with the peaceful acquiescence and tolerance of Severus Alexander only 15 years before. During Decius repressions Christians were forced to celebrate polytheistic rituals under the penalty of death, if they refused, the priests were jailed and the Roman emperor even sentenced the Pope Fabianus to death. Valerian went few steps further, as he forced the clergy to take part in libations for the Roman gods and due to his edict, the bishop Ciprianus of Carthage was sentenced to death. Nevertheless, M. Cary and H. Scullard[4] rightly mention that because the Empire's subjects wanted to live in peace with Christians and perhaps, the people had been endeavoring the concept of one god, those events occured rarely. We should recall here the short yet official cult of Elagabal established by the mad emperor Elagabalus and the one of Sol Invictus introduced by Aurelianus.

Who were Paul and Anthony? Jerome writes that Paul was an educated man, fluent in Greek and Egyptian, who together with his sister was supposed to inherit a substantial wealth after the death of their mother and father.[5] Now, it is not explained whether his parents died as victims of persecution or not, however, we can suspect that, as in fear of persecution he left himself for some time to a more secure place, later betrayed by the greedy husband of his sister. And for this reason, Paul fled to inaccessible mountains to wait till *the storms* would finish. This is how his transformation and journey to sanctity began. As for Anthony, we don't have such a brutal reality in Athanasius's story. Anthony was an orphan with one sister just like Paul, wealthy as Paul, yet he wasn't drawn into the eremite path the same way the one already described. Anthony had always been very

2 Kevin Roddy, "Paul the Hermit" in *The Holy People in the World. Vol III: Entries from H to P*, edited by Phyllis Jestice, (United States of America: ABC-CLIO, 2004), 679.

3 *During the persecutions of Decius and Valerian [...] many churches in Egypt and the baid were laid waste by the fury of the storm*, Jerome, *Life of St Paul*, 2.1-6.

4 Max Cary, Howard Hayes Scullard, *A history of Rome down to the reign of Constantine.* Vol. II (United Kingdom: Bedford, 1976), 418-419.

5 Jerome, *op. cit.*, 5.1-10.

devoted to Church and it was by the words of Gospel,[6] he decided to give his wealth to the villagers due to find his path to Eternal Life in Heaven.

2. Few Steps Backwards and then Back to the Future

I think, in order to understand the phenomenon of living a solitary life chosen by monks of the Late Antiquity, we should learn more about them from authentic sources and authors. Their life inspired many people to follow the life of an ideal eremite, after the example of Paul and Anthony. Perhaps, studying the ancient texts we can investigate how the term of *ideal eremite* was perceived. According to Jerome, it was a very modest life; Paul lived for hundred thirteen years, surviving on water from the inside spring, fruits from the palm tree, half a loaf of bread brought by a raven, and wearing clothes made of palm leaves, and the most important on prayers. For those of little faith, Jerome recalls examples of such similar eremites and claims that *all things are possible to him that believeth.*[7] By God's power, Paul is able to tame fantastic mythical creatures like centaurs[8] or satyrs[9] and bring them onto the path of God as a symbol of the human victory over the pagan deities, symbol of deceiving Satan.

Anthony, on the contrary, had his own disciples before departing to the desert life and his struggles with devil are mostly of different nature from what we can see on the dramatic paintings or prints by the Renaissance masters, such as Michelangelo,[10] Bernardino Parenzano,[11] Hieronymus Bosch,[12] or Martin Schongauer,[13] which present the most shocking aspects of life of the saint eremite. Athanasius often describes them as those of a frequent human struggle, like hunger, temptations towards the needs of flesh, worries about the family[14] and desire of restoring wealth.[15] Generally, the story of Athanasius seems to be much more human than the idealistic picture of Jerome. His problems are much closer to ours, being enticed with things that all the humans are struggling

6 *If you would be perfect, go and sell that you have and give to the poor*, Athanasius, *op. cit.*, 2.12-14.

7 Jerome, *Life of St Paul*, 5.8-18, 6.1-12.

8 *Ibid.*, 7.21.

9 *Ibid.*, 8.17-20.

10 Michelangelo Buonarotti, *The Torment of Saint Anthony.* Oil and tempera on panel (Fort Worth: Kimbell Art Museum, 1487-1488).

11 Bernardino Parenzano, *Temptations of Saint Anthony.* Oil on panel (Rome: Galleria Doria Pamphilj, 1494).

12 Hieronymus Bosch, *Triptych of Temptation of Saint Anthony.* Oil on panel (Lisbon: Museu Nacional de Arte Antiga, 1501).

13 Martin Schongauer, *The Temptation of Saint Anthony.* Copperlate engraving. (London: British Museum, 1470).

14 Athanasius, *op.cit.*, 5.

15 *Ibid.*, 12.

with during their lives. Anthony is neither a stationery ascetic, he moves his locations from tombs where his friend would bring him bread,[16] to the Nile fort, where he would deny the entrance to other people,[17] finally to the cave inside of the mountain[18] that remained his shelter and most beloved place. He would weave baskets to provide himself alimentation,[19] which in my opinion, only emphasizes the human face of Anthony that Athanasius presents in his writings. Fighting with demons looks rather like a combat against the wildness of the rough land that he chose for ascetic life though the demons approached him in the shape of wild animals, natural disasters.[20] These are the ferocious beasts and hostile conditions that want to interfere in his sacred mission.

And I think, that at this point we should reconsider of what the evilness and the demons were and what did the desert really meant to Anthony, Paul and other men, like Hilarion,[21]Moses the Ethiopian,[22] and many other followers of their deeds. Just to recall, we should remember that the desert was the arena of life of the John Baptist, it was where Jesus was tempted by the devil but also, as a Biblical term, it meant *the wilderness*,[23] so no wonder that we see the passages in Athanasius and Jerome that relate to the wild beasts that attacked our eremites. These places have had a great spiritual meaning to these men, who went there to search for the enlightment. The word *eremite* itself means *someone, who lives in the desert/ wilderness*[24] and according to me, it should be understood metaphorically and literally as *the God's warrior*; one who goes to the wilderness, the place which should be bereft from God, to find Him there.

16 *Ibid.*, 8.

17 *Ibid.*, 13.

18 *Ibid.*, 49-50.

19 *Ibid.*, 53.

20 *Ibid.*, 9-10, 51.

21 William Harmless, *Desert Christians. An Introduction to Literature of Early Monasticism* (United States of America: Oxford University Press, 2004), 432.

22 *Ibid.*, 203.

23 Matthew George Easton, "Desert", in *The Ultimate Bible Dictionary: Extended Annotated Version*, (Germany: Jazzybee Verlag, 2012); Stephen Renn, "Desert", in *Expository Dictionary of Bible Words: Word Studies for Key English Bible Words Based on the Hebrew and Greek Texts*, (United States of America: Hendrickson Publishers, 2005), 267; Bernd Janowski, "Wild Beasts", in *Dictionary of Deities and Demons in the Bible*, edited by Karel van der Toorn, Bob Becking, Pieter van der Horst, (United States of America: William B. Erdmans Publishing Company, 1999), 897; James Douglas, Merrill Tenney, Moises Silva, "Desert", in *Zondervan Illustrated Bible Dictionary*, (United States of America: Zondervan, 2011).

24 Mostyn John Armstrong, *History and Antiquities of the Country of Norfolk. Vol. X*, (United Kingdom: Gale Ecco. Print Editions, 1781), 284; Dimitri Gondicas, *et al.*, *Greek Today: A Course in the Modern Language and Culture*, (United States of America: University Press of New England, 2004), 334; Arnold Toynbee, David Sommervell, *A Study of History. Abridgement of Volumes VII-X* (United States of America: Oxford Paperbacks, 1957), 110.

It was to prove His almightiness in assisting the triumph over the devil[25] and the warriors,[26] having the desert as an exercise field. The desert had been attested as this miraculous place in the Bible already in The Book of Isaiah,[27] or Deuternomy[28] and the famous passage from The Gospel of John[29] could be an analogy of raven that brought bread to Paul, or the date tree, water springs and oasis found among the land of endless sands that were the testimonies of Lord and helped Paul and Anthony to sustain their worldly being. And above all, the desert as the place of seclusion, shouldn't be just taken for the physically known desert; Martin of Tours (ca. 316/336-397) installed his hermitage outside the city of Ligugé[30] because of obvious desert lands scarcity. So, the place itself needed to follow the idea of inaccessibility and harshness.

As a novice in archaeologist, I would like to adduce archaeological data from some hermitages found in Egypt and to compare their relevance to the ideal eremite system found in Athanasius and Jerome. As mentioned before, the literary data is important to understand the mentality of then Christians, to create a perfect archetype of an eremite that prevailed in people's minds. Yet, we are ought to be aware about how ideals differ from the reality and in this case we should be attentive too. Studying hermitage from Naqlun I would present my perception of truth in the anchoresis now and then basing on my research studies.

Naqlun is a hermitage complex carved inside the hill slopes located within the Fayum Oasis in Egypt. It has been excavated by the University of Warsaw since 1988 and consists of hermitages in number of 89 that were inhabited from the 5th century to the Late Medieval times. From around 200 years after Paul's and

25 *This was Anthony's first struggle against the devil, or rather this victory was the Saviour's work in Anthony*, Athanasius, *op.cit.*, 7.1-2.

26 *Ibid.,* 10.5-9.

27 *They did not thirst when He led them through the deserts; He made water flow for them from the rock; He split the rock, and water gushed out*, Holman Christian Standard Bible, Isa. 48:21; *A voice of one crying out: Prepare the way of the LORD in the wilderness; make a straight highway for our God in the desert*, Isa. 40:3.

28 *For the LORD your God has blessed you in all the work of your hands. He has watched over your journey through this immense wilderness. The LORD your God has been with you this past 40 years, and you have lacked nothing*, Deut. 3:7.

29 *Our fathers ate the manna in the wilderness, just as it is written: He gave them bread from heaven* to eat, John 6:31.

30 Marylin Dunn, *Emergence of Monasticism: From the Desert Fathers to the Early Middle Ages,* United Kingdom: Blackwell Publishing, 2003) 62; Clifford Lawrence, *Medieval Monasticism: Forms of Religious Life in Western Europe in the Middle Ages*, (United Kingdom: Routledge, 2000)12; William Harmless, "Monasticism", in *The Oxford Handbook of Early Christian Studies*, edited by: Susan Ashbrook Harvey, David C. Hunter, (United States of America: Oxford University Press, 2008), 496.

Anthony's estimated life. It is located in the vicinity of 6-7th century cemetery and Nekloni (Naqlun) monastery[31] that lived according to Anthony's rules.

The oldest among all was Hermitage 44[32] which could be dated even to the 5th century. This monastery is located 1000 m from the Neklo monastery, inside of a small valley. The complex is another rock-carved construction and consists of seven rooms that could be entered from the courtyard, each room having a separate entrance.[33] The excavators claim that the complex wasn't used for a long time, perhaps just before the roof fell down. Some of its rooms were executed with care, their walls being plastered, some other were done rather carelessly. There were two bread ovens found in the courtyard, which could prove the self-sufficiency of the eremites.[34] According to the Polish archeologists that excavated the hermitages of Naqlun, it appeared that Hermitage 44 was inhabited by one or two eremites. One of them, probably named Phoibammon,[35] was rather an educated and wealthy man speaking either Greek and Coptic, which would have followed Paul's and Anthony's pattern, if not for the remains of opulence found inside of his dwelling. This hermitage adapted to the natural landscape, yet it brought up questions of how ascetic was life of its dweller. Namely, though, these cells were maybe not as elaborate as the others listed by Darlene Hedstrom,[36] she points out finds from Unit B[37] such as golden coins, glass vessels and wares from Cyprus or North Africa. Except questioning the modest lifestyle, there should also be questioning of how distant from the temporal life was an inhabitant of this complex. In Jerome's text, one of the first questions St Paul asked Anthony when he just met him was about the situation of the world he had known before,

31 Iwona Zych, "Cemetery C in Naqlun: Preliminary Report on the Excavation in 2006", in *Polish Archaeology in the Mediterranean XVIII. Reports 2006*, edited by Michał Gawlikowski, Wiktor Daszewski, (Poland: University of Warsaw Publishers, 2006), 231.

32 Włodzimierz Godlewski, "Naqlun. Excavations 1995", in *Polish Archaeology in the Mediterranean VII. Reports 1995.*, edited by Anna Witecka, (Poland: University of Warsaw Publishers, 1995), 82.

33 Darlene Hedstrom, "Divine Architects: Designing the Monastic Dwelling Place", in *Egypt in the Byzantine World. 300-700*, edited by Roger S. Bagnall, (United Kingdom: Cambridge University Press, 2010), 376.

34 Włodzimierz Godlewski, Ewa Parandowska, "Naqlun. Excavations 1996", in *Polish Archaeology in the Mediterranean VIII. Reports 1996*, edited by Anna Witecka, (Poland: University of Warsaw Publishers, 1996), 88-89.

35 *Ibid.*, 90-91; Włodzimierz Godlewski, "Naqlun (Nekloni). The Hermitages, Cemetery and the Keep in the early 6th century", in *Graeco-Roman Fayum-Texts and Archaeology: Proceedings of the Third International Fayum Symposion*, edited by Steffen Lippert and Maren Schentuleit, (Germany: Harrasowitz Verlag, 2008), 103-105.

36 Darlene Hedstrom, *op.cit.*, 376.

37 *Ibid.*, 377.

the political changes and civilization.[38] The other units[39] in the complex weren't as wealthy as Unit B, but were still provided with some fine objects, like glass or pottery objects.[40]

Hermitage 89[41] followed same rock-carving technique of construction as Hermitage 25 and consisted six units.[42] One of the rooms (A2) had an evidence of a long occupation according to alterations being made. In one of its phases, it had been equipped with a bed with profile headrest[43] and most probably it had communication with Unit B.1. through a large window, which again arises same questions of the factual life of eremites in that times. Furthermore, Włodzimierz Godlewski states that Unit B.1. might have been used as an oratory[44] of a kind, and graffiti on its walls belonged to the people, who visited it. Olaf Kaper wrote in his report[45] that there were some Arabic inscriptions there but most of it belonged rather to Coptic pilgrims. We can observe names and the origin of the visitors of hermitage. However, most probably this hermitage produced[46] natural fiber products, such as mats, ropes or baskets and pottery objects, the finds suggest. This brings us back to Saint Anthony weaving the baskets in an exchange for food. There are papyri[47] appearing that officials sent their donations to Naqlun's anachorites. This hermitage, as the finds suggest, was one of those inhabited in the Late Medieval times.

---

38 *Tell me therefore, I pray you, how fares the human race? Are new homes springing up in the ancient cities? What government directs the world? Are there still some remaining for the demons to carry away by their delusions?* Jerome, *op.cit.*, 10.3-5.

39 *Ibid.*, 377; Włodzimierz Godlewski, "Polish Excavations at Naqlun (1988-1989)", in *Polish Archaeology in the Mediterranean. Reports 1988-1999,* edited by Rafał Koliński, (Poland: University of Warsaw Publishers, 1989), 31.

40 *Ibid.*, 32.

41 Włodzimierz Godlewski, "Deir el-Naqlun,1990", in *Polish Archaeology in the Mediterranean II. Reports 1990.*, edited by Rafał Koliński, (Poland: University of Warsaw Publishers, 1990), 48.

42 Tomasz Derda, "Polish excavations at Deir el-Naqlun 1986-1991", in *Proceedings of the 20th International Congress of Papyrologists. Copenhagen, 23-29 August, 1992,* edited by Adam Bulow-Jacobsen, (Denmark: Museum Tusculanum Press, 1992), 126.

43 *Ibid.*, 49.

44 *Ibid.*, 50.

45 Olaf Kaper, "Arabic Papyri and Inscriptions from Naqlun, Hermitage 89", in *Polish Archaeology in the Mediterranean II. Reports 1990,* edited by Rafał Koliński, (Poland: University of Warsaw Publishers, 1990), 57.

46 Włodzimierz Godlewski, "Deir el-Naqlun,1990", in *Polish Archaeology in the Mediterranean II. Reports 1990,* edited by Rafał Koliński, (Poland: University of Warsaw Publishers, 1990), 51-53.

47 Tomasz Derda, "Polish excavations at Deir el-Naqlun 1986-1991", in *Proceedings of the 20th International Congress of Papyrologists. Copenhagen, 23-29 August, 1992,* edited by Adam Bulow-Jacobsen, (Denmark: Museum Tusculanum Press, 1992), 126.

We shall now look at some contemporary eremites according to the theory of convergent evolution,[48] which is originally a biological theory but can be applied to many disciplines of science. It is important to understand the archeological tradition of Paul and Anthony or the traditions of Naqlun or maybe they found a balance between two? The case studied and presented is of so-called The Eremite Melsztyn from (Poland) and Rachel Denton from Lincolnshire (England).

There are two eremites near Melsztyn, who live in two small houses (according to media,[49] each 2x2m big) near the Dunajec river. Their names are Marian and Grzegorz and one of them lives in a total seclusion, the other doesn't prohibit the entrance to those who seek for shelter or help. Both hermitages aren't located in the absolute wilderness, but the witnesses to lives of these two eremites claim that you can hear the sounds of cars passing on the nearby roads.[50] As Grzegorz states in his story, he came to his hermitage spot in 1995, after he had been casted away[51] from his monastery due to reasons, he doesn't remember anymore. Yet, he never held a grudge and wanted to continue his service to Jesus in another way. His main reason[52] to continue to live in seclusion was that the world heads towards something contrary to good. When he came to Melsztyn, Marian had already been living his anachorite life there for few years, allegedly coming during the time of Martial law in Poland. He claims that he built his small hermitage with his own hands. His diet[53] is combined of fresh vegetables, eggs produced by his hens and honey made by bees he breeds himself. Occasionally, he eats meat but also, from time to time, he tends to fast for the whole day. His days are filled mostly with prayer and work but he doesn't avoid contacting with humans. Grzegorz lets people visiting his hermitage, he is a very respect persona in his local community and he contacts with the world through the computer[54] and doesn't abstain from doing small jobs to earn his living. He uses sun battery installed on the top of his dwelling. Undoubtedly, in many cases he isn't standard eremite but according to

48 Elizabeth Browne, "Convergent Evolution", in *Dictionary of the History of Science*, edited by William Bynum, Elizabeth Browne, Roy Porter, (United States of America: Princeton University Press, 1981), 79.

49 Marta Paluch (2012), "Pustelnik z Melsztyna", *Gazeta Krakowska Online,* December 25, 2012, available: http://www.gazetakrakowska.pl/artykul/726347,pustelnik-z-melsztynazdjecia,id,t.html?cookie=1

50 *Ibid.*

51 *Ibid.*

52 Daria Jaworska, "Pustelnik z Melsztyna: "Cudów jeszcze nie czynię"", *Kolory i cienie życia. Historie dobrze opowiedziane,* January 29, 2015, available: http://www.koloryicienie.pl/ludzie/pustelnik-z-melsztyna/.

53 Marta Paluch, *op.cit;* Daria Jaworska, *op.cit.*

54 *Ibid.*

him[55] Jesus doesn't claim in Gospels that we should mortify ourselves, he teaches about loving the others and loving God.

Rachel Denton is a 50 year old lady living a red brick house in Lincolnshire. She is one of the British eremites and has spent 14 years living with dedication to sacrum sphere. Just like Grzegorz, she relies on crops she grows and poultry she looks after. Furthermore, she shares a monastery background[56] just like The Eremite from Melsztyn and earns her own living. Rachel sells her hand-made cards[57] and other stationery in an on-line shop and sustains contact with people through the internet, having her own Twitter[58] account. She admits that she would prefer to dwell in a cave,[59] or mountain and seclude herself completely from the society like the ancient hermits used to, but she is also aware that in the world we live in, one must do their living.

The Lincolnshire Eremite named her home St Cuthbert's House after St Cuthbert (ca. 634-687), bishop of Lindisfarne whose body had been uncorrupted eleven years after he died. He was a very popular preacher and allegedly bore a talent of prophecy and healing. David Farmer[60] writes that St Cuthbert became one of the Northern England's most popular saints. Therefore, it is quite understandable that Rachel chose him as the patron of her hermitage. She says that she has valued solitude[61] as a little girl and that she had thought about getting married and establishing family when she had been younger, but somehow the vocation has always been present in her life. One of her words strikes me the most, literally her observation, that an anchorite life is a little bit like death[62] either fascinating and frightening people, because it is something unknown but something that people would like to taste just to experience it, thus I think that this sentence also describes my interest in this subject.

3. Final Conclusion

Anachoresis is a phenomenon present in the Christian world since antiquity. Through the pages of this article we have followed its forms in different times and geographical areas and discussed it in various aspects, making it not strictly

55 M. Paluch (2012), *op.cit* [original text: A Pan Jezus nie mówi w Ewangelii, żeby się umartwiać, tylko uczy miłości względem innych i Boga. A umartwienia to dodatek]

56 Rebecca Sandiford, "The modern hermit living in an end-of-terrace house", *BBC online*, October 11, 2013, available: http://www.bbc.co.uk/religion/0/24367826

57 http://www.stcuthbertshouse.co.uk/index_files/Page2231.htm

58 https://twitter.com/hermitrachel

59 Rebecca Sandiford, *op.cit.*

60 David Farmer, *The Oxford Dictionary of Saints, Fifth Edition Revised*, (United States of America: Oxford University Press, 2011), 108.

61 Rachel Denton, "I am a hermit", *the Guardian Online*, June 20, 2009, available: http://www.theguardian.com/lifeandstyle/2009/jun/20/experience-hermit

62 Rebecca Sandiford, *op.cit.*

historical or archaeological work but also philosophical and theological. My question formed in first paragraphs and reiterated throughout the whole article, is if the ideal pattern of anachorite has been sustained by its followers and how actual is it nowadays. Let me give my last remarks according to examples I have used in my work.

Personally, I have chosen such subject of an article not without the reason. Even though, I am not a member of any order, there has been a time in my life in which I considered being, living, and becoming an eremite and spend my life committed to prayer and meditation. I have always seen anachorite life as ***The Great Escape***. Escape from the turpistic world preoccupied by money and triggered by wars to the sanctuary of mind and solitude. Escape to a place, where one doesn't need to bear many goods to feel happy or fulfilled and can test oneselves on survival based on their co-relation with the world of nature. Finally, escape from materialism and secularism into spiritual rapprochement.

We can observe many analogies studying the lives of St Paul and St Anthony, the prototypes for eremitism set in the Late Antiquity and comparing them with the Naqlun eremites or the modern anachorites from Poland and England. Jerome's *Vita Pauli Primi Eremitae* is a more idealistic vision of hermitage than the one by Athanasius, yet it seems to be closer to the Biblical vision of the desert; life on it and concept of manna from heaven derived from the Bible and as whole, should be rather taken theoretically. Thus, at the point where the ideologies of Anthony and Paul partially meet; literally refusing contact with people and the outer world, we can agree that we can't see the same feature in the monks from Naqlun, having the evidence of them having guests, and in Grzegorz from Poland or Rachel from England, who keep in touch with *the outer world* through the internet or the direct contact.

The model of Anthony can be easily seen in many aspects, especially in the emphasize of work as the way of survival having Naqlun and modern hermits selling things they produce with their own hands. Another similarity is the human face that Athanasius gave to his hero, the natural fears and temptations; Rachel claims that she had been thinking about setting up a family, Grzegorz had been suffering from cold and inconveniences before he built his hermitage. As for the concept of *wilderness* that I devoted a fair portion of text to, we should recall the roof that collapsed in Hermitage 44 or point out one of the memories of Grzegorz that we can find in Marta Paluch's article I used before, about the eremite's goats that froze to death due to a harsh weather. The analogies are many, but can we truly say that eremites have kept the same ancient understanding of anachoresis since the 4th century to this day?

Both Athanasius and Jerome set their stories in the time of Christian persecutions, but only Jerome uses it as a reason for Paul to start his ascetic path. Athanasius states clearly about the vocation received by Anthony, same goes for the examples from Poland and England. Yet, I think that to understand the complexity of problem arisen in my work, we should ask ourselves if such total isolation from the outer world was possible and therefore, if both stories shouldn't just be understood as a wishful thinking rather than factual situation? The question of seclusion appeared when I spoke about Naqlun and Grzegorz and Rachel admitted without hesitation that they do not refuse contact with people. According to this, it seems most probable that *Vita Pauli Primi Eremitae* and *Vita Antonii* were spiritual manuals to how should one lead their life in seclusion written with idealistic and unrealistic features of mentality, especially that the one by Jerome was written around the same time as Naqlun monastery started to function. The real image of anachoresis as phenomenon being shown rather by the dwellers from the Fayum Oasis and the modern ones, they were "more or less modest, more or less wealthy. Nevertheless, the idea of the Great Escape remains inside of our beings. Tempting and tantalizing.

Bibliography

Armstrong, Mostyn John. *History and Antiquities of the Country of Norfolk. Vol. X.* United Kingdom: Gale Ecco. Print Editions, 1781. Athanasius, *Life of St Anthony.*Becking, Bob and Van der Toorn, Karel and Van der Horst, Pieter. *Dictionary of Deities and Demons in the Bible.* United States of America: William B. Erdmans Publishing Company, 1999. Bien, Peter and Gondicas, Dimitri and Rassias, John and Karanika Andromache and Yannakou-Bien Chrysanthi. *Greek today: A course in the Modern Language and Culture.* United States of America: University Press of New England, 2004. Bosch, Hieronymus. *Triptych of Temptation of Saint Anthony.* Oil on panel. Lisbon: Museude Arte Antiga, 1501. Browne Elizabeth. "Convergent Evolution" in *Dictionary of the History of Science,* edited by Elizabeth Browne, William Bynum and Roy Porter, (United States of America: Princeton University Press, 1981), 79. Buonarotti, Michelangelo. *The Torment of Saint Anthony.* Oil and tempera on panel. Fort Worth: Kimbell Museum, 1487-1488. Cary, Max and Scullard, Howard Hayes. *A History of Rome Down to the Reign of Constantine. Vol. II* Kingdom: Bedford/ St Martin's, 1976. Denton, Rachel. "I am a hermit", *the Guardian Online,* available: http://www.theguardian.com/lifeandstyle/2009/jun/20/experience-hermit Derda, Tomasz. "Polish excavations at Deir el-Naqlun 1986-1991" in *Proceedings of the 20th International Congress of Papyrologists. Copenhagen, 23-29 August, 1992,* edited by Adam Bulow-Jacobsen, (Denmark: Museum Tusculanum Press, 1992), 124-131. Douglas, James and Tenney, Merrill and Silva, Moises. "Desert" in *Zondervan Illustrated Bible Dictionary,* (United States of America: Zondervan, 2011). Easton, Matthew George. "Desert", in *The Ultimate Bible Dictionary: Extended Annotated Version,* (Germany: Jazzybee Verlag, 2012).

Farmer, David. *The Oxford Dictionary of Saints, Fifth Edition Revised.* United States of America: Oxford University Press, 2011.

Godlewski, Włodzimierz. "Polish Excavations at Naqlun (1988-1989)" in *Polish Archaeology in the Mediterranean. Reports 1988-1999,* edited by Rafał Koliński, (Poland: University of Warsaw Publishers, 1990), 29-34. Godlewski, Włodzimierz. "Naqlun. Excavations 1995" in *Polish Archaeology in the Mediterranean VII. Reports 1995,* edited by Anna Witecka, (Poland: University of Warsaw Publishers, 1995), 82-88.Harmless, William. *Desert Christians. An Introduction to Literature of Early Monasticism.* United States of America: Oxford University Press, 2004. Harmless, William. "Monasticim" in *The Oxford Handbook of Early Christian*

Studies, edited by Susan Harvey Ashbrook and David C. Hunter, (United States of America: Oxford University Press, 2008), 493-521.

Hedstrom, Darlene. "Divine Architects: Designing the Monastic Dwelling Place" in *Egypt in the Byzantine World, 300-700*, edited by Roger S. Bagnall, (United Kingdom: Cambridge University Press, 2010), 766-806. Jaworska, Daria. "Pustelnik z Melsztyna: "Cudów jeszcze nie czynię"" in *Kolory i cienie życia. Historie dobrze opowiedziane*, available: http://www.koloryicienie.pl/ludzie/pustelnik-z-melsztyna/Jerome, *Life of St Paul.* Kaper, Olaf. "Arabic Papyri and Inscriptions from Naqlun, Hermitage 89" in *Polish Archaeology in the Mediterranean II. Reports 1990*, edited by Rafał Koliński, (Poland: University of Warsaw Publishers, 1995), 57-59. Lawrence, Clifford. *Medieval Monasticism: Forms of Religious Life in Western Europe in the Middle Ages*. United Kingdom: Routledge, 2000. Paluch, Marta. Pustelnik z Melsztyna, *Gazeta Krakowska Online,* available: http://www.gazetakrakowska.pl/artykul/726347,pustelnik-z-melsztynazdjecia,id,t.html?cookie=1 Parenzano, Bernardino. *Temptations of Saint Anthony*. Oil on panel. Rome: Galleria Doria Pamphilj, 1494.

Renn, Stephen. "Desert" in *Expository Dictionary of Bible Words: Word Studies for Key English Bible Words Based on the Hebrew and Greek Texts*, (United States of America: Hendrickson Publishers, 2005). Roddy, Kevin. "Paul the Hermit" in *The Holy People in the World. Vol III: Entries from H to P*, edited by Phyllis Jestice, (United States of America: ABC-CLIO, 2004), 679. Sandiford, Rebecca. "The modern hermit living in an end-of-terrace house", *BBC online*, available: http://www.bbc.co.uk/religion/0/24367826 Schongauer, Martin. *The Temptation of Saint Anthony.* Copperlate engraving. London: British Museum, 1470. Sommervell, David and Toynbee, Arnold. *A Study of History. Abridgement of Volumes VII-X*, United States of America: Oxford Paperbacks, 1957. *The Holy Bible*. United States of America: Holman Bible Publications, 2003. Zych, Iwona. "Cemetery C in Naqlun: Preliminary Report on the Excavation in 2006" , in *Polish Archaeology in the Mediterranean XVIII. Reports 2006* , edited by Michał Gawlikowski and Wiktor Daszewski, (Poland: University of Warsaw Publishers, 1995), 230-247.

Chapter 9

Death Inspires Life
A Perspective in Medical Anthropology

Marina D'Costa

1. Introduction

Originally death appears to us as something which comes from the outside and strikes us down, something over which we have no control; and it is precisely this feature of our original reaction to death, which produces the greatest terror and drives us mostly surely into an attitude of inauthenticity.[1] Embedded in most people's conception of a good life is avoiding an early death. Life expectancy takes account of the credits as well as the debits: it embodies all the behavior, circumstances and interventions that promotes health or detract from it.[2] A health system encompasses many areas: perceptions and classifications of health problems, prevention measures, diagnosis, healing (magical, religious, scientific, healing substances) and healers. Ethnomedicine has expanded its focus to include topics such as perceptions of the body, culture and disability and change in indigenous or traditional healing systems, especially as resulting from globalization.[3] Anthropologist have turned in increasing numbers to the cross- cultural study of medical systems and to the biological and socio-cultural factors that influence

1 Robert. G. Olson, *An Introduction to Existentialism* (New York: Dover Publications Inc, 1962), 200.

2 *Alistair Woodward, Tony Blakely, The Healthy Country?: A History of Life and Death in New Zealand* (Auckland: University Press, 2014), 8.

3 Barbara Miller, *Cultural Anthropology* (United States of America: Content Technologies Inc, 2014), 164.

the incidence of health and disease now and throughout human history.[4] Along with the Physiological and Psychological aspect of humans, one cannot ignore the three dimensions of body, soul and spirit. Body is the outer being, soul connects to mind and emotions and spirit the inmost part of individuals that relates to God. All three parts are co-existent, interdependent and complimentary.[5] Scripture gives plenty of ink to depicting a worldly fear that diminishes human life. Cain has sown the blood of Abel, and he shrinks from the consequences of his sin. In a world ruled by sin and death, we seem doomed to fear our fellow man.[6] Unlike animals, humans think, ask questions and seek answers. If they do not get the answer to their questions, they are disturbed.[7] This chapter highlights the perceptions of death that has constantly inspired humans to seek answers to life.

2. Culture of Death

One of the areas that anthropologist have been curious to study is the area of life and death. To understand how it occurs to humans in general or in various cultures, paying keen attention to the rituals and behaviors that are associated with the matter of life and death.[8] It is true that all humans share the experiences of being born and the fact that everyone will eventually die. The culture of death inspiring life is beautifully given in the life of Jesus, where he raised Lazarus to life and asked him to walk out of the tomb (John11:38- 43). Jesus by dying on the cross and being resurrected after three days has a message for life. The culture of life always encompasses the culture of death. The term 'culture of death' in the church documents was made famous in the 1993 encyclical, *Evangelium Vitae* by Pope John Paul II.[9] Where, culture of death is expressed in forms of evil behaviors that devalue human lives, leading to an explosion of all types of sins. Paradoxically, much work in the anthropology of death is life centered instead of death centered. Death is regarded as a disturbance of the social order, a laceration of the social body and a gap in social and family networks, which has led many

---

4 George M. Foster and Barbara G. Anderson, *Medical Anthropology* (New York: John Wiley K Sons, 1978), 1.

5 Robert Foster Rusell, *Answers to Life* (United States of America: Xulon Press, 2004), 66.

6 Russell Reno, "Fear of the Lord accessed from," accessed from www.baylor.edu/content/services/document.php/79879.pdf (27 October, 2014).

7 B. P. Pai, *Why Do We Live?: A Simple Answer to a Complex Question* (Houston: Strategic Book Publishing and Rights Co, 2013), 70.

8 Casey Golomski, "Life and Death," accessed from http://www.culanth.org/articles/browse/themes/43-life-and-death, (23 October, 2014).

9 John, "What is the Culture of Death?" accessed from http://www.solemncharge.com/post/2012/10/19/What-is-the-Culture-of-Death-The-Catholic-Meaning.aspx (23 October, 2014).

communities to set systems for health or systems for healing especially that of mind and body.[10]

Most humans do not willingly accept the idea of death either it can be their own or the death of their loved ones, whereas some find death as a blessing and end of their sufferings. In fact, the most common reaction to the thought of dying is fear. Becker is among the many theorists who believes that the fear of death is a major conflict of psychopathological conditions.[11] Different religions and cultures have given context to death. For example among the Maori's of New Zealandit is believed that the spirit continues to exist after death and that the deceased will always be part of the *marae,*[12] making their way to the spirit world.[13] Muslims believe there will be a day of judgment (Yawm ad-Din) by Allah (God). Until then, the deceased remain in their graves.[14] Buddhists believe that doing good karma (action) will help them escape the cycle of life and death leading to nirvana.[15] Scientologists believe that humans are immortal spiritual beings called 'thetans' who live several lives. Each 'thetan' has a body and a mind, which exists from lifetime to lifetime. When a person dies they simply move into a new life.[16] Thus these varied conceptions of death have comforted the loss of lives giving a whole new purpose to life. One of the responses to death anxiety can be that of positive reinforcement, that is, people who are afraid of dying tend to do whatever it takes to ensure that they stay alive. Staying alive, in turn, contributes to the continuity and socialization of the species because people so driven are more likely to want to have children and to raise them according to their society's acceptable standards. However, the same death anxiety, if not properly handled, can become a destructive force and could even result in both physical and mental problems.[17] Here, lies my understanding of 'death inspires life' which is articulated in the context of medical anthropology.

---

10 Antonious C. G. M. Robben, *Death, Mourning and Burial: A Cross Cultural Reader* (Victoria: Blackwell Publishing, 2004), 13.

11 Ernest Becker, *The Denial of Death* (New York: Free Press. 1973), 16.

12 Marae is the traditional meeting place of the Maori indigenous community Ref: Hirini Moko Mead, *Tikanga Maori: Living by Maori Values* (Wellington: Huia Publishers, 2003), 110.

13 Margaret R. Orbell, *The Illustrated Encyclopedia of Maori Myth and Legend* (Australia: University of New South Wales Press, 1996), 48.

14 Gerardo Eastburn, *The Esoteric Codex: Zoroastrianism* (Online Self Publication in United States of America : Lulu Press Inc, 2015), 155.

15 Jesudas M. Athyal, "Dharma/Dhamma," *Religions in South East Asia: An Encyclopedia of Faith and Cultures* (California: ABC-CLIO, LLC, 2015), 65.

16 L. Ron Hubbard, *Scientology: A New Stan on Life* (California: Bridge Publications, 2007), 27.

17 James T. Gire , "How Death Imitates Life: Cultural Influences on Conceptions of Death and Dying" accessed from http://www.wwu.edu/culture/gire.htm (30 October, 2014).

3. Medical Pluralism

In medical anthropology the term medical pluralism is referred to an adoption of more than one medicinal system, or the simultaneous integration of both orthodox medicine with complementary and alternative medicine.[18] There are evidences in the Indus civilization that show the traces of yoga, these same yoga postures are found in the Brahmanical, Buddhist and Jain philosophy.[19] Likewise there are traditional medicines like Arabic Unani medicine, Chinese medicine, Ayurvedic medicine, Chinese acupuncture therapy and other various traditional medicines that are interconnected under some philosophy or the other. These forms of traditional medicines and therapies are widely used and are rapidly growing in the mainstream health systems. The counter practice in health practices has also been that of shamanism[20] or exorcism[21] in various indigenous communities.[22] Most of the indigenous communities incorporate the idea of man, nature and God in the medicinal practices.[23] Thus, these aspects of medical pluralism gives immense opportunities to humans to get acculturate in different medical practices, also that of the mainstream health systems. It is a paradigm shift if we see ethnomedicines[24] and mainstream health systems as a constant attempt to win life over death. Ancient societies believed that events and people were controlled by the supernatural and when individuals in the community acted outside of what was considered 'normal' they were then placed at the mercy of evil spirits or also terming them as witches.[25] It is also interesting to know medical issues arising

18 Carol R. Ember and Melvin Ember, "Medical Pluralism," in *The Encyclopedia of Medical Anthropology : Health and Illness in the World's Cultures,* Volume I & II (New York: Kluwer Academic, 2004), 110 & 111.

19 James Mallinson, "Yogic Identities: Traditions and Transformation," accessed from http://www.asia.si.edu/research/articles/yogic-identities.asp (27th October, 2014).

20 Shaman is a person believed to achieve various powers through trance or ecstatic religious experience. Mircea Eliade, "Shamanism," accessed from http://www.britannica.com/topic/shamanism (23 October, 2014).

21 Exorcism is attempted expulsion of a supposed evil spirit from a person or place. See also. Benjamin Radford, "Exorcism: Facts and Fiction About Demonic Possession," accessed from www.livescience.com/27727-exorcism-facts-and-fictional.html (27 October, 2014).

22 Published by World Health Organization, "WHO Traditional Medicine Strategy 2002-2005," accessed from www.wpro.who.int/health_technology/book_who_traditional-medicine-strategy_2002_2005.pdf (28 October, 2014).

23 Ndenecho Emmanuel Neba, "Traditional Health Care System and Challenges in Developing Ethnopharmacology in Africa: Example of Oku, Cameroon," *Studies on Ethnomedicines,* 2/5 (2011), 132.

24 Ethnomedicine is a study of traditional medicine practices by various ethnic groups, especially by indigenous communities. Pamela I. Erickson, *Ethnomedicine* (United States of America: Waveland Press, 2008), 1.

25 Pamilla Ramsden, "Understanding Abnormal Psychology : Clinical and Biological Perspectives" (New York: Sage Publications, 2013), 4.

from funerary practices like that of 'kuru'. Kuru is an incurable degenerative neurological disorder endemic to the Fore tribe of Papua New Guinea. It is now widely accepted that Kuru was transmitted among members of the Fore tribe via cannibalism. The Fore people contracted the disease by performing cannibalism during funeral rituals.[26] Traditional Chinese medicines represent a special case of the central concept of Chinese cosmology, "the dual forces of yin and yang, whose continuous interaction lies behind all natural phenomena, including the constitution and functioning of the human body". The proper balance of yin (negative elements – developed by internal forces) and yang (positive elements – developed by external forces) is essential for good health.[27] These beliefs and practices set the grounds for medical anthropologist to intervene to understand the health beliefs and health seeking behavior that humans in various cultures have defined.

In cross-cultural studies, belief has both 'objective' and 'subjective' aspects. In other words belief has a propositional and a psychological nature. As an objective, propositional issue, a belief constitutes a 'truth claim', an assertion about something 'real' in the world. If a person is said to 'believe in something', that means that the person takes it to be true. But such a belief is no guarantee of reality and does not necessarily depend on thereality of what is believed. As subjective or psychological issues, beliefs are additionally and necessarily constructed as mental states of individuals.[28] One of the clear distinctions given in medical anthropology is that of disease and illness, where disease is seen as a pathological concept and illness as a cultural concept.[29] Let us consider oneself to be diseased when in fact one is fearing darkness which is causing mental blocks, after visiting the doctor with unending complaints of body ache, sleepless nights, weakness etc, the doctor diagnosis that the individual is suffering from a psychological stress. The doctor though wishes to cure diseases, lands up treating illness, for usually it is impairment of function and not the presence of a disease that causes us to seek aid. Thus, medical anthropology takes into consideration various medical practices along with beliefs that are attached to such practices.

Symbolic Understanding of the Human Body

A 'cultural account' of the body is a method, it is a way of imagining how the body carries symbolic significance in social life and how people experience their

---

26 K. B. Kotade, et al., "Kuru: A Neurological Disorder" *International Journal of Current Trends in Pharmaceutical Research* 2/2 (2014), 405.

27 Anderson, *Medical Anthropology*, 63.

28 Ellet D. Jack, *Introducing Anthropology of Religion* (New York: Routledge Taylor and Francis Group, 2007), 29.

29 Anderson, *Medical Anthropology*, 40.

own bodies and the bodies of others as socially or culturally significant objects.[30] Let us use an analogy for instance to conceptualize the body as a machine which is engine or battery driven, where the doctor refers to your body as a machine by saying, 'your heart isn't pumping so well' or 'you will have a nervous breakdown'. If assuming that the modern world perceives human body just as a machine, there is a traditional world that considered human body as a core aspect of their spirituality, which eventually manifested into good or bad spirits. This also can be seen in many funerary practices where a dead body becomes symbolic for the entire community to reflect over life and death. As modern doctors would say, 'recharge your body with good food or fuel your body'. Other societies would fast or harm their body to please God, human sacrifice could also be one of them. This shows that human body exists in time and space; this is partly due to the cultural concepts of the development and changes of the body as it travels from life to death.[31]

4. Understanding Human Body in Indigenous Cultures

In the course of human prehistory and continuing to the present day, culture has played a prominent role in transforming the human form. From birth to death, the body serves as a medium and metaphor of cultural expression.[32] Human body in traditional cultures is defined in terms of the cosmology of that culture. The body symbolizes nature, its various parts are metaphor of different parts of nature.[33] The human body is symbolic where the individual's status is physically written on surface of their body through tattooing, circumcision, piercing of ears or lips etc. Among the Arabs in Iraq it is found that tattooing is divided into two kinds, broadly speaking: ornamental or decorative tattooing and tattooing applied for magic or therapeutic reasons. Generally the therapeutic and magic designs are simple and crude in form, with curative tattooing applied to the seat of pain or injury, whereas the tattooing done for the sake of beauty is more extensive and elaborate.[34] Tattooing among the Nagas, a tribe in North East India pay great significance to body marking to identify clans and also to differentiate who is a friend and a foe.[35] For Maori (indigenous community) warriors of New Zealand a full body tattoo was a type of spiritual amour that protected them and also an

30 Victor Pitts-Talylor, "Introduction – Cultural Accounts of the Body," *Cultural Encyclopedia of the Body* 2 (2008), 18.

31 Helman G. Cecil, *Culture, Health and Illness* (New York: Arnold Publishers, 2001), 32 & 33.

32 John. W. Burton, *Culture and the Human Body: An Anthropological Perspective* (United States of America: Waveland Press, 2001), 132.

33 Soheila Shahshahani, *Body as Medium of Meaning* (Münster: LIT Verlag, 2004), 2.

34 Winifred Smeaton, "Tattooing among the Arabs of Iraq," *American Anthropologist Journal* 39/1 (2009), 54.

35 Iris Odyuo, "The Various Aspects of Naga Art," *Journal of Humanities and Social Science (IOSR-JHSS)* 9/4 (2013), 20.

expression of deeper cultural and religious beliefs. Interestingly to Anthropologist Claude Levi Strauss the purpose of these tattoos was not only to imprint a drawing onto their flesh but also to stamp onto the mind all the traditions and philosophy of the group.[36] Likewise, Wilfred in his book 'The History of Tattooing'[37] brings forth various impressions of indigenous societies on tattooing, through the eyes of anthropologists and the perspectives of people themselves. However, the theories concerning the origin and impetus of tattooing necessarily vary according to the particular area studied. These tattoos in today's society may have lost significance in the community, but many youngsters in the modern world have them with a craving for a fixed and permanent identity.[38]

On the others hand, tribes in the Democratic Republic of Congo, Kenya, Nigeria, Sudan, the Ivory Coast and Ethopia use scarification which has long been considered a sign of beauty for women. Girls receive scars at puberty to demonstrate that they are ready to be married and that they are strong enough to bear children. The scars are seen as beautiful to touch and look at.[39] In many cultures cases of measles, mumps, chiken pox are rarely reported in hospitals or clinics, as they are considered as "compulsory diseases" for the body, something that is inevitable and perhaps normal of the process of growing up.[40] Isolation, home remedies, various bathing patterns, food patterns and rituals are associated with individual who suffer from chicken pox or measles. Indigenous people in the past sometimes mummified and displayed the bodies of their ancestors or symbolically represented them in the form of marks, statues and other forms of human body representation.[41]

5. Understanding the Human Body Biblically

The gospels of Mathew, Mark, Luke and John speak about the human body. It means that in some way the human body is a sign and instrument of the same message of our salvation in Christ.[42] In the bible we find different responses to diseases and illnesses, where we find God testing the faith of Job in the old testament by making his body diseased multiple times, and after he pleads for

36 Helman. G. Cecil, *Culture, Health and Illness* (New York: Arnold Publishers, 2001), 25.

37 Wilfrid D. Hambly, *The History of Tattooing* (New York: Dover Publication Inc, 2009), 15-18.

38 Desley Hennessy, "Ankhs and Anchors: tattooing as an expression of identity – exploring motivation and meaning," accessed from http://ro.uow.edu.au/cgi/viewcontent.cgi?article=4481&context=theses (23 October, 2014).

39 Margo DeMello, *Inked: Tattoos and Body Art around the World* (California: ABC-CLIO, LLC, 2014), 583.

40 Anderson, *Medical Anthropology*, 41.

41 Richard J. Chacon and David H. Dye, *The Taking and Displaying of Human Body Parts as Trophies by Amerindian* (New York: Springer, 2007), 374.

42 Christopher West, *Theology of the Body Explained: A Commentary on John Paul II's "Gospel of the Body"*. (England: Gracewing Publishing, 2003), 2.

mercy he is cured. Also, the word 'leprosy' has caught my attention many times in the bible. Leviticus records "the leprous person who has the disease shall wear torn clothes and let the hair of his head hang loose, and he shall cover his upper lip and cry out, 'Unclean, unclean.' He shall remain unclean as long as he has the disease. He is unclean. He shall live alone. His dwelling shall be outside the camp" (Leviticus 13:45-46). Thereby, treating lepers as unclean physically and spiritually. "Jesus heals a leper" (Mathew 8:2-4). It is interesting to note how menstrual problem was healed by Jesus in a crowd, which was on the basis of faith. The bible verses say, "There was a woman who had had a discharge of blood for twelve years, and who had suffered much under many physicians, and had spent all that she had, and was no better but rather grew worse. She had heard the reports about Jesus and came up behind him in the crowd and touched his garment. For she said, "If I touch even his garments, I will be made well" (Mark 5: 24-29). If we note later what Jesus said to the woman, is something that can be connected to the concept of illness. Jesus said to her, "My daughter, your faith has made you well. Go in peace and be healed of your trouble" (Mark 5: verse 34). It was her faith that healed her.

In Christianity the entire spirituality is surrounded around the body of Jesus and the resurrected Jesus. The bible says, 'the word was made flesh and dwelt among us' (John 1:14). The Apostle's Creed[43] speaks of the birth of Jesus, the suffering and death of Jesus and the resurrection on the third day. Thomas had to touch the body of Jesus, put the finger in his wound to believe (John 20:27). The last supper where the body of Christ was broken and today received in the form of holy communion is a symbolic act which many have failed to understand. 'Lord I am not worthy that you should entre my roof, but only say the word and my soul shall be healed' (Mathew 8:8), is a sign of faith that we profess. God made the womb of Mary instrumental in giving birth to the saviour of the world. Even the story of creation had encompassed human body beautifully, where Eve was made from the rib of Adam (Genesis 2:22). How then one can ignore the human body, when the bible says, 'Do you not know that your body is a temple of the Holy Spirit who is in you, whom you have from God, and that you are not your own. For you have been bought with a price, therefore glorify God in your body' (1 Corinthians: 19-20). Therefore, in this perspective of medical anthropology the human body becomes symbolic which requires to be contextualized in every segment of the phenomena of life in different cultures.

6. Understanding Human Body in the Modern World

An anthropological perspective on the human body, gained through an appreciation of millions of years of evolution and thousands of years of rise and fall of civilization, emphatically suggests the necessity of the co-existence of different

43 Apostles' Creed (*Symbolum Apostolorum*) accessed from https://blog.faithlife.com/blog/2015/04/the-apostles-creed-its-history-and-origins, on 23 October, 2014.

cultural lives. Aggression towards the human body will therefore be destructive to the life of the species at large, whether imposing lethal ways, with holding medication, food and care necessary for the protection of human bodies, body traffic, slavery, cheap labour and other aggressive acts that cause harm to human body.[44] Thus, the modern world provides many dimensions to reflect on the human body, it can be in terms of lifestyle, sexual practices, pregnancy, cancerous diseases and various factors that awaken us to see human body as one's sacred identity.[45] Sex workers who are trafficked are forced to work under hazardous conditions, it is crucial to understand how they would perceive their own body image. Their health is always questioned, where they are vulnerable to various diseases like HIV/AIDS and the worst would be the social stigma that would keep them aloof from addressing many of their health problems.[46] Likewise, sexual abuses, rape, genocide and other violent acts that harm human body externally and internally becomes a huge concern for health. It is also important to acknowledge the efforts made for health promotion by World Health Organization (WHO) and other health care institutions. Health promotion is the process of enabling people to increase control over, and to improve, their health. To reach a state of complete physical, mental and social well-being, an individual or group must be able to identify and to realize aspirations, to satisfy needs, and to change or cope with the environment. Health is, therefore, seen as a resource for everyday life, not the objective of living. Health is a positive concept emphasizing social and personal resources, as well as physical capacities. Therefore, health promotion is not just the responsibility of the health sector, but goes beyond healthy life-styles to well-being.[47]

7. Culture of Poverty

The world had faced severe health problems during the post colonial period, as the newly emerging nations related to violence, wars and military coups. The concern for health arise right from the refugees to displaced communities in internal migration, highlighting issues of hunger, nutrition and other aspect of national calamities that are not predictable.[48] Anthropologist Oscar Lewis in his book *Five Families: Mexican Case Studies in the Culture of Poverty* (1959), created

---

44 Soheila Shahshahani, *Body as Medium of Meaning* (Münster: LIT Verlag, 2004), 5.

45 Desda Zukerman, *Your Sacred Anatomy: An Owner's Guide to the Human Energy Structure* (United States of Amercia: Spiritway Press, 2012), 3.

46 World Health Organization, "Sex Workers," accessed from http://www.who.int/hiv/topics/sex_work/en/ (30 October, 2014).

47 World Health Organization, "The Ottawa Charter for Health Promotion," accessed from http://www.who.int/healthpromotion/conferences/previous/ottawa/en/ (30 October, 2014).

48 Carol R. Ember, Melvin Ember, "Colonialism, Early Post Colonialism and Health," *Encyclopedia of Medical Anthropology: Health and Illness in the World's Cultures* Volume I & II (New York: Kluwer Academic/ Plenium Publishers, 2004), 185.

the theory of 'Culture of Poverty' where the theory states that living in conditions of pervasive poverty will lead to the development of a culture or subculture adapted to those conditions. This culture is characterized by pervasive feelings of helplessness, dependency, marginality and powerlessness.[49] Irrespective of all that the world has achieved today in the area of medical sciences there is one aspect we need to question that is 'affordability'. Approximately 1.2 billion people in the world live in extreme poverty which is less than one US dollar per day. Poverty creates ill-health because it forces people to live in environments that make them sick, without decent shelter, clean water or adequate sanitation.[50] This is partly due to the costs of seeking health care, which include not only out-of-pocket spending on care such as consultations, tests and medicine, but also transportation costs and any informal payments to providers.[51]

8. Inspiration for Life

Life is a gift, which many fail to appreciate. Human body is designed in the image and likeness of God (Genesis 1:26-27), where Jesus Christ, who is God, came to earth as a man, lived a sinless life, and then died to pay the penalty for our sins.[52] A canvas of brutal deaths can be seen in the world wars, ethnic conflicts, natural calamities and other instances where humanity is questioned. The mystery of life evokes awe and concern, while the art of dying includes naturalistic interpretations of life and health that foster a great sense of the legitimacy of death, however reluctantly accepted.[53] It is often the fear of death that draws us close to God.[54] Renowned theologian Pierre Teilhard de Chardin writes, "However far science pushes its discovery of the 'essential fire' and however capable it becomes some day of remodeling and perfecting the human element, it will always find itself in the end facing the same problem: how to give their final value to all and to each of these elements in grouping them within the unity of an organized whole".[55] So as far as death is accidental and unpredictable, our life cannot be for us a meaningful totality. We do not claim to know the full meaning of a particular battle until the

---

49 David Dietrich, "Culture of Poverty" accessed from http://www.encyclopedia.com/topic/Culture_of_Poverty.aspx (30 October, 2014).

50 World Health Organization, "Poverty and Health," accessed from http://www.who.int/hdp/poverty/en/ (30 October, 2014).

51 World Bank, "Poverty and Health," accessed from http://www.worldbank.org/en/topic/health/brief/poverty-health (30 October, 2014).

52 Dr. Tommy Mitchell, "Why Does God's Creation Include Death and Suffering?" accessed from https://answersingenesis.org/suffering/why-does-gods-creation-include-death-and-suffering/, (30 October, 2014).

53 Anderson, *Medical Anthropology*, 296.

54 Russell Reno, "Fear of the Lord accessed from," accessed from www.baylor.edu/content/services/document.php/79879.pdf (28 October, 2014).

55 Pierre Teilhard de Chardin, *The Phenomenon of Man* (New York: Harper and Row, 1959), 284 & 296.

war is over; it is only when everything is ended we see a perspective.[56] This is the process of death that we encounter each day as we live and thus, death inspires life.

Bibliography

Books

D. Hambly, Wilfrid. *The History of Tattooing*. New York: Dover Publication Inc, 2009.

D. Jack, Ellet. *Introducing Anthropology of Religion*. New York: Routledge Taylor and Francis Group, 2007.

DeMello, Margo. *Inked: Tattoos and Body Art around the World*. California: ABC-CLIO,LLC, 2014.

Eastburn, Gerardo. *The Esoteric Codex: Zoroastrianism*. United States of America: Lulu Press Inc, 2015.

F. Rusell, Robert. *Answers to Life*. United States of America: Xulon Press, 2004.

G. Cecil, Helman. *Culture, Health and Illness*. New York: Arnold Publishers, 2001.

G. Olson, Robert. *An Introduction to Existentialism*. New York: Dover Publications Inc, 1962.

Hubbard, L. Ron. *Scientology: A New Stan on Life*. California: Bridge Publications, 2007.

I. Erickson, Pamela. *Ethnomedicine*. United States of America: Waveland Press, 2008.

J. Chacon, Richard and H. Dye, David. *The Taking and Displaying of Human Body Parts as Trophies by Amerindian*. New York: Springer, 2007.

Miller, Barbara. *Cultural Anthropology*. United States: Content Technologies Inc, 2014.

M. Foster, George and G. Anderson, Barbara. *Medical Anthropology*. New York: John Wiley K Sons, 1978.

Ramsden, Pamila. *Understanding Abnormal Psychology: Clinical and Biological Perspectives*. New York: Sage Publications, 2013.

Shahshahani, Soheila. *Body as Medium of Meaning*. Münster: LIT Verlag, 2004.

Teilhard de Chardin, Pierre. *The Phenomenon of Man*. New York: Harper and Row, 1959.

Woodward, Alistair and Tony Blakely. *The Healthy Country?: A History of Life and Death in New Zealand*. Auckland: University Press, 2014.

W. Burton, John. *Culture and the Human Body: An Anthropological Perspective*. United States of America: Waveland Press, 2001.

West, Christopher. *Theology of the Body Explained: A Commentary on John Paul II's "Gospel of the Body"*. England: Gracewing Publishing, 2003.

Zukerman, Desda. *Your Sacred Anatomy: An Owner's Guide to the Human Energy Structure*. United States of Amercia: Spiritway Press, 2012.

Journal Articles

Emmanuel Neba, Ndenecho."Traditional Health Care System and Challenges in Developing Ethnopharmacology in Africa: Example of Oku, Cameroon," *Studies on Ethnomedicines*, 2/5 (2011): 132.

56 Robert. G. Olson, *An Introduction to Existentialism* (New York: Dover Publications, 1962), 209.

Kotade, K. B. et al., "Kuru: A Neurological Disorder". *International Journal of Current Trends in Pharmaceutical Research* 2/2 (2014): 405.

Odyuo, Iris. "The Various Aspects of Naga Art". *IOSR Journal of Humanities and Social Science (IOSR-JHSS)* 9/4 (2013): 20.

Smeaton , Winifred, "Tattooing among the Arabs of Iraq". *American Anthropologist Journal* 39/1 (2009*)*: 54.

Encyclopedia

Religions in South East Asia: An Encyclopedia of Faith and Cultures, "Dharma/Dhamma" (2015): 65.

The Encylopedia of Medical Anthropology: Health and Illness in the World's Cultures, Volume I & II. "Medical Pluralism" (2004): 110 & 111.

Cultural Encyclopedia of the Body 2. "Introduction – Cultural Accounts of the Body" (2008): 18.

Encyclopedia of Medical Anthropology: Health and Illness in the World's Cultures, Volume I & II. "Colonialism, Early Post Colonialism and Health" (2004): 185.

Net Articles

Apostles' Creed (*Symbolum Apostolorum*) accessed from https://blog.faithlife.com/blog/2015/04/the-apostles-creed-its-history-and-origins, on 23 October, 2015.

Dietrich, David. "Culture of Poverty" accessed from http://www.encyclopedia.com/topic/Culture_of_Poverty.aspx, on 30 October, 2015.

Eliade, Mircea. "Shamanism," accessed from http://www.britannica.com/topic/shamanism, on 23rd October, 2015.

Hennessy, Desley. "Ankhs and Anchors: Tattooing as an expression of identity – exploring motivation and meaning," accessed from http://ro.uow.edu.au/cgi/viewcontent.cgi?article=4481&context=theses, on 23 October, 2015.

John. "What is the Culture of Death?" accessed from http://www.solemncharge.com/post/2012/10/19/What-is-the-Culture-of-Death-The-Catholic-Meaning.aspx, on 23 October, 2015.

Mallinson, James. "Yogic Identities: Traditions and Transformation," accessed from http://www.asia.si.edu/research/articles/yogic-identities.asp, on 27th October, 2015.

Mitchell, Tommy. "Why Does God's Creation Include Death and Suffering?" accessed from https://answersingenesis.org/suffering/why-does-gods-creation-include-death-and-suffering/, on 30 October, 2015.

Radford, Benjamin. "Exorcism: Facts and Fiction About Demonic Possession," accessed from www.livescience.com/27727-exorcism-facts-and-fictional.html, on 27 October, 2015.

Reno, Rusell. "Fear of the Lord" accessed from www.baylor.edu/content/services/document.php/79879.pdf, on 27 October, 2015.

T. Gire James, "How Death Imitates Life: Cultural Influences on Conceptions of Death and Dying" accessed from http://www.wwu.edu/culture/gire.htm, on 30 October, 2015.

World Bank, "Poverty and Health," accessed from http://www.worldbank.org/en/topic/health/brief/poverty-health, on 30 October, 2015.

World Health Organization, "WHO Traditional Medicine Strategy 2002-2005," accessed from www.wpro.who.int/health_technology/book_who_traditional-medicine-strategy_2002_2005.pdf, on 28 October, 2015.

World Health Organization, "Sex Workers" accessed from http://www.who.int/hiv/topics/sex_work/en/, on 30 October, 2015.

World Health Organization, "The Ottawa Charter for Health Promotion," accessed from http://www.who.int/healthpromotion/conferences/previous/ottawa/en/, on 30 October, 2015.

World Health Organization, "Poverty and Health," accessed from http://www.who.int/hdp/poverty/en/, on 30 October, 2015.

Chapter 10

Certitude in Newman's *Grammar of Assent*

Albert Kumar

Ever since humanity began its intellectual quest for the 'unknown' whether natural or supernatural, some of the dimensions of the 'unknown' remain so far unfathomed and vague.[1] Today the quest for certitude in knowledge gets all the more intensified. Man perceives the realities like God, universe and human beings from multiple assessments to arrive at certitude. Thus, the concept of certitude gets no exception from the perception of human intellectual inquiry even today. The concept of truth or certitude has been the focus of discussion and discourse since the dawn of humankind in history. John Henry Newman,[2] Oxford scholar and convert to Catholicism (1801-1890), in *An Essay in Aid of a Grammar of Assent*,[3] written after his conversion to Roman Catholicism, has also contributed

1 Sebastian Karotemprel, *God and Secular Man: A Study of Newman's Approach to the Problem of God and its Implications for Secular Man.* (Calcutta: Firma Klm Private Limited, 1977), 1. Cf. Jonas, "Faith 'And' or 'Versus' Philosophy," *The Divine Shepherd's Voice*, 4, 3 (2013), 151. Cf. Sekar Sebastin, "The Ethical Conception of God: A Levinasian Implication," *Sacred Perspectives*, 3, 2 (September 2013 - February 2014), 48. Henceforth, in the subsequent references for Karotemprel's book, I will be using only the main title of the book: *God and Secular Man.*

2 Newman, an English religious thinker and Cardinal of the Roman Catholic Church, was born in the city of London on 21 February 1801. He is known for his conversion from Anglicanism to Catholicism. He spent his complete in defending the faith of the Church. This conversion of Newman to the Roman Catholic Church, in 1845, was doubtless a surprising and sensational event. See J. H. Walgrave, *Newman the Theologian* (London: Geoffrey Chapman, 1960), 13. Cf. John Henry Newman, *John Henry Newman Autobiographical Writings*, ed. Henry Tristram (London: Sheed and Ward, 1956), 10 & 29.

3 For many years, Newman cherished the ambition of writing a treatise in philosophy. In 1859, he began to compile a notebook on philosophical topics in preparation for this venture. He even gave it a tentative title, namely *Discursive Enquiries on Metaphysical Subjects.* Unfortunately,

to the concept of 'certitude'. His contribution is much appreciated by the history.[4] It is demanding to comprehend his notion on 'certitude' devoid of studying the term 'assent'.

1. What is Assent?

In several chapters of the *Grammar of Assent*, Newman gives the definition of assent. Assent is "the absolute acceptance of a proposition without any condition."[5] "To assent to is to acquiesce in it as true."[6] Assent is an "absolute adhesion of the mind to a proposition."[7] Newman makes it abundantly clear that our acts of assent are always given in an unconditional way. Apart from affirming it throughout the *Grammar of Assent*, he also dedicates a separate chapter to this topic. In the opening paragraph, he states his position: "The circumstances of an act, however necessary to it, do not enter into the act; assent is in its nature absolute and unconditional, though it cannot be given except under certain conditions."[8]

1.1 Simple and Complex Assent

Newman introduces the distinction between simple and complex assent. The distinction is based on whether our assent is made after a conscious intellectual

---

this enterprise never came to realization. Nevertheless, much of his complete philosophical thought did come to light with the publication of his *Grammar of Assent.* Although, the prime aim of this work was theology, its argument rests on a firm philosophical foundation. This is the context in which I find *Grammar of Assent* as the primary source for his philosophy. The book is divided into two parts: the first part is entitled 'Assent and Apprehension' and the second part is entitled 'Assent and Inference'. Both the parts deal with the subject 'assent'. See. *AW*, 269. Cf. Laurence Richardson, *Newman's Approach to Knowledge* (Gracewing, 2007), xiii. Newman's basic approach to philosophy is that of Aristotle. He confesses that Aristotle is his master. This is reflected in the *Grammar of Assent*, for instance, by the fact that he adopts in broad terms, the three operations of the intellect as envisaged by Aristotle, namely, apprehension, illative sense and reasoning. See John Henry Newman, *An Essay in Aid of a Grammar of Assent* (London: Longmans, Green and Company, 1870), 430. Henceforth, it will referred as *GA*.

4 Ludwig Wittgenstein (1889-1951 A.D), the great linguistic, has taken Newman as his guide for his book *On Certainty*; in the beginning of the first section of Wittgenstein's *On Certainty* Newman's name is found. See. Wittgenstein, *On Certainty*. eds. G. E. M. Anscombe and G. H. Von Wright (Oxford: Basil Blackwell, 1977), 1. It is significant to note that the *Grammar of Assent* had the greater influence on Bernard Joseph Francis Lonergan (1904-1984 A.D), a philosopher-theologian was a Canadian Jesuit priest. See Richard M. Liddy, *Transforming Light: Intellectual Conversion in the Early Lonergan* (Collegeville: The Liturgical Press, 1993), 16.

5 *GA*, 13. Henceforth, it will be referred to as *GA*. Cf. John Henry Newman, *The Theological Papers of John Henry Newman on Faith and Certainty*, ed. J. Derek Holmes (Oxford: Clarendon Press, 1796), 11. Henceforth, it will be referred as *TP*.

6 *GA*, 14.

7 *GA*, 16.

8 *GA*, 157.

reflection or not. Simple assent is made unconsciously and without deliberation, whereas the complex assent[9] is consciously and deliberately elicited;[10] he refers to the latter as certitude.[11] In our constant mental operations, all kinds of propositions will come into our minds and we very often assent to them unexpectedly.[12] He says that many of our assents are given 'unconsciously', in a spontaneous way without us being aware of any intellectual reflection. They are the consequences of our already acquired mental habits. He describes these as 'simple' assents. Conversely, those "made consciously and deliberately"[13] he refers to as "complex or reflex assents."[14]

The mode of assent, which is exercised unconsciously, is what Newman calls as 'simple assent'. However, one can always move from the simple assent to complex assent. For instance, if one holds absolutely that Great Britain is an island, concerning this belief one has no doubts at all. Yet one may still look for reasons, which support this belief if one has been challenged to do so. For example, one might reflect that no serious person has ever cast doubt upon Great Britain's island status; that it would be impossible for all the mapmakers to be wrong on this point; that it is a basic presumption of English history that Great Britain is an island. Having put together all of these separate reasons, which in themselves are only probabilities, one reaffirms ones original assent to the truth of the proposition that Great Britain is an island. In other words, one gives complex assent to this proposition. Here we have the process of moving from simple assent to complex assent. Simple assents are given without much reflection. Complex assents are given only after reflection.[15]

By focusing on such examples such as Britain being an island, we have gained more insight into how simple assent leads to complex assent. When one sees all the reasons which, though each only probable in themselves, converge upon the truth of a particular belief like Britain being an island, one should accept the belief as if it were demonstrated. Here probable inference leads to definite belief.[16]

2. What is Certitude?

After the discussion on simple and complex assent in the *Grammar of Assent*, Newman introduces the concept of certitude. The question of certitude is an essential element in *Grammar of Assent*. Newman explains clearly what certitude is and how it is distinguished from assent. Certitude for Newman "is the perception

---

9 Newman also sometimes calls complex assents also as reflex assents. See *GA*, 189-190.

10 *GA*, 189.

11 *GA*, 183.

12 *GA*, 189-190.

13 *GA*, 189.

14 *GA*, 189-190. Cf. *TP*: I, 64.

15 *GA*, 189. Cf. *TP*: I, 64.

16 *GA*, 190.

of a truth with the perception that it is a truth, or the consciousness of knowing, as expressed in the phrase, "I know that I know," or "I know that I know that I know," - or simply "I know"."[17] In his *Apologia* Newman affirms this, "To be certain is to know that one knows."[18] For him, all certitude is assent, but not all assents are certitude; for simple assent, that is, assent without reflection, is only certitude in a popular sense. Newman prefers to call simple assent as material, virtual or interpretative certitude. Simple assent has potentiality for certitude and it could be interpreted. As soon as reflection is exercised upon simple assent, it is converted into actual certitude.[19] Hence, Newman clearly states that mere assent is not certitude, and must not be confused with it.[20] Reflex assent differs from simple assent in that it is explicit and deliberate. It is not only an assent of 'P' but it is an assent to the claim of 'P' as true. Hence, Newman says that certitude is an assent to an assent or conviction. It is a species of assent namely, complex assent.[21] He affirms this in his 'Papers in Preparation for a *Grammar of Assent*' written during the years 1865-1869. He says, "Certitude is an assent deliberate, unconditional, and conscious, to a proposition as true."[22] We shall see his concept of certitude in more detail using three characteristics that he gives for certitude. They are: certitude follows investigation and proof, certitude is indefectible, and certitude causes a sense of repose and triumph.

2.1 Certitude Follows Investigation and Proof

According to Newman, most men pass through life with neither doubt nor certitude, but only with simple assents, which are virtual certitudes. Very often, we give our assent to propositions in an almost unconscious way. All our assents are generally simple assents and we assert that we are certain of them. Nevertheless, these propositions are but "expressions of our personal likings, tastes, principles, motives, and opinions, as dictated by nature, or resulting from habit."[23] They are "acts and manifestations of self." The kernel of Newman's theory lies in this assertion: what we call certitude in everyday life, is often no certitude at all, instead, they are simple assents or material certitudes, and they are not certitudes in the strict sense of the word. Therefore, for Newman certitude is not only an assent to a proposition but it is an assent to an assent, it is a complex and reflex act, and it is certitude in the full sense of the word. As we have seen above "it is a perception

17 *GA*, 197.

18 *Apologia*, 228. Cf. Richardson, *Newman's Approach to Knowledge*, 85.

19 *GA*, 210-212.

20 *GA*, 203.

21 *GA*, 221-222.

22 *TP*: I, 122.

23 *GA*, 188.

of a truth with the perception that it is a truth."[24] Hence, the first characteristic of certitude is conscious and deliberate investigation and proof.[25]

2.2 Certitude as Indefectible

According to Newman, the object of certitude is truth. There are right and wrong convictions and certitude is a right conviction of truth. He says, "[T]ruth cannot change; what is once truth is always truth; and the human mind is made for truth, and so rests in truth, as it cannot rest in falsehood... therefore once certitude always certitude."[26] Assents may and do change from simple to complex and real to notional but certitudes endure.[27] Hence, for Newman certitude does not fail, and failure is an exception for it. If the certitude is unfounded or has fault then it is the reasoning, which is at fault not the certitude, for it is a deliberate conviction or assent given after reasoning or investigation.[28] Hence, Newman argues that once a person attains certitude about a truth it never fails him but always remains certitude. In other words, once a certitude, always a certitude.[29] We may think this claim of Newman's is too extreme. Indeed, one may wonder how Newman himself could make this claim, since after all he himself was a convert from Anglicanism to Roman Catholicism. Newman deals with the problem of certitude presented by the conversion of people from one religion to another at great length in *Grammar of Assent*.[30] He says that even in religious matters certitudes remain undamaged. When a person changes from one religion to another, there is no change in the certitude; instead, it means that person was not holding certitude at all.[31] A Jew or a Muslim on becoming a Catholic does clearly prove that certitude is indefectible.[32] Hence, according to Newman, certitude by nature is indefectible and it does not change.

2.3 Certitude Causes a Sense of Repose and Triumph

We have so far considered two characteristics of certitude; 'reflexivity' and 'indefectibility'. Now let us turn to its third and most important condition, 'repose'. Repose is the spontaneous rejection of doubt. Assent cannot co-exist with hesitation or doubt. Repose is the mark of certitude as self-approval. When a man says that he is certain, he means that he is conscious of himself of having the specific feeling of self-approval. "It is a feeling of satisfaction and self-congratulation, of

24 *GA*, 197.

25 *GA*, 194-195 & 197. Cf. *TP*: I, 36.

26 *GA*, 221.

27 *GA*, 220.

28 *GA*, 222 & 229. Cf. Richardson, *Newman's Approach to Knowledge*, 88.

29 *GA*, 221.

30 *GA*, 240-255.

31 *GA*, 250-252. Cf. *TP*: I, 4.

32 *GA*, 252.

intellectual security, arising out of a sense of success, attainment, possession, finality."[33] As the fulfilment of duty causes peace of mind and enjoyable self-approval, in the same way the attainment of truth causes a feeling of intellectual security and self-repose. He also says that simple assent and inference do not cause this satisfaction; instead, this satisfaction of repose is the characteristic that Newman gives only for certitude, that is, assent after reflection.[34]

Newman, therefore, summarizes that there are three characteristics for certitude: firstly, certitude follows investigation and proof; secondly, certitude is indefectible; and thirdly, certitude is accompanied by a specific sense of intellectual satisfaction and repose.[35] These characteristics are not to be found in simple assent and therefore it cannot be called as certitude.

3. How do we Arrive at Certitude or Complex Assent in Concrete?

In *Grammar of Assent*, Newman distinguishes three phases of inference:[36] Formal, Informal and Natural.[37] And he says that only through informal inference one can arrive at certitude and therefore, let us try to understand the differences between the inferences.

3.1 Formal Inference

Formal inference contains verbal reasoning, which proceeds by means of major or minor premises and generally with the aid of well-formulated propositions. Newman defines formal inference as a process of verbal reasoning; it is an attempt to express reasoning in words.[38] Logic and syllogistic reasoning are scientific expression of this type of inference.[39] For example, all men are mortal; Kumar is a man, and therefore Kumar is mortal. The more abstract and notional the propositions involved in this type of reasoning process are, the more effective does this reasoning become.[40] The expressions of formal inference are probably found in mathematics and it is at home in the realm of mental abstractions. However,

33 *GA*, 204. Cf. *TP*: I, 34.

34 *GA*, 204-206.

35 *GA*, 258.

36 Inference in general is characterized by Newman as the conditional acceptance of a proposition. Inference is also defined by Newman as a process of reasoning, either implicit or explicit, whereby the mind proceeds from premises to conclusions. He defines the reasoning in general as holding to something as true, in virtue of something else. Reason is an act of mind by which one proceeds to know from known. For example, if one says that one knows x because of y, then one makes an act of inference. See *GA*, 8, 59, 75, 172 & 189. Cf. Gerard Casey, *Natural Reason: A Study of the Notions of Inference, Assent, Intuition, and First Principles in the Philosophy of John Henry Cardinal Newman* (New York: Peter Lang, 1951), 2. Cf. *GA*, 259-260.

37 *GA*, viii.

38 *GA*, 263-264. Cf. Richardson, *Newman's Approach to Knowledge*, 94.

39 *GA*, 264.

40 *GA*, 265.

since the "abstract can only conduct to abstract,"[41] this reasoning process breaks down in the matter of ascertaining concrete facts. In concrete facts, for Newman, formal inference can only conclude probabilities for two reasons: "first because its premises are assumed, not proved; and secondly, because its conclusions are abstract, and not concrete."[42] Thus for Newman, formal inference cannot lead the mind to certitude in concrete matters.[43]

3.2 Informal Inference

Informal inference is a reasoning process by which man becomes certain of what is concrete.[44] For Newman this method consists:

> [In] the cumulation of probabilities, independent of each other, arising out of the nature and circumstances of the particular case which is under review; probabilities too fine to avail separately, too subtle and circuitous to be convertible into syllogisms, too numerous and various for such conversion even were they convertible.[45]

Newman describes informal inference as "unwritten summing up" of many probable arguments. Informal reasoning is a convergence of many probabilities towards the same point, as absolute assent to the truth of the fact. If belief with certitude has any rational foundation, it must be based on informal reasoning about converging probabilities. The premises of this mode of reasoning are concrete and individual, varying with different minds,[46] and they cannot be reduced or converted to the abstract premises upon which formal inference is based.[47] In this reasoning process, the conclusion is not actually attained, but, as it were, foreseen and predicted;[48] its premises do not "touch it logically, [but] converge to it."[49]

Newman lists three characteristics of informal inference. Firstly, though informal inference reaches truth in the 'concrete', it, however, is no longer in the realm of abstraction, but reaches into the realities of the concrete and individual case.[50] Secondly, informal inference is not only a mental act; instead, it also

41 Newman points out that even mathematics can be subject to imperfections in its process of investigation. See *GA*, 268.

42 *GA*, 268-269.

43 *GA*, 279-281.

44 *GA*, 288.

45 *GA*, 288.

46 *GA*, 293.

47 *GA*, 288.

48 *GA*, 321.

49 *GA*, 321.

50 *GA*, 292.

includes the sense experience. Thirdly, informal inference like any other formal inference is 'conditional'. It is conditioned by the premises.[51]

3.3 Natural Inference

Natural inference is an unconscious transition from the known to the unknown. Newman describes this kind of reasoning as dealing directly with things, not so much with words and concepts. He says that this mode of natural reasoning is not from propositions to propositions, but from things to things from concrete to concrete.[52] It is possible in both, for uneducated men and men of genius, for this mode needs no intellectual aids and rules, or any mental discipline.[53] For example, a woman may not trust a particular stranger because she senses an unpleasant character behind the charming exterior. If she has had a great deal of experience in noting the way that men speak, dress and carry themselves, she has acquired a great deal of knowledge which comes to bear upon the particular man in front of her. Thus, her intuition will often prove to be correct.[54]

4. Certitude and Informal Inference

Informal inference is the most adequate process of arriving at truth in the concrete; however, since it remains conditional, it is not assent, for assent is always unconditional. This being the relationship between inference and assent, how then does the mind, in concrete matters, move through informal inference, which is conditional to an assent, which is unconditional and certain? Now, how does the mind arrive at truth in the concrete? Newman began the *Grammar of Assent* with this question. Assent in concrete matters is preceded by informal inference whose conclusions are conditional to the extent that they are probabilities converging toward a truth. In making a judgment of truth in the concrete, the mind moves from the evidence of converging probabilities to an assent, which is unconditional and certain. Obviously, the evidence, which is only conditional, cannot by itself produce a certain assent. The connection between conditional inference and unconditional assent is found in the activity of the living mind called Illative sense.[55]

51 *GA*, 293.

52 *GA*, 330.

53 *GA*, 331. Cf. A. J. Boekraad, *The Personal Conquest of Truth According to J. H. Newman* (Louvain: Editions Nauwelaerts, 1955), 140-142.

54 This example employed to illustrate is mine.

55 Philip Flanagan, *Newman: Faith and Believer* (London: Sand & Company Limited, 1946), 95.

5. Illative Sense: The Way to Certitude

Newman refers to illative sense as the intellective power of judging and concluding a proposition with its perfection.[56] It is a rational faculty,[57] a valid function of the mind. In simple words, Newman calls illative sense as a natural faculty by which the mind arrives at truth in concrete matters. He says that it is the sole 'criterion' for discerning truth in the concrete.[58]

Ultimately, there are two functions of illative sense. Firstly, illative sense supervises the whole argument or process of reasoning about some concrete matter and judges the truth. Secondly, it provides the key to man's selection of his first principles. Concerning the first point, Newman gives an extended example of how various historians argued about the pre-historic situation of Greece and Rome. To assent the pre-historic situation true, the historian during his inquiry should consider the following: What are the marks of truth? What are falsehoods? What is probable? What is suspicious? What are the possibilities for discriminating facts from fictions? What are the things to consider and interpret it as mythical or as allegorical, or to hold so much to be trustworthy? What cannot be disproved? How much of the tradition, analogy, isolated testaments and records, ruins, vague reports, legends, the facts, language, popular verbs, to be told in the inquiry? Then, arguments have to be balanced against each other, and then lastly the decision is to be made, whether any conclusion at all can be drawn.[59] All that Newman tries to say through this example is that illative sense directs and supervises the reasoning process about any concrete matter.

Newman then gives a brief review of first principles, which have determined the cultural history of modern man. He is not trying to determine the right and the wrong but merely describing what has happened. Clearly first principles are the single most important factor controlling any judgments a man might make in the concrete matter. Newman gives the example of Francis Bacon. Up until Bacon's time, the typical approach to the study of nature was through Aristotle's notion of the four causes, particularly the final cause. The first principle was that 'the world was a thing of design'. Bacon initiated the practice of leaving out the final cause and concentrating only upon the efficient or moving causes and then checking the results by experiment. Newman does not elaborate on this matter. However he does give the background of modern times in which Aristotle's quest for intelligibility was tossed aside in favour of the use of reason which has given man great power over the physical world.[60]

---

56 *GA*, 353.

57 *GA*, 345.

58 *GA*, 345. Cf. Zeno, *John Henry Newman Our Way to Certitude*, 30.

59 *GA*, 363-364.

60 *GA*, 372-378.

The next point I would like to comment upon is Newman's discussion of the place that 'doubt' has in philosophy. For Rene Descartes (1596-1650)[61] doubt was everything and he tried to rebuild the world on new foundations.[62] In another example, Newman speaks about the first principle of Protestants. For Protestants, the first principle is Bible. All religious truth is to be found in the 'Bible.'[63] In all these examples, if the first principle is mistaken, Newman does not consider the illative sense to be wrong, instead, the use of illative sense is wrong and the reasoning process is wrong.[64]

6. Conclusion

It was while immersed in research for my master's thesis on *Grammar of Assent* that I came to realize the possibility of certitude through the act of rationality called 'Illative sense'. What struck me at the first reading of Newman's works, especially *Grammar of Assent* is the intellectual integrity (experience and reason) without these being in conflict, he develops arguments to arrive at certitude. This approach to certitude of Newman is a personal approach; one arrives at certitude through one's own experiences and Illative sense. Many books and articles have been published on Newman's life–long commitment to truth and certitude. However, the overall intention of this article is to show that Newman, apart from his deserved fame as a theologian, also merits universal recognition as a significant philosopher as his thinking on Certitude possesses all the necessities for a philosophical argument. Hence, let us figure out as one of our major tasks to give Newman his room in the history of philosophy.

Bibliography

Boekraad, A. J. *The Personal Conquest of Truth According to J. H. Newman.* Louvain: Editions Nauwelaerts, 1955.

Casey, Gerard. *Natural Reason: A Study of the Notions of Inference, Assent, Intuition, and First Principles in the Philosophy of John Henry Cardinal Newman.* New York: Peter Lang, 1984.

Flanagan, Philip. *Newman: Faith and the Believer.* London: Sands and Company Limited, 1946.

Jonas. "Faith 'And' or 'Versus' Philosophy." *The Divine Shepherd's Voice* 4, 3 (2013): 151-159.

Kaipan, Joy. *Love of Wisdom: A Beginner's Guide to Philosophy.* Bangalore: Kristu Jyoti Publications, 2008.

---

61 Rene Descartes (1596-1650 A.D), a French philosopher, mathematician and founding father of modern philosophy, was born in a village near Tours in France and was educated at a Jesuit college. His famous works include *The Passion of the Soul, Mediations on the First Philosophy, Rules for the Direction of the Mind,* and *Discourse on Method.* He is known for his famous statement, *cogito ergo sum* (I think therefore I am). See Kaipan, Love *of Wisdom: A Beginner's Guide to Philosophy*, (Bangalore: Kristu Jyoti Publications, 2008), 110-111.

62 *GA*, 376-377.

63 *GA*, 379.

64 *GA*, 381.

Karotemprel, Sebastian. *God and Secular Man: A Study of Newman's Approach to the Problem of God and its Implications for Secular Man.* Introduction by Cardinal John Wright. Calcutta: Firma Klm Private Limited, 1977.

Liddy, M Richard. *Transforming Light: Intellectual Conversion in the Early Lonergan.* Collegeville: The Liturgical Press, 1993.

Newman, John Henry. *The Theological Papers of John Henry Newman on Faith and Certainty.* Vol. I. Selected and Edited by J. Derek Holmes. Oxford: Clarendon Press, 1976.

Newman. John Henry. *John Henry Newman Autobiographical Writings.* Edited with an Introduction by Henry Tristram. London: Sheed and Ward, 1956.

Newman, John Henry. *An Essay in Aid of a Grammar of Assent.* London: Longmans, Green and Company, 1870.

Richardson, Laurence. *Newman's Approach to Knowledge.* Leominster: Gracewing, 2007.

Sebastin, Sekar. "The Ethical Conception of God: A Levinasian Implication." *Sacred Perspectives* 3, 2 (September 2013 - February 2014), 48-59.

Walgrave, J. H. *Newman the Theologian.* London: Geoffrey Chapman, 1960.

Wittgenstein, Ludwig. *On Certainty.* Edited by G. E. M. Anscombe and G. H. Von Wright. Oxford: Basil Blackwell, 1977.

Chapter 11

Paradigm Shift
Ecological Crisis to Ecosophical Care

Romero D' Souza

1. Introduction

The contemporary ecological crisis is increasingly recognized as the greatest challenge that the *Homo sapiens sapiens* have had to face, ever since their emergence nearly two hundred thousand years ago. For the first time in the history of the modern humans, the conditions for the flourishing of human and other forms of life in the common planetary home are endangered in an unprecedented way today. It is evident in some of the important manifestations of the ecological crisis like climate change, biodiversity loss, pollution and the fast depletion of natural resources.[1] The ecological crisis is indeed about the precarious state of our common home. Significantly the term 'ecology' derives from two Greek words '*oikos*' denoting *home* and '*logos*' meaning *discourse*. To talk about the ecological crisis is to refer to the alarming state of our planetary home. The contemporary ecological crisis raises huge challenges to the course of our current civilization and to human society at large.

The manifold impacts of the ecological crisis are being felt all around the globe. One of the most tragic truths about the contemporary ecological crisis is that those who have contributed least to causing the crisis are the ones most affected by it.[2] The unfortunate tales of the world grappling with the consequences

1 Christian Aid, "Warning Signs: The Science and Impacts of Climate Change" (June 2010), 5.

2 Rachel Baird, *The Impact of Climate Change on Minorities and Indigenous Peoples* (London: Minority Rights Group International, 2008), 2.

of changing weather patterns, natural calamities like droughts and floods, land degradation and increasing desertification and other manifestations of the contemporary ecological crisis, are steadily on the increase around the globe.

Yet, ironically those staying in the middle-east regions and areas are the among those most affected by the degradation of ecosystems, changing weather patterns, depletion of natural resources, and other manifestations of the contemporary ecological crisis. The present article is precisely about the significant role of a paradigm shift from the ecological crisis to ecosophical care and wisdom in accomplishing such a transition. The article will unfold in two parts.

The First part will deal with the **2014 Faith and Ecology Conference in Jerusalem** and the second part will basically reflect on **the paradigm shift from the ecological crisis to ecosophical care** the understanding shift that needs to be implemented for a better future. We shall examine how wisdom – the quintessence of the knowledge and praxis of ecosophy is a step to care. Along these lines, I intend to offer a path forward for humanity in terms of a rediscovery of a harmonious and sustainable relationship with the physical world, a re-emphasis of understanding human existence in terms of interrelatedness and interdependence, and a reawakening to the sacred dimension of all creation.[3]

PART I: 2014 Faith and Ecology Conference in Jerusalem

2. Faith and Ecology

The Interfaith Center for Sustainable Development[4] organization and the Konrad Adenauer Stiftung organization, organized a conference on the Faith and Ecology in Jerusalem. Despite differences in theology and practice, one tenet that faith members of the Abrahamic traditions have in common is the importance of being stewards of God's creation. As current and emerging faith leaders, one has a unique and powerful ability to guide and influence one's community. Religious teachings reach a substantial percentage of humanity, and as such, can serve as a powerful vehicle through which society can address the environmental and climate crisis. The objectives of the conference were: to provide tools, resources, and inspiration to integrate ecological awareness into religious education; to help participants plan for integrating ecology into their own teaching with clear ideas and tangible action steps; to cultivate coexistence and religious tolerance across the three monotheistic religions based on a shared goal of environmental stewardship. At the end of the sessions, we identified resource persons from different institutions

---

3 C. Sobre-villa, *The Role of Indigenous Peoples in Biodiversity Conservation: The Natural But Often Forgotten Partners* (Washington, DC: World Bank, 2011).

4 The Interfaith Center for Sustainable Development (ICSD), based in Jerusalem, accesses the collective wisdom of the world's religions to promote co-existence, peace, and sustainability through education and activism. I invite you to visit www.interfaithsustain.com, where you will find a wealth of resources on faith and ecology, including the most extensive online video collection of religious leaders speaking out on ecological sustainability.

to continue collaboration with other representatives from this conference. The idea behind this was to create a sustained effort across different faiths in education, advocacy, and practical application of "greening" religious institutions in this city and elsewhere.

At a deeper level, why is the religious community so important in this regard? Because the environmental crisis conveys a deeper message: the widespread human degradation of the natural world indicates that our way of life is out of balance. Thus the environmental crisis is a spiritual crisis. It is not a problem of the birds and the bees, the trees and the toads. Rather, it is a crisis of the human being and how we live as spiritual beings in a material world. Ecological disruptions reflect the inner imbalance within billions of human beings. The change required of us to correct this is primarily of a spiritual nature, and centers on becoming givers instead of takers. This is where religions come in, to be a force for positive change in the world. People of many faiths can draw inspiration from their respective traditions to live sustainably, and these efforts cross-pollinate each other and encourage co-existence on our shared planet and in this land. The earth can be in balance, and a more conscious, aware human society is key to making the change. The organization Religion for Peace notes how "As some of the most numerous and well-organized members of civil society, religious communities have a key leadership role to play. Not only do religious communities have ethical and moral principles to draw from, they also possess multiple assets and networks for practical action. They are also significant landholders, operate millions of schools, run media outlets and hold billions of dollars in financial assets. Using their broad networks and influence, religious leaders and communities have the potential to mobilize millions of people and influence policy makers to address climate change."[5]

["Our common future is an issue on which we can all come together. Our local and global environmental challenges represent an opportunity for people of faith to unite in a new way and put aside our differences. There is no better place to begin than with religious leaders and seminary students here in the Holy Land. And there is no better time to do it–a month before the UN climate negotiations in Lima, Peru, when representatives from 180 nations gather to try to agree on a plan for how to live more sustainably. As the Jewish sage Hillel taught, "If not now, when?"] We hope that your experience here today and your continued efforts will catalyze a shift in consciousness that will ripple outward within and across communities of faith.[6] The planning and participation was done because of the collaborative work of the *Konrad Adenauer Foundation*, the *Julia Burke*

5 From the *Handbook for Faith and Ecology Conference Jerusalem, October 2014* in *Religion for Peace*, 2011.

6 Words from the *Rabbi Yonatan Neril*, the Founder and Executive Director of The Interfaith Center for Sustainable Development.

Foundation, the *Salesian Pontifical University* – Jerusalem Campus and Bina – *Jerusalem Secular Yeshiva*.

Climate change is an all-encompassing threat to human development and habitat on earth. The increase in global temperatures, according to most scientists, is a direct result of our fossil fuel driven economy and the excessive emissions of carbon dioxide and greenhouse gases. The effects of climate change are already felt around the world, and are projected to increase. If action is not taken now, the world will witness a dramatic decline in global health, security, the environment and human development. To meet the challenges of climate change, people must curb their over-reliance on fossil fuel, and stop the exploitation of the environment. As some of the most numerous and well-organised members of civil society, religious communities have a key leadership role to play. In recent years, prominent leaders of the world's major religions have publicly called for global action to prevent the effects of climate change. From tiny houses of worship in rural villages, to the most hallowed sanctuaries in the world's major cities, religious leaders and people of faith are in an ideal position to mobilize their communities for action and advocacy on climate change. Stewardship of the earth is a principle found in all of the world's major religions. From a basic belief in nature as divine creation, to scriptural commands to care for the earth, the collective sacred texts of all faiths speak of caring for the earth in diverse ways.[7]

The effects of climate change range from rising sea levels and melting glaciers to catastrophic weather events like floods, droughts and storms, to seemingly small changes that affect the entire ecosystems of forests, mountains and oceans. People who depend on the land for their livelihoods, such as indigenous peoples, subsistence farmers and fishermen, will face the harshest impacts of climate change and have the least resources available to adapt to them. By 2050, an estimated 200 million people could be displaced due to climate change.[8] Extreme storms, floods and mudslides will force people living in low-lying areas and places susceptible to drought to leave their homes. Over the past two decades, recorded natural disasters have doubled, with seven out of ten reported as 'climate related.'[9] Poor mega-cities in Asia and Africa are especially vulnerable to changing weather patterns because of their geography and the lack of necessary infrastructure to cope with disasters. Rising sea levels will also force people living in low-lying coastal areas and small islands to migrate. Economic pressures are another result of climate change, and include loss of farmland, damage to crops from drought, depletion of fish

7 From the *Introduction* of *Religions for Peace*, 9.

8 UN Framework on Climate Change: Adaptation. See fn. 4 of *Religions for Peace*.

9 Church World Service: International Adaptation Funding Resource. See fn. 5 of *Religions for Peace*.

stocks from over-fishing, scarce water supply and even famine. These also trigger migration,[10] and may also result in conflict, even war, and increase suffering.[11]

Responding to climate change requires coordinated global solutions driven by appropriate government policy that is backed by legislation. It also requires local community action that promotes sustainable development. Scientists and policy makers agree that there are two approaches in responding to climate change: mitigation, which means reducing emissions of greenhouse gases through practical measures, and adaptation, which means helping communities adjust their lifestyles to the effects of climate change.[12]

Advocacy is a process to bring about change in the policies, laws and practices of influential individuals, groups and institutions. The focus of this section is to prepare religious leaders and communities for advocacy, particularly with government decision-makers. However, advocacy can be practised at many levels, including within households, with community or local authorities, by engaging with the private sector, or at the national, regional or international level. For many faith communities, advocacy is often initially internal, focused on changing the sustainability practices of the community. Such internal advocacy is an important first step. External advocacy can take many forms, such as: letter writing campaigns, peaceful marches, media outreach, or private meetings with policy makers. Using their broad networks and influence, religious leaders and communities have the potential to mobilize millions of people and influence policy makers to address climate change.[13]

3. Faith and Ecology Conference: Report and Reflection

The Conference began with the opening words of Dr. Michael Borchard (Head of Israel Office, Konrad Adenauer Foundation) who introduced the dual role and responsibility of the conference, that is, a *necessity* and a *provocation*. An invitation to a personal and societal vocation, to interreligious dialogue, to possess the nature of ecological thinking as ecological fundamentalism, for a better future, for a sustainable future.

4. Faith and Science on Ecology

The Panelist for this session was Bishop William Shomali, Imam Wisam Barhum, Rabbi Yuval Cherlow, and Dr. Nurit Hashimony Yaffe who briefed the participants with their knowledge and wisdom from their own perspective on 'ecology.' The moderater for this session was a former member of Knesset Rabbi

10 Data of the 8th Market Mechanisms Sub-Committee, Environment Committee, Industrial Structure. See fn. 6 of *Religions for Peace.*

11 Ms. Despina Namwembe from Coperation Circle of United Religions Initiative Uganda, email message, July 19, 2010. See fn. 7 of *Religions for Peace.*

12 *Religions for Peace*, 24.

13 *Ibid.*, 29.

Michael Melchoir. This session began with **Melchoir** reflecting on Religion as the biggest NGO the world has ever produced and a calling that we need to make the right and proper use of this by motivating the people to take *responsibility* of their *identity* and their *existence.* He also elaborated the essence of the world as a temporary residence which is entrusted to us (Judea-Christian-Muslim understanding of Creation).

Shomali presented the reality of the present state of the world and creation. He reflected on Creation from Genesis and offered valuable suggestion to counter the high-rising risk such as pollution, deforestation, global warming, etc. **Barhum** presented the relationship of religion and the reality of nature from the basis of Quran. He later elaborated on the importance and significance of Man being responsible to worship and cultivate, to protect and care what the Lord has given (especially, land) to man. **Cherlow** presented the role to examine religion in connection with the world and God and whether religion is a solution to the problem of ecological crisis. **Yaffe** presented the state of environment and its relationship with global warming. In the latter presentation she offered a common responsibility, that of, socio-eco-politico-scientifico-religious corporation.

5. Perspective of Rabbi Yonatan Neril on Jewish Teachings on Ecology

At different times in history, Jews have engaged in growing crops, tending fruit trees, and shepherding animals in the Land of Israel. These activities were critical to provide food to sustain Jews living in the Land. Yet they also may have presented challenges to environmental sustainability in the Land of Israel. Jewish tradition can teach us about sustaining the Land over time, both in pre-modern times and today. People living in consumer society relate to material objects in a vastly different way than people did in previous times. Age-old Jewish teachings reveal a Jewish vision for 'holy use' of the material world and relate deeply to today's need for sustainable resource use. Beyond the physical causes, the widespread degradation of the natural world indicates that our way of life is out of balance.[14] Thus *the environmental crisis also reflects a spiritual crisis.*[15]

14 In our times we are beginning to witness the planet's ecological balance weakening due to human influence: rainforests shrinking, deserts expanding, hurricanes intensifying, the planet heating. What is driving the deterioration of the natural world? To be sure, there are physical reasons, yet to answer 'fossil fuels' or 'wood use' or even 'consumerism' would provide only partial answers. In order to truly understand a problem, we need to look under its surface to understand the root causes.
This resource is part of Canfei Nesharim's Year of Jewish Learning on the Environment, in partnership with Jewcology.com, with support from the ROI Community, a community of young Jewish innovators founded by Lynn Schusterman, and the Shedlin Outreach Foundation. Yonatan Neril, "Learning Resources: Jewish Environmental Teachings on 18 Core Topics," accessed from http://www.jewishecoseminars.com/learning-resources/#sthash.xCOH8WXf.dpuf, on 5th November 2014.

15 Rabbi Yonatan Neril (*Executive Director*, The Interfaith Center for Sustainable Development) made use of the analogy of the boat in order to explain his concept of the ecological sustainability

Human-caused disruptions to the natural world emerge from the inner imbalance within billions of human beings. The change required of us to correct this is, to a significant degree, of a spiritual nature.[16]

6. Perspective of Father Biju Michael sdb on Christian Teachings on Ecology

Faith and Ecology are closely interlinked. The responsibility and duty to care for the environment is an integral part of the Christian faith. This is so first, because of the faith in a creator God who created all things and entrusted the environment as a gift to human beings to be cared for in recognition of the love that bestowed it upon them as a home. This gift is to be used with holiness and righteousness (cf. Wis 9:3). Secondly, the recognition of the effects of human sin - both personal and social - calls attention to the possible use and misuse of the trust that God put in human beings. Thirdly, because the salvation expected at the end of times includes the environment since all things will be reconciled in Christ the Lord (cf. Col 1: 19-20; 2 Pt 3:13). The natural law (recognition of the grammar of creation) understanding that guides Christian morality is also a factor that unites faith and ecology.[17]

7. Perspective of Yasmin Barhum on Muslim Teachings on Ecology

The right and need of every human is to have access to plants. Nourishing both our souls and bodies, the relationship we have with plants is essential to well being. All people should have access to growing, nurturing, harvesting and appreciating plants. However, in the modern world, particularly in large built-up areas or areas exposed to pollution or desertification, local people often do not enjoy this "right to plants". Their living conditions deny them access to plants that could be grown, harvested and traded to feed the local community, for instance, or perhaps planted simply to improve and beautify their immediate environment.

---

and invited us in the session to become 'givers' and 'sharers' and not 'takers.'

16 For many ecological issues, the root issues beyond the physical symptoms lie in the spiritual health of human beings. *Prayer* is one of the key tools that God has given us to change the world. As we will see, it is our responsibility and opportunity to pray for the health of the earth and human civilization living on it and with it. Today's environmental movement seems to focus strongly on doing. There are things to buy, actions to take, petitions to sign, policies to advocate. It is rare for environmentalists to think of prayer as a tool for change. Many people in today's society think of prayer as a passive, contemplative activity – a break from action. The first two chapters of Genesis contain teachings with profound relevance for ourselves and our world today. "Be fruitful and multiply, fill the earth and subdue it, and have dominion over the fish of the sea, and over the birds of the sky, and over every living thing that moves upon the earth." What does it mean for humans to subdue the earth and have dominion over other creatures?

17 Father Biju Michael sdb (*President*, **Salesian Pontifical University**, Jerusalem Campus) elaborated the reality ecological crisis and the utmost need for moral responsibility and human care of the eco-system as Christians from the faith aspect with a Biblical background.

There exists in planning and environmental policies a cynicism towards and in some instances a complete denial of integrating plants and nature back into people's lives. This is only emphasized by the driving force of capitalism that affects all political decisions. Thus, leading to a collective bias in politics that removes us from, rather than engages us with, our natural environment. Therefore, an urgent call to respond to the cause of environmental justice, the right-to-landscape and the right-to-plants for all people is needed immediately! Change is needed to promote environmental values as the driving force for all policy decisions world-wide! As some of the advocates for this change those of us who follow a faith, firstly should understand the blessing that this planet is, and should also take on the serious responsibility we all dare to protect, enjoy and crucially share our living environment. By developing our personal relationship with plants and the natural environment and by influencing and drawing the attention of others to this crucial cause we all have a role to play in initiating and demanding this change. [18]

PART II: The Paradigm Shift from the Ecological Crisis to Ecosophical Care

8. The Ecological Crisis[19]

The multiple manifestations of the contemporary ecological crisis will exacerbate the sufferings and deprivations already faced by all around the world. Climate change, biodiversity loss, ruthless extraction and rapid depletion of natural resources, mega developmental projects like dams and highways which lead to the eviction of many of them from their native territories, loss of biodiversity, reckless mining and resource extraction, deforestation and conversion of forest land for agribusiness projects, massive developmental projects like the construction of hydroelectric dams, and the rapidly increasing amount of land being converted into plantations of bio-fuel crops especially in tropical forest areas, threaten the way of life, and at times the very existence of some traditional cultures,[20] and floods

18 Jessica Yasmin Barhum (british/swiss origin, Gardener, Landscape Architect, Jerusalem & Housewife) shared her experience of what environment/land/resource means to the local people staying in families which are underprivileged.

19 The entire section on Ecological Crisis are snippets (eclectically) taken from: Joshtrom Isaac Kureethadam, "From Victims to Leaders: Tapping Indigenous Wisdom for the Stewardship of Creation," in Parte Terza: Saggezza Etica E Antropologica: (411-441). Maurizio Marin, *Sapienza, Saggezza E Filosofia: Teoria E Pratica Come Vertice Umano Aperto Al Divino*. Libreria Ateneo Salesiano (Las) – Roma, 2014.

20 Farah Mihlar, *Voices that Must Be Heard: Minorities and Indigenous People Combating Climate Change* (London: Minority Rights Group International, 2008), 1 & 4.

facilitate the proliferation and spread of infectious diseases as well as respiratory and diarrhoeal diseases.[21]

An estimated 1.3 billion people, or 40 percent of the economically active people worldwide, work in agriculture, fishing, forestry and hunting and gathering. The depletion of natural resources will affect in particular the indigenous communities around the world. While they constitute only about 5 percent of the world's population, they own, occupy or use up to 22 percent of the world's land, which holds 80 percent of the planet's biodiversity, and an estimated 60 million of them depend totally on forest resources for their livelihood.[22] Against such a background, we need a real change of paradigm today in order to acknowledge and promote the leadership role of stewardship of the natural world, of care for creation and sustainability in the protection of life on earth, and of earth itself. In recent years there has been a rapidly growing interest and increasing recognition of the potential role of indigenous wisdom in responding to the contemporary ecological crisis.[23] It is recognized that native peoples have often developed sustainable environmental practices and can contribute to mitigating climate change thanks to their traditional knowledge and practices.[24] Joshtrom quotes here: As stewards of the world's biodiversity and cultural diversity and with our traditional livelihoods and ecological knowledge, we can significantly contribute to designing and implementing more appropriate and sustainable mitigation and adaptation measures.[25]

It is the holistic and comprehensive nature of such wisdom which makes it appropriate and relevant in responding to the contemporary ecological crisis which is itself complex and multifaceted. The ecological cri-sis is not just a physical problem. It is also a moral problem since its disproportionate victims are the poor and vulnerable communities, who have contributed least to cause the problem in the first place. Further, the eco-logical crisis is a spiritual crisis as the degradation of the Earth, entrusted to human stewardship, is a defilement of creation permeated and sanctified by the presence of the Divine. The crisis is indeed a cry of the Earth, of the poor and of the gods.[26] Wisdom, in response to the

21 United Nations Development Programme, *Human Development Report 2011*, 53; D. Green - U. King - J. Morrison, "Disproportionate burdens: The multidimensional impacts of climate change on the health of indigenous Australians" in *Medical Journal of Australia* 190 (1), 4-5.

22 United Nations Development Programme, *Human Development Report 2011*, 54.

23 J. Salick - N. Ross, "Traditional peoples and climate change" in *Global Environmental Change* 19 (2009), 137-9; D. Riedlinger - F. Berkes, "Contributions of traditional knowledge to understanding climate change in the Canadian Arctic" in *Polar Rec* 37 (2001), 315-328.

24 Lars Otto Naess, "The role of local knowledge in adaptation to climate change" in *WIREs Climate Change* 4 (2013), 99.

25 Quoted by Lindroth - Sinevaara-Niskanen, "At the crossroads of autonomy and essentialism," 284.

26 See in this regard Joshtrom Isaac Kureethadam, *The Ecological Crisis: A Triple Cry of the Earth, of the Poor and of the Gods* (forthcoming).

ecological crisis, hold a triple promise in terms of the rediscovery of a harmonious existence with the physical world, a reemphasis of the communitarian dimension of human existence, and a reawakening to the divine presence in all of creation.

The declaration stated:

> Human beings and the natural world are on a collision course. Human activities inflict harsh and often irreversible damage on the environment and on critical resources. If not checked, many of our current practices put at serious risk the future that we wish for human society and the plant and animal kingdoms, and may so alter the living world that it will be unable to sustain life in the manner that we know. ... A great change in our stewardship of the earth and the life on it is required if vast human misery is to be avoided and our global home on this planet is not to be irretrievably mutilated.[27]

Today, as the 2012 Planet Under Pressure Conference notes, "humans have become a prime driver of change at the planetary level, significantly altering Earth's biological, chemical and physical processes. There is increasing evidence that humans are driving the Earth system towards dangerous thresholds or tipping points."[28] As Lynn White noted already in 1967 in his epoch-making article: "surely no creature other than man has ever managed to foul its nest in such short order."[29]

At its core, the contemporary ecological crisis stems from a disharmonious relationship between humanity and the rest of the natural world. The crisis from the amnesia of our profound connectedness with the natural world that engendered us and sustains humans and the rest of the living entities. The modern humans forget that they belong to and are situated in the natural world. With the aid of modern technology, we have created a global satellite-driven digital media world – a media culture – that quite literally isolates us from the natural world that we participate in daily. We have insulated our everyday lives from the living planet that sustains us.[30] We forget that our own lives depend on a complex web of life in which everything is interrelated and interconnected. Instead, "we are killing ourselves by ending the lives of many of our other-than-human relatives on which our own lives depend."[31] The ecological crisis results from our dis-connection from the rest of the natural world. As Daniel R. Wildcat points out with regard to climate change, "the incredibly high cost of this climate change to our Mother

---

27 "The World Scientists' Warning to Humanity" in Paul Ehrlich - Anne Ehrlich, *Betrayal of Science and Reason: How Anti-Environmental Rhetoric Threatens Our Future* (Washington, D.C.: Island Press, 1998), 242 & 244.

28 International Conference Planet Under Pressure, *Rio+20 Policy Brief* (London - 26-29 March 2012), 1.

29 Lynn White, "The historical roots of our ecologic crisis," *Science* 155 (1967), 1204.

30 Daniel R. Wildcat, *Red Alert: Saving the Planet with Indigenous Knowledge* (Golden, Colorado: Fulcrum, 2009), 10 & 29.

31 Wildcat, *Red Alert*, 39.

Earth must be understood as related to humankind's development of societies and cultures disconnected in fundamental ways from the landscapes and seascapes, the places where they are situated."[32]

In the face of the contemporary ecological crisis, we need to live in harmony with the natural world that engendered and sustains us. This requires that we need to see, appreciate and protect Earth as our very home. In May 2011, the Pontifical Academy of Sciences published a report on mountain glaciers.

The Opening Declaration of this report is worth quoting in this regard:

> We call on all people and nations to recognise the serious and potentially irreversible impacts of global warming caused by the anthropogenic emissions of greenhouse gases and other pollutants, and by changes in forests, wetlands, grasslands, and other land uses ... aware that we all live in the same home. By acting now, in the spirit of common but differentiated responsibility, we accept our duty. to one another and to the stewardship of a planet blessed with the gift of life. We are committed to ensuring that all inhabitants of this planet receive their daily bread, fresh air to breathe and clean water to drink as we are aware that, if we want justice and peace, we must protect the habitat that sustains us.[33]

In the rediscovery of Earth as our home and in the responsible stewardship of our common home, indigenous wisdom has indeed much to offer to humanity. The ethnic populations that have lived in harmonious relationship with the physical world in the past can offer humanity precious as we mentioned earlier, the contemporary ecological crisis is not just merely a physical problem. The contemporary ecological crisis reveals how we have ruptured our bonds of fellowship with the natural world but also among ourselves. The ecological crisis is, in fact, brewed within the crucible of inequality. The injustices leading to a divided world are especially evident in the ecological and carbon footprints of individuals and com-munities on our common home planet and on its atmosphere. While the carbon footprint analysis indicates the huge disparities between nations in the emissions of greenhouse gases that lead to global warming and cause climate change, the ecological footprint analysis reveals profound inequalities in the consumption of the natural resources.[34] Against the global ecological apartheid that humanity is drifting into we need to discover unity not only with the natural world but also establish solidarity with our fellow brothers and sisters. It appears that wisdom which is not only about interrelatedness between humanity and the natural world but also about harmonious relationships within native communities can

32 Wildcat, *Red Alert*, 61.

33 Pontificia Academia Scientiarum, *Fate of Mountain Glaciers in the Antrhopocene: A Report by the Working Group Commissioned by the Pontifical Academy of Sciences* (5 May 2011), 2, 15.

34 The Ecological Footprint Analysis was pioneered by William Rees and Mathis Wackernagel. See William Rees and Mathis Wackernagel, *Our Ecological Footprint: Reducing Human Impact on the Earth* (Philadelphia, PA: New Society Publishers, 1996).

provide some valuable resources here. The clue to the harmonious relationship of different communities is in sharing and caring with the wisdom about stewarding the very natural resources from where we all draw sustenance. In the wake of the contemporary ecological crisis humanity needs to rediscover and reemphasize the communitarian dimension of human existence if we are to live in harmony with the physical world. In this way, future generations will have to bear the heaviest burden for the present generation's irresponsibility.[35] It also means that "we are taking the greatest of gambles with our children's and our grandchildren's futures – indeed, the future of the next fifty generations."[36]

In the face of the contemporary ecological crisis we need to rediscover not only our bonds with the natural world but also among humans themselves. At a deeper level, the contemporary ecological crisis is paradigmatic of the amnesia of a profound truth, namely, that the physical world is above all God's creation, is permeated with the divine presence, and entrusted to human beings who are called to be its responsible guardians. The ecological crisis is the outcome, above all, of our incapacity to look at the physical world as God's creation, as God's own home (oikos), and respect its sanctity and integrity. A certain 'de- sacralisation' of nature, it may be claimed, has been one of the contributing factors of the present day ecological crisis.[37]

In the wake of Modernity, all natural phenomena were held to be explicable in mechanical terms; a conceptual advance which ignited the first sparks of the Scientifico-Politico-Religious Evolution-Revolution. Modern philosophy enthroned the rational human being, the *res cogitans*, at the pinnacle of reality, thereby dethroning all other absolutes.

9. The Ecosophical Care

Ecosophy and ecophilosophy are neologisms formed by contracting the phrase ecological philosophy. The Norwegian philosopher Arne Naess (1912-2009), professor at University of Oslo, introduced this term 'ecosophy' into environmental literature. Focus on deep experience, questioning, commitment, dedication and above all an ecological wisdom. Felix Guattari (1930-), a psychoanalyst, poststructuralist philosopher and political activist, refers ecosophy to a field of practice. Ecosophy is a science of ecosystems, mental and social ecosystems. 'Deep Ecology,' is also connected to Ecosophy. The phrase 'Deep Ecology' was also coined by Arne Naess. What is meant by 'Deep Ecology' is that like human beings, the

35 Mayer Hillman - Tina Fawcett - Sudhir Chella Rajan, *How We Can Save the Planet: Preventing Global Climate Catastrophe* (New York: Thomas Dunne Books, 2008), 2.

36 Marlowe Sam, "Ethics from the land: Traditional Protocols and the Maintenance of Peace" in *Original Instructions: Indigenous Teachings for a Sustainable Future*, ed. Melissa K. Nelson (Rochester, Vermont: Bear & Co., 2008), 40.

37 Dora Marinova - Margaret Raven, "Indigenous knowledge and intellectual property: A sustainability agenda" in *Journal of Economic Surveys* 20 (2006), 587.

living environment as a whole has the same right to live, grow and develop. Deep Ecology claims to be 'deep' because it asks deep questions like 'why' and 'how'. Ecosophy and Deep Ecology are propagated by Arne Naess (1912-2009), Warwick Fox (1954-), David Abram (1957-), Felix Guattari (1930-) and Thomas Berry (1914-2009). Philosopher-Theologian who goes beyond Ecology, Deep Ecology and Ecological Concerns is none other than Raimon Panikkar (1918-2010).

10. Raimon Panikkar's Understanding of Ecosophy

According to Raimon Panikkar,[38] 'Ecosophy' is a new word for a very ancient 'Wisdom'. For Panikkar, Ecosophy implies the following aspects: the human consciousness that the earth is a living being, as a whole and in all its members;

---

38 Raimon Panikkar was born in Barcelona, Spain, November 3, 1918, to a Spanish Roman Catholic mother and an Indian Hindu father. [Pascaline Coff, "Biography of Raimon Panikkar," accessed from, http://monasticdialog.com/a.php?id=666, accessed on January 26 2011]. Raimon Panikkar had from the beginning an openness to these two religions (Christianity and Hinduism). His work as a Roman Catholic Priest ('He was ordained in 1946. After his ordination he left Spain in 1953 and lived in India until 1960, where he taught Indological subjects in the universities of Mysore and Banaras.' [E. H. Cousins, "Introduction: The Panikkar Symposium at Santa Barbara," *Cross Currents*, 29/2 (1979), 132]. In the diocese of Varanasi enabled him to come in close contact with the people of India, with their culture and their religions, particularly with the religion of his father. He held three doctorates – in Science, Philosophy and Theology. His doctorate in philosophy is likewise from the University of Madrid, 1946 '*El Concepto de Naturaleza. Análisis Histórico e Metafisico de un Concepto,*' the title of his dissertation which earned him the *Menéndes y Pelayo* prize; and his doctorate in theology from the Lateran University, with a dissertation on, "the Relation of Christianity and Hinduism." After a scientific and industrial experience he became professor of philosophy and took active part in the cultural life of Europe immediately after the World War II, mainly, in Spain. Please note here that the title of Panikkar's dissertation is not mentioned in English, due to the lack of resources and research. [Dominic Veliath, *Theological Approach and Understanding of Religions: Jean Daniélou and Raimundo Panikkar A Study in Contrast* (Bangalore: Kristu Jyoti College, 1987), 81-82.] The bulk of his writings are mainly concerned with comparative cultures, the history of religions, comparative religion, theology and hermeneutics. (Panikkar has published more than thirty books and over three hundred major academic articles. An additional updated note to this footnote is that there have been nine hundred articles written by Panikkar till the year 2010. "Raimon Panikkar," accessed from http://www.iemed.org/publicacions/quaderns/14/qm14_pdf/8.pdf, accessed on January 26, 2011). As one who had grown up and worked both in the East and in the West he has had the rare opportunity of internalizing the essence of both Christian and Hindu traditions. His involvement in other religions was so deep that he could rightly say that he started as a Christian, went through Hinduism and returned to Christianity, but only passing through Buddhism. [Raimundo Panikkar, *The Unknown Christ of Hinduism: Towards an Ecumenical Christophany* (London: Darton, Longman and Todd, 1981), x]. See also.[Peter Slater, "Hindu and Christian Symbols in the Work of R. Panikkar," *Cross Currents*, 29/2 (1979), 169-182 passim]. He last lived in Tavertet, Catalonia outside Barcelona and passed away on August 26, 2010.["Raimon Panikkar, "Life," accessed from "http://avidpdf.com/viewer?url=http://raimonpanikkar.org/pdf%20stampa/National_Catholic_Reporter_2010-08-31.pdf, accessed on January 18, 2011].

the approach to matter and the physical world whose names, physics, nature, *bhumi* (earth), etc. reveal that she is begotten and is alive; life is not the privilege of humans alone; in fact, humans share in the life of the universe which has unity, a living principle and a soul; contemporary ecological crisis cannot be just reduced to ecological or technical. A radical conversion in human thinking and cultural mutation are necessary. Man's desire is to eradicate its exploitation and for these simple ecological considerations will not suffice, a pragmatic approach remotely subtle and indirect ways of exploiting the earth is essential. Man as lord and master can still keep exploiting the earth in spite of the precautionary measures, recycling and others. What is required is to go beyond ecology to ecosophical vision of reality. Ecosophy calls for a renewal in our attitudes and perceptions to look deeply at the collective identity and destiny of the three dimensions of reality, i.e., cosmic, human and divine.

Beyond a simple ecology, ecosophy is a wisdom-spirituality of the earth. "The new equilibrium" is not so much between man and the earth, as between matter and spirit, between spatio-temporality and consciousness. Ecosophy neither a mere 'science of the earth' (ecology) nor even 'wisdom about the earth', but rather a 'wisdom of the earth herself' that is made manifest to man when he knows how to listen to her with love. Panikkar speaks of not only of communion of the human kind, but also of communion between all entities. His idea of dialogue holds a vision whole reality in terms of "pure communicability." Man should therefore have dialogue with the Earth itself. Mere "eco-logy" is not enough. There must also be room for "ecosophy," which adopts a dialogical attitude towards the Earth, seeing it as a Thou. In Panikkar's ecosophy, the Earth has a certain revelatory meaning since man's task is disclosed in dialogue with the Earth. This idea of dialogue with the Earth runs parallel with Panikkar's fundamental view that man's task is to participate in reality and its cosmic rhythms.[39]

11. Christophany and Ecosophy

Christophany invites us to listen to the wisdom of the earth or as Panikkar calls it ecosophy. It is the awareness that ecology based on Man's reason and effort to "save the earth." Man cannot save the earth rather Man has to learn to listen to the wisdom of the Earth (ecosophia). Hence it would be more appropriate to say, "to serve the earth" rather than "save the earth". Man has to listen if a healthy attitude is to be developed to Mother Earth. In a word, ecology (science of the earth) is a problem that also belongs to Christophany[40] and in its light

39 Raimon Panikkar, *Christophany: The Fullness of Man*, trans. Alfred DiLascia (Maryknoll: Orbis Books, 2004), 173.

40 Christophany, as Panikkar states, is not a simple extension of Christology that attempts to explain—and even understand—the "fact" of Christ. Since it is more experiential, christophany concentrates its attention on the light in which Christ manifests himself to us. In this way we discover that not only do many of Jesus' statements create scandal by shaking our habits, but they seem to originate in a different vision of the world. Christophany is the manifestation of

becomes 'eco-sophy' (wisdom of the earth, not just our wisdom of the earth).[41] Panikkar speaks of "the harmony with nature that must be restored by something other than simple ecological cosmetics. Ecosophy is a contemporary imperative of human consciousness (cosmic brotherhood). Awareness of the inter independence of all beings makes it imperative to assimilate a vision wherein Man is part, of the whole. Ecosophy promotes an attitude of wholeness, an attitude of interiority and an attitude of belonging to the Earth. Man's consciousness has to be of the nature of a response to what the Earth is to us, and what she is shouldering, saying, and showing. Most importantly, ecosophy implies a Cosmotheandric spirituality, where the whole world is revered as a temple and every action becomes as it were a prayer because its intentionality is for the welfare of all.[42]

Man's relationship with the Earth should be like cultivating "her as one would a friendship or a garden, not as one would plunder a mine." In fact, Panikkar even understands the Earth to be "our own Body" and "part of ourselves – of our own Self." On this point, modern science and technology have fatally deviated, thus disclosing their distorted nature. He stresses that science should not be separated from theology and cosmology. At the slight risk of over-simplifying, it could be said that his holisitic way of thinking gives obvious preferentiality to the philosophy of nature and eschews the modern scientific approach.[43]

12. Cosmotheandric Vision and Ecosophy

I think that Panikkar's cosmotheandric vision unfolds to us the primordial and mystical vision of reality that is crystallized on a meta-epistemo-onto-mystical level. Panikkar's ecosophy message calls for the reclamation of the natural order of the universe as a whole, not only through an awareness of the rights and equality, justice and stability but to consider the earth as a subject. We are invited to keep open an inter-trans-disciplinary dialogue between science, philosophy and theology, as disciplines belonging to the same cosmological context, critically emancipating our thinking to approach a paradoxical logic in order to combine the analytical vision (rational) with the vision of the whole (intuition), a uni-pluriversal way, to protect knowledge, environment and cultural and ethnic relations, for a sustainable future.[44] All over the world there are imitations in our times that a

---

the mysterious union of the divine, human, and cosmic 'dimension' of Reality. The conjunction of three is search for a Cosmotheandric reality. The task of Christophany is not to defend or criticize any Christology but to find adequate answers to the basic human and ecological questions and the goal of Christophany is to build and not to destroy and to work for the wholeness and integration of human, divine, and cosmos. Panikkar, *Christophany*, 168.

41 Panikkar, *Christophany*, 168.

42 *Ibid.*, 170.

43 Cheriyan Menacherry, *Christ: The Mystery in History – A Critical Study on the Christology of Raymond Panikkar* (New York: Peter Lang, 1996), 174.

44 Maria Roberta Cappellini, "Between Intercultural Philosophy and Complexity: Ecosophy, The Wisdom of Dwelling," *Cirpit Review: Rivista Internazionale On-line* (December, 2010): 13.

common concern (however minimal) as regards the world is emerging. It is not the magnitude of this concern-community that we are witnessing. Cutting across the board we have movements from all kinds of scientific-religio-politico-socio-eco-cultural groups showing awareness of the urgency for care of the environment. A common horizon is on the way.[45] It is a wakeup call for depth-dimension, for divine-dimension.[46]

Every being bears in itself the stamp of the divine, the human, and the cosmic. To signify this inseparable relation, Panikkar coins a new term – cosmotheandric[47] in which cosmos (universe), theos (God), and ander (human) are not simply three dimensions of a whole, but all the three are present in every single being. The principle of radical relativity–which conceives the ontological nature of the whole reality as a web of relationships – can be seen in the deeper law that governs it. Panikkar calls it '*ontonomy*.'[48] Ontonomy is neither *heteronomy*[49] nor *autonomy*.[50] For heteronomy indicates the state of being governed from without, implying a tilt towards the pole of theos. On the other hand, autonomy refers to the state in which beings are self-ruled without relatedness to other beings. This frees the reality from the pole of theos and orients it towards the cosmic and the human. Both heteronomy and autonomy cause polarization, whereas ontonomy is that state of consciousness which overcomes both individualism of autonomy as well as monolithism of heteronomy, as ontonomy is the realization of the nomos – the law of being. The same vision of unity leads Panikkar to link also time and

45 Francis X. D'sa, "The Significance of Panikkar's Cosmotheandric Vision," *Cirpit Review: Rivista Internazionale On-line* (December, 2010): 33

46 Raimon Panikkar, *The Rhythm of Being: The Gifford Lectures* (Maryknoll: Orbis Books, 2010).

47 Raimon Panikkar, *A Dwelling Place for Wisdom* (Delhi: Motilal Banarsidas Publishers, 1993), 98.

48 By *ontonomy* we mean that degree of awareness, which having overcome the individualistic attitude as well as the monolithic view of reality, regards the whole universe as unity so that the regulation of a particular being is neither self-imposed nor dictated from above, but a part of the whole discovering or following its destiny. Ontonomy is the realization of the *nomos*, the law of the *on*, being, at that profound level where unity does not impinge upon diversity, but where the latter is rather the unique and proper manifestation of the former. It rests on the specular character of reality, in which each part mirrors the whole in a way proper to it. Raimundo Panikkar, *Worship and Secular Man* (Maryknoll: Orbis Books, 1973), 29-30.

49 By *heteronomy* we understand a worldview, as well as an anthropological degree of consciousness, which relies on a hierarchical structure of reality, which considers that a regulations in any sphere of being come from a higher instance, and are in each case responsible for the proper functioning of that particular being or sphere of being. Panikkar, *Worship and Secular Man*, 31-33.

50 By *autonomy* we understand the world as well as the human being to be *sui iuris*, that is self-determined and determinable, each being a law unto its self. This autonomy means that any injunction from outside, or from above, is regarded as an imposition. Panikkar, *Worship and Secular Man*, 33-36.

eternity expressed in his another neologism – *tempiternity* (unity of time and eternity). Tempiternity is the indissoluble unity of all reality, which bears in itself some dimension of transcendence as well as some dimension of temporality.[51] Participation and in a certain way mysticism could be the key words from a cosmological angle expressing the ontonomic experience. The latter stands for the twofold conviction that (a) reality has a hidden and invisible dimension, which in one way or another can be brought to light or to the surface of the real, and that (b) only when one is aware or takes into account (even if in an unconscious way) this dimension of reality does an authentic human life emerge. The word participation is meant to convey that cosmological vision which sees the interdependence and interpenetration of all things and their mutual relationship as the deepest web of reality.[52]

13. Cosmotheandric Spirituality and Ecosophy

Panikkar suggests some milestones for this new awareness of a terrestrial spirituality. For heuristic purposes, he divides into paragraphs what is simple and corresponds to a single and simple vision. And, for the sake of brevity, he does not elaborate all the ramifications of this insight.

First, this cosmotheandric insight has to emerge spontaneously. A new innocence is required here. Legal impositions or moral constraints will not suffice, important as these human disciplines may be on their own terrains. But spirituality cannot, ultimately, be legislated or commanded. It has to germinate freely in the very depths of our being. The proper soil is the myth.

Second, such spontaneity entails that this spirituality keep itself independent, so far as possible, from philosophical and scientific hypotheses. The criterion for the authenticity of a myth is its meta-philosophical and meta-scientific character. A myth is polyvalent and polysemic. For many people today, God and science are no longer myths, but ideologies, i.e., it will function whether we follow one ideology or another.

Third, the Earth is neither inferior to Man nor superior. Man is neither the boss of this World, nor just a creature, the product of a cosmic Womb. The Earth is also not "equal" to Man. Equality assumes a higher genus of which the two species are precisely equal specimens. Man and the cosmos, to the contrary, are ultimates, and thus reducible neither one to the other nor to a higher entity. The relation is non-dualistic. Both are distinct, but not separable. My head is distinct from me, yet cannot be separated from me. It would cease to be what it is, and so would I. The head is essentially the head of a body. The metaphor of the body may still be powerful: we do not treat our bodies as something other, although we discover their otherness: *aliud non alius.*

---

51 Panikkar, *Worship and Secular Man*, 41-46.

52 *Ibid.*, 46-47.

Fourth, our relation with the Earth is part of our self-understanding. It is a constitutive relationship. To be entails being *in* and *with* the World. I do not treat my stomach independently of my body, or of myself. I am convinced that what is best for my stomach is also best for me-although sometimes I may set my sights on the maximum instead of the optimum and overeat or drink too much. Our relationship with the Earth is similar, once this total awareness has dawned. We don't so much need a pragmatic recycling as a living symbiosis, a mutual rejuvenation, a spiral movement. If there are entropic phenomena in the universe, there are equally syntropic ones-the vital ones.

Finally, this spirituality would heal another open wound for modern Man: the chasm between the material and the spiritual and, with this, between the secular and the sacred, the inner and the outer, the temporal and the eternal. It is not a question of blurring differences, but of realizing interrelations and becoming conscious of interdependencies and correlations. Man does not have a double citizenship, as it were-one here below and another above, or for later on. He or she is here and now the inhabitant of an authentic reality that has many mansions and presents many dimensions, but which does not slice human life into sections, either in time or in space, or for the individual or for society. Service to the Earth is divine service, just as the love of God is human love.

14. Transhistorical Consciousness and Ecosophy

The novelty of the phenomenon is the increasingly societal aspect of this transhistorical consciousness on the contemporary scene. It is no longer some few individuals who attempt to overcome historical consciousness by crossing to the other shore and experiencing the *transtemporal*, the *tempiternal*. There are increasing numbers of people in the historical world impelled to this breakthrough in their consciousness out of sheer survival necessity, due to the stiffing closeness of the system and the universal strictures of the modern predicament.[53]

Man wants the fulfillment of life not only here and now for the select few, but for everybody. This means that there is now emerging a new myth that is the fullness life. It is this impasse that fosters the emergence of *transhistorical* consciousness.[54] The world of transhistorical Man, his environment, is the

---

53 Raimon Panikkar, *The Cosmotheandric Experience: Emerging Religious Consciousness*, ed. Scott Eastham (Delhi: Motilal Banarsidass, 1998), 125.

54 Transhistorical consciousness pierces through history to its transtemporal core. The mystic has a transhistorical experience. Theirs is a vision which includes the three times: past, present and future. Human life is more than just an accretion from the past and a projection into the future. It is both (and together) the ex and sistence which constitute our being. This is why only by in-sisting on the ex-sistence are saved. They live in the present in all its intensity and in this tension discover the in-tentionality and in-tegrity of life, the tempiternal, ineffable core which is full in every authentic moment. The novelty of the phenomenon is the increasingly societal aspect of this consciousness. The emerging myth of transhistorical Man assumes a more or less conscious theanthropocosmic vision of the universe: he finds himself,

cosmotheandric universe.[55] Love is the supreme principle, the linking force which brings everything together.[56] Man is embarking upon a new venture, about which we know only what we shall act the more freely the more we allow the internal dynamism of our deepest being to express itself, without projecting beforehand what we are to do and to be. We are creatively participating in the very existence of the cosmotheandric reality.

15. Wisdom and Ecosophy

In a word, the primary dwelling place of wisdom is our universe, our world, and still more concrete, our Mother Earth. One might interpret it as a *fuga mundi* (flight from the world); however, such a trip would not be a departure from earth but an escape from self. It is a place to stay where we can settle down, a home where we can be ourselves, where we can have a human relationship with things. We do not need to hide this wisdom; neither do we have to protect or defend it. Sacred writings tell us that wisdom has a double dwelling place. On the one hand, it is the human heart (Hebrew *leb*) that is a dwelling place of wisdom (Prov. 2:1); here heart symbolizes the totality of a person. The heart is understood in an intellectual, spiritual, and physical sense; it follows the rhythm of nature, being at the same time in contact and symbiosis with other hearts. On the other hand, it is the entire earth that is a dwelling place of wisdom (Prov. 8:22-31) Hence, a dwelling place is neither just a small house nor a certain community or civilization but the human heart and the earth at large. "In the good heart of Man (lies) wisdom," the Bible says (Prov. 14:33), and the Earth is its dwelling place (Prov. 8:2).[57] Panikkar states: the climax of life is, in my opinion, to participate in the life of the universe, in both the cosmic and divine symphonies to which even we mortals are invited. It is not only a matter of living but also of letting life be-this life, offered to us as a gift so that we may sustain and deepen it.[58] Religion,

---

in varying degrees of harmony and tension, within a cosmotheandric reality in which all forces of the universe are intertwined. It concentrates on building and bringing to completion the microcosm that is Man, both individually and collectively: mirroring and transforming the macrocosm altogether. The cosmotheandric vocation is a calling to the inner discovery of a lifestyle. It is a consciousness which reaches the fullness of time, since the three times are simultaneously experienced. My individuality touches everything and everybody and yet I am: *aham Brahman*. Sharing in the unfolding of Life, assisting at the cosmic display of all the forces of the universe, feeling the very assimilation and dissimilation of the cosmos on both the macro- and micro-cosmic scales, just to be, to live, to exist on all the planes of existence at the same time: the tempiternal explosion of the adventure of Be-ing this is transhistorical existence. Panikkar, *The Cosmotheandric Experience, passim* 120-133.

55 Panikkar, *The Cosmotheandric Experience*, 128.

56 *Ibid.*, 128-129.

57 Raimon Panikkar, *A Dwelling Place for Wisdom,* trans. Annemarie S. Kidder (Westminster: John Knox Press, 1993), 15-17.

58 Panikkar, *A Dwelling Place for Wisdom,* 79.

philosophy and culture are three "elements" of the human reality. If the first could be compared to the feet with which Man journeys towards his destiny, philosophy could represent the eyes that scrutinize that journey, and culture, the earth on which Man is walking during his concrete pilgrimage. Interculturality represents the relativity (not the relativism) of everything human, and therefore of these three notions. The question of the nature of philosophy is already a philosophical question, and intimately connected with life.[59]

16. Cosmology and Kosmology

Although the modern scientific cosmology has triumphed over the old cosmologies, the modern vision has not corrected many errors of the old cosmologies, but rather seems to have merely displaced or found functional substitutes for certain key elements. Therefore, in order to stress continuity, on the one hand, and novelty, on the other, Panikkar has chosen to change the ordinary spelling of the new cosmology (to Kosmology) instead of introducing any new name. By Kosmology, Panikkar understands science in the holistic sense. Kosmology is a kosmos-legein, a "reading" of the kosmos, the disclosure of the world to our human consciousness by means of all forms of knowledge we may possess. It is mainly understood here in the sense of the subjective genitive: the logos, the word of the kosmos that Man should try to hear and to understand by attuning himself to the music of this world, to the mysteries of the kosmos. We are aware that the kosmos speaks differently to different cultures and that Man hears and interprets this logo in many ways. It deals with how Man envisions the universe, with how the kosmos displays itself to Man, and with the experience that Man has of the universe of which we happen to form part and that leads us to discover the real universe in which we live. It aspires to a knowledge of the kosmos in a manner similar to the way theology aspired to a knowledge of God and thus claimed to have saving power. The novelty of this cosmotheandric kosmology is that it also claims to possess saving power for the fullness of Man, a microcosm. It tries to understand and interpret, more or less profoundly, whatever enters into the field of our consciousness.

Laudato si (Praised be to you, my Lord and my God) – Ecological Care: A Response of Pope Francis to Ecological Crisis.

Ecology studies the relationship between living organisms and the environment in which they develop. This necessarily entails reflection and debate about the conditions required for the life and survival of society, and the honesty needed to question certain models of development, production and consumption. It cannot be emphasized enough how everything is interconnected (Laudato si,

59 This text reproduces, with some variations, the inaugural address of the first Congress of Intercultural Philosophy, held in Mexico City in March 1995, address whose title was "Filosofía y cultura: unarelaciónproblemática". It was published in: *Ilu. Revista de Ciencias de lasReligiones* 1 (1996), 125-148.

138). An integral ecology includes taking time to recover a serene harmony with creation, reflecting on our lifestyle and our ideals, and contemplating the Creator who lives among us and surrounds us, whose presence "must not be contrived but found, uncovered" (Laudato si, 225).

"The external deserts in the world are growing, because the internal deserts have become so vast." For this reason, the ecological crisis is also a summons to profound interior conversion. It must be said that some committed and prayerful Christians, with the excuse of realism and pragmatism, tend to ridicule expressions of concern for the environment. Others are passive; they choose not to change their habits and thus become inconsistent. So what they all need is an "ecological conversion," whereby the effects of their encounter with Jesus Christ be-come evident in their relationship with the world around them. Living our vocation to be protectors of God's handiwork is essential to a life of virtue; it is not an optional or a secondary aspect of our Christian experience (Laudato si, 217).

Greater investment needs to be made in research aimed at understanding more fully the functioning of ecosystems and adequately analyzing the different variables associated with any significant modification of the environment. Because all creatures are connected, each must be cherished with love and respect, for all of us as living creatures are dependent on one another. Each area is responsible for the care of this family. This will require undertaking a careful inventory of the species which it hosts, with a view to developing programmes and strategies of protection with particular care for safeguarding species heading towards extinction (Cf. Laudato si, 42). Today, however, we have to realize that a true ecological approach always becomes a social approach; it must integrate questions of justice in debates on the environment, so as to hear both the cry of the earth and the cry of the poor (Laudato si, 49).

Caring for ecosystems demands far-sightedness, since no one looking for quick and easy profit is truly interested in their preservation. But the cost of the damage caused by such selfish lack of concern is much greater than the economic benefits to be obtained. Where certain species are destroyed or seriously harmed, the values involved are incalculable. We can be silent witnesses to terrible injustices if we think that we can obtain significant benefits by making the rest of humanity, present and future, pay the extremely high costs of environmental deterioration (Cf. Laudato si, 36).

Care for nature is part of a lifestyle which includes the capacity for living together and communion. Jesus reminded us that we have God as our common Father and that this makes us brothers and sisters. Fraternal love can only be gratuitous; it can never be a means of repaying others for what they have done or will do for us. That is why it is possible to love our enemies. This same gratuitousness inspires us to love and accept the wind, the sun and the clouds, even though we cannot control them. In this sense, we can speak of a "universal fraternity." We must regain the conviction that we need one another that we have a shared responsibility for others and the world, and that being good and decent are worth it. We have had enough of immorality and the mockery of ethics, goodness, faith and honesty. It is time to acknowledge that lighthearted superficiality has done us no good. When the foundations of social life are corroded, what ensue are battles over conflicting interests, new forms of violence and brutality, and obstacles to the growth of a genuine culture of care for the environment (Cf. Laudato si, 228, & 229).

Love, overflowing with small gestures of mutual care, is also civic and political, and it makes itself felt in every action that seeks to build a better world. Love for society and commitment to the common good are outstanding expressions of a charity which affects not only relationships between individuals but also "macro-relationships, social, economic and political ones." That is why the Church set before the world the ideal of a "civilization of love." Social love is the key to authentic development: "In order to make society more human, more worthy of the human person, love in social life – political, economic and cultural – must be given renewed value, becoming the constant and highest norm for all activity." In this framework, along with the importance of little everyday gestures, social love moves us to devise larger strategies to halt environmental degradation and to encourage a "culture of care" which permeates all of society. When we feel that God is calling us to intervene with others in these social dynamics, we should realize that this too is part of our spirituality, which is an exercise of charity and, as such, matures and sanctifies us (Cf. Laudato si, 231).

17. Conclusion

In this article I have sought to realize a transition from the contemporary ecological crisis to ecosophical care. It is an invitation to make a shift from the materialistic reasoning to a spiritualistic understanding. It is a progressive movement from the action to a proactive contemplative-action reality. The truth of creation is seen from a deeper level, a moral level, a mystical level. I would call it a movement from progress to being proactive. The person/people can become truly beacons of hope in a world that faces the spectre of an ecological breakdown. We need a new cosmic alliance today, in the wake of the contemporary ecological crisis, between the physical world, humanity, and the very Creator. We need to realize that the cosmotheandric vision of Panikkar can be actualized only if we accept this paradigm shift of ecological crisis to ecosophical care.

Bibliography

Books

Baird, Rachel. *The Impact of Climate Change on Minorities and Indigenous Peoples.* London: Minority Rights Group International, 2008.

Ehrlich, Paul and Anne Ehrlich. "The World Scientists' Warning to Humanity" in *Betrayal of Science and Reason: How Anti-Environmental Rhetoric Threatens Our Future.* Washington, D.C.: Island Press, 1998.

Hillman, Mayer, Tina Fawcett and Sudhir Chella Rajan. *How We Can Save the Planet: Preventing Global Climate Catastrophe.* New York: Thomas Dunne Books, 2008.

Marin, Maurizio. *Sapienza, Saggezza E Filosofia: Teoria E Pratica Come Vertice Umano Aperto Al Divino.* Libreria Ateneo Salesiano (Las) – Roma, 2014.

Menacherry, Cheriyan. *Christ: The Mystery in History – A Critical Study on the Christology of Raymond Panikkar.* New York: Peter Lang, 1996.

Mihlar, Farah. *Voices that Must Be Heard: Minorities and Indigenous People Combating Climate Change.* London: Minority Rights Group International, 2008.

Panikkar, Raimon. *A Dwelling Place for Wisdom.* Delhi: Motilal Banarsidas Publishers, 1993.

_____. *A Dwelling Place for Wisdom.* Translated by Annemarie S. Kidder. Westminster: John Knox Press, 1993.

_____. *Christophany: The Fullness of Man.* Translated by Alfred DiLascia. Maryknoll: Orbis Books, 2004.

_____. *The Cosmotheandric Experience: Emerging Religious Consciousness.* Edited by Scott Eastham. Delhi: Motilal Banarsidass, 1998.

_____. *The Rhythm of Being: The Gifford Lectures.* Maryknoll: Orbis Books, 2010.

_____. *The Unknown Christ of Hinduism: Towards an Ecumenical Christophany.* London: Darton, Longman and Todd, 1981.

_____. *Worship and Secular Man.* Maryknoll: Orbis Books, 1973.

Sam, Marlowe. "Ethics from the land: Traditional Protocols and the Maintenance of Peace" in *Original Instructions: Indigenous Teachings for a Sustainable Future.* Edited by Melissa K. Nelson. Rochester, Vermont: Bear & Co., 2008.

Slater, Peter. "Hindu and Christian Symbols in the Work of R. Panikkar." *Cross Currents,* 29/2 (1979): 169-182.

Sobre-villa, C. *The Role of Indigenous Peoples in Biodiversity Conservation: The Natural But Often Forgotten Partners.* Washington, DC: World Bank, 2011.

Veliath, Dominic. *Theological Approach and Understanding of Religions: Jean Daniélou and Raimundo Panikkar A Study in Contrast.* Bangalore: Kristu Jyoti College, 1987.

Wildcat, Daniel R. *Red Alert: Saving the Planet with Indigenous Knowledge.* Golden, Colorado: Fulcrum, 2009.

William Rees and Mathis Wackernagel. *Our Ecological Footprint: Reducing Human Impact on the Earth.* Philadelphia, PA: New Society Publishers, 1996.

Articles

Cappellini, Maria Roberta. "Between Intercultural Philosophy and Complexity: Ecosophy, The Wisdom of Dwelling." *Cirpit Review: Rivista Internazionale On-line* (December, 2010): 13.

Christian, Aid. "Warning Signs: The Science and Impacts of Climate Change" (June 2010), 5.

Cousins, E. H. "Introduction: The Panikkar Symposium at Santa Barbara." *Cross Currents,* 29/2 (1979), 132].

D'sa, Francis X. "The Significance of Panikkar's Cosmotheandric Vision." *Cirpit Review: Rivista Internazionale On-line* (December, 2010): 33.

Green, D. U. King - J. Morrison. "Disproportionate burdens: The multidimensional impacts of climate change on the health of indigenous Australians" in *Medical Journal of Australia* 190 (1): 4-5.

International Conference Planet Under Pressure, *Rio+20 Policy Brief* (London - 26-29 March 2012): 1.

Isaac Kureethadam, Joshtrom. "From Victims to Leaders: Tapping Indigenous Wisdom for the Stewardship of Creation." in *Parte Terza: Saggezza Etica E Antropologica*: 411-441.

Lindroth - Sinevaara-Niskanen. "At the crossroads of autonomy and essentialism," 284.

Marinova, Dora - Margaret Raven. "Indigenous knowledge and intellectual property: A sustainability agenda" in *Journal of Economic Surveys* 20 (2006): 587.

Otto Naess, Lars. "The role of local knowledge in adaptation to climate change" in *WIREs Climate Change* 4 (2013): 99.

Panikkar, Raimon. "Filosofía y cultura: unarelaciónproblemática." *Revista de Ciencias de las Religiones* 1 (1996): 125-148.

Pontificia Academia Scientiarum, *Fate of Mountain Glaciers in the Antrhopocene: A Report by the Working Group Commissioned by the Pontifical Academy of Sciences* (5 May 2011): 2 &15.

Riedlinger, D. - F. Berkes, "Contributions of traditional knowledge to understanding climate change in the Canadian Arctic" in *Polar Rec* 37 (2001): 315-328.

Salick, J. - N. Ross. "Traditional peoples and climate change" in *Global Environmental Change* 19 (2009): 137-139.

White, Lynn. "The historical roots of our ecologic crisis," *Science* 155 (1967): 1204.

Other Sources

From the *Handbook for Faith and Ecology Conference Jerusalem, October 2014* in *Religion for Peace*, 2011.

Rabbi Yonatan Neril. The Interfaith Center for Sustainable Development.

United Nations Development Programme. *Human Development Report 2011.*

Internet Articles

"Raimon Panikkar." accessed from http://www.iemed.org/publicacions/quaderns/14/qm14_pdf/8.pdf, on January 26, 2011.

Coff, Pascaline. "Biography of Raimon Panikkar." accessed from http://monasticdialog.com/a.php?id=666, on January 26, 2011.

Panikkar, Raimon. "Life." accessed from "http://avidpdf.com/viewer?url=http://raimonpanikkar.org/pdf%20stampa/National_Catholic_Reporter_2010-08-31.pdf, on January 18, 2011.

Yonatan Neril, "Learning Resources: Jewish Environmental Teachings on 18 Core Topics," accessed from http://www.jewishecoseminars.com/learning-resources/#sthash.xCOH8WXf.dpuf, on November 5, 2014.

The Epilogue

A Christian Philosophical Anthropological Outlook of Saint Pope John Paul II's View on the Human Person

1. Introduction

Why this Topic

The person of Pope John Paul II fascinated me from my childhood days and ever since he became the leader of the Catholic Church from 1978-2005. In the light of his thinking on the human person, the most interesting 'thing itself' which is precisely the human being as subject.[1] Hence I have formulated my paper – an epilogue, "A Christian Philosophical Anthropological Outlook of Pope John Paul II's View on the Human Person." Firstly, the word 'Christian' is for me is an identity that I live everyday of my life. It is the very foundational base and fundamental potion of *what I am* and *who I am*. Secondly, the word 'Philosophical' is for me a search for a deep and radical meaning of life. It is in these years of my living, that the love for knowledge and wisdom has grown within me and this is where I began to grapple with the questions related to life. It is here, that I began to push my thinking and live my thinking as a human being. Thirdly, the word 'Anthropological' for me is the study of human beings. It has not only motivated but also created the interest within me to know the different realities related to humankind. Fourthly, the 'Human Person' is that which summarizes the whole reality of what Pope John Paul II lived his entire life for that is, reflecting on the person. Lastly, the person of 'Pope John Paul II' the reason why I chose him is because I like the person that he was. His thoughts and writings simply fascinate me and my thinking. When I pick up his book and begin to read, it overwhelms and inspires me to live an authentic life to learn from experience and be a conscious being with will and freedom always seeking to transcend and search for truth and live in this truth.

1 Karol Wojtyla, *The Acting Person*, ed., Anna-TreasaTymiennieecka and trans., Andrzej Potocki (London: Reidel Publishing House, 1979), xiv.

Therefore, with all eagerness and interest I decided to write my epilogue on the thoughts of Karol Wojtyla/Saint Pope John Paul II. He went on to become the third longest reigning pontiff having guided the church for 27 years. He struck me as someone very fascinating and capturing. My admiration for this talismanic man has been growing since. His thoughts have shed light on my awareness of the knowing and understanding of the human person. At the outset, his biographical sketch will help us to know the person whose thought will be elaborated in the subsequent pages.

A Biographical Sketch of Saint Pope John Paul II

Saint Pope John Paul II's original name was Karol Wojtyla. He was born on May 18, 1920, in Wadowice, Poland, to Karol Wojtyla and Emila Kaczorowska. His mother passed away in 1924 when he was just nine years old and then his elder brother Edmund in the year 1932. In the year 1938, he moved with his father to Krakow to study at Jagiellonian University. In the year 1941, his father passed away and in the following year he was accepted by the Archdiocese of Krakow as a clandestine seminarian. He was ordained a priest in the year 1946 and began his further studies.[2] He was then ordained as auxiliary Bishop of Karkow in 1958 and in the year 1963, Pope Paul VI appointed him as Archbishop of Krakow. In the year 1967, he was elevated as Cardinal.[3] On October 16, 1978 he was elected as 264th Pope and took the name John Paul II.[4] On April 5, 2005 he peacefully passed away to eternity.[5] He has gone down in history as one of the most important leader in the second half of the twentieth century. He changed the course of history in the Church as well as the world.[6] When it came to the writing world, he was simple and lucid, and had a flair of conveying his thoughts in a very convincing and personal manner. His character and personality spoke out in his writings. He had an extraordinary number of writings to his credit. The numerous studies on his thought bear witness to the profound influence he had over the course of the last few decades. He was indeed an enigma!

2 Garry O'Connor, *Universal Father: A Life of Pope John Paul II* (London: Bloomsburg, 2005), 393.

3 O'Connor, *Universal Father*, 394.

4 *Ibid.*, 395.

5 Nany Gibbs, "A Pilgrim Journey: Pope John Paul II, 1920-2005," *Time* 43/1(2005), 26.

6 Nick Bakalar and Richard Balkin, *The Wisdom of John Paul II: The Pope on Life's Most Vital Questions* (London: Routledge, 2002), xix.

Philosophical Anthropology and Personalism

Philosophical Anthropology is the study of human being in his subjectivity. It aims at arriving at a philosophical understanding of the human person. It is concerned with the uniqueness of each person in his subjective reality as a conscious but free-willing being.[7] Personalism is that in which everything is studied from the viewpoint of the person. It is an important trend in philosophical anthropology. It gives the highest value to the human person. According to St Thomas Aquinas (1225-1274), the personal mode constitutes the highest form of existence in nature.[8]

The Philosophical Formation of Saint Pope John Paul II

Saint Pope John Paul II was an intellectual. He was not only a professor of philosophy, but also a moralist.[9] His publications show the influence of Maurice Blondel (1861-1949), Marechal's (1878-1944) Transcendental Thomism and Marcel's (1889-1973) Personalistic Philosophy on his thought.[10] The influence of Jacques Maritain (1882-1973) is also evident in his phenomenological study of the person.[11] He did his doctoral thesis which was concerned with the possibility of grounding a Christian ethics upon Scheler's (1874-1928) philosophy. This study stimulated the enterprise of a reform of phenomenology.[12] One can conjuncture that his interest is St John of the Cross and in Carmelite spirituality led to his discovery of the philosophical works of Sr Benedicta of the Cross, more publicly known as Edith Stein (1891-1943). His interest in phenomenology was also sparked off through his encounter with Roman WitoldIngarden, one of the greatest and most novel of Husserl's (1859-1938) disciple, a prominent personality in the cultural milieu of Krakow. Ingarden was also responsible for acquainting him with the philosophy of Immanuel Kant (1724-1804). In Lubin, he gained an international reputation for his synthesis of Thomism and phenomenology.[13]

---

7 Jean L. Mercier, *Being Human: Basic Elements of Philosophical Anthropology* (Bangalore: Asian Trading Corporation, 1998), 8.

8 Mercier, *Being Human*, 11.

9 Ronald Lawler, *The Christian Personalism of John Paul II* (Illinois: Franciscan Herald, 1982), 2.

10 Gerard A. McCool, "From Leo XIII to John Paul II: Continuity and Development," *International Philosophical Quarterly* 40/2 (2000), 171.

11 Lawler, *The Christian Personalism of John Paul II*, 17.

12 Buttiglione, *Karol Wojtyla*, 36.

13 *Ibid.*, 54.

The Anthropology of Saint John Paul II

The central thesis of Saint Pope John Paul II is that God dwells within each person. It forms the basis of human life as a subject. This fundamental theme of the human person permeates the entire corpus of his works although there may be a few variations. The efforts to plumb the depths of the person have taken him into almost every area of philosophy and theology. He has an original and unique role to play, precisely because it discards any partial vision of man. As Rocco Buttiglione, writes in his book, *Karol Wojtyla: The Thought of the Man who became John Paul II* (1997): "John Paul II's true originality is in producing a view of the person that arises from faith, the foundation of a renewed and deeper comprehension of the human reality, gained through an essentially rational method. Faith illuminates the intelligence without violating the natural way in which it proceeds."[14]

Pope John Paul II's understanding of the human person is the foundation upon which his anthropology stands. An analysis of *The Acting Person* (1979) brings to light the existence of the human person and all that concerns life. This brings us to the first chapter wherein I have consciously focused on *the basic aspects of the human person* according to the author. In the second chapter I have made an effort to reflect in this perspective of the human person of the *experience* and *consciousness*. The third chapter brings to light *will* and *freedom* that articulates the human activity in everything thought and done. Finally, in the fourth chapter, we shall see how *transcendence* and *truth* enables a person to transcend the transitory mode and makes one participate and cultivate love in a personal way, in the light of faith, to God.

The Pope writes in *Crossing the Threshold of Hope* (1994), 'the concept of person is not only a marvelous theory; it is at the centre of the human ethos.'[15] *The Acting Person* is in fact a sharp investigation of what it means to be a person. It is strictly anthropological, by means of an ontological hermeneutics that integrates the dynamic function of the person, through self-possession and self-governance which emphasizes the irreducible transcendence of the human person.[16] An investigation of the human subject that unravels the network of man's constitutive tendencies and strivings in his experience and in being conscious, it reveals to himself his status in the world, the meaning of freedom and the willingness to will in reaching the transcendence and ultimately the fulfillment in finding the truth.

---

14 Rocco Buttiglione, *Karol Wojtyla: The Thought of the Man who became John Paul II*, trans., Paolo Gutietti and Francesca (Cambridge: Eerdmans, 1997), 93.

15 John Paul II, *Crossing the Threshold of Hope*, ed., Vittorio Messori (London: Jonathan Cape, 1994), 97.

16 Wojtyla, *The Acting Person*, xxii.

Present Situation of the Person

The scientific and technological growth in the world today, on one hand, has broadened the general outlook towards the human person, but on the other hand, it has limited and narrowed down the knowledge about the human person. The crisis of the human person has grown at the same breakneck pace as that of the scientific and technological development. This seems to be the logical conclusion because, as we know, man[17] is a complex being. In addition, Karol Wojtyla says, "The problem of man's subjectivity is today of paramount importance of philosophy."[18] Man's subjectivity, for Wojtyla is "his very existence, his crisis and confrontations, and the nature and meaning of his being."[19] Hence, there arises the need to deal with the problems of man's subjectivity.

The study of the human person is not only relevant but exigent because of the present postmodernism trends that are affecting the world at large and are causing a great crisis. Such an undertaking and understanding of the human person re-emphasizes its value and reinstates its dignity. Our knowledge and awareness of such values helps us to respect other human persons for who they are, why they are, what they are and how they are. It helps us to treat them as ends and not as means for our vested interests and selfish desires. Today, more than ever, humanity is struggling to regain the pristine beauty and value of the human person. Anywhere one glances, one finds the moral values are at a great risk in our society due to the degradation of the human person. This is so conspicuous in the undermining of the very infra-structure of the social life of a person, viz., divorce, abortion, murder, suicide, violence, abuse of power and position, competition, corruption, conflicts (cultural, caste, class), spiritual crisis, emotional breakdown, war, terrorism and the like. And the reason is not far to seek. It is due to the lack of respect and ignorance of living and letting live of the human person and for human life. With growing technology and science, the quality of life has increased in various ways. With this growth, there has also been a threat to the life of human beings. However, the most dangerous threat to human life is that which has originated from the ancient to the postmodern culture. Some believe that they can control life and death by taking the decision about the matter into their own

17 The word Man means the androgynous human being and not the male element which has hitherto monopolized it – although when using pronouns I follow common usage, the new gender which encompasses both masculine and feminine without reducing either to a non-human neuter. It is not that the masculine stands for the whole Man, but that the whole Man has allowed this untoward domination by the male. The solution is not juxtaposition (he/she), but integration. For this reason the word Man is used when referring to the *anthropos* of the *the anthropocosmic* vision, just as capitalize World and God.

18 Karol Wojtyla, "The task of Christian Philosophy Today," *The American Catholic Philosophical Association* LIII (1979), 3.

19 Wojtyla, "The Task of Christian Philosophy Today," 3.

hands. What really happens here is that the individual is overcome and crushed by death, deprived of any prospect or meaning or hope (EV, 48).[20]

Definition given by Boethius (c.475-524) in *De Persona etduabusnaturis* where he says that the person is, "an individual substance possessed of a rational nature."[21] In this view, "to be a person means, to be a particular kind of living being, despite the individual and cultural differences between the cannibal and the Wall Street business man."[22] St. Thomas Aquinas carried forward the definition of a person when he described the person as "an individual substance of a rational nature," a definition actually given by Boethius. The way in which Aquinas explained it, constitutes a new definition. By 'individual substance,' he means, a substance that is complete, which subsists by itself, and which is separated from others. According to him, the term 'person' signifies something complete, subsisting in its own right, of rational nature. So, he held the objective view of the human person as a member of the human species and according to him 'person' means that which is most perfect in the whole of nature.[23]

The Exposition

Journeying with Pope John Paul II has brought me to a realisation that the journey within oneself as well as with the other is the best way to know and understand reality and truth. Therefore I have, in my short study on the person of Pope John Paul II, studied his writings, both the Pre-Papal and the Papal periods. In this work, I would like to present his thoughts and writings on the human person. I have in my paper used the name 'Wojtyla' because it pertains to the works of his pre-papal time and the name 'Pope John Paul II' of his Papal period.

To begin with the journey of understanding or rather coming to an understanding of the human person in Wojtyla/Pope John Paul II one needs to reflect on the basic aspects of the human person according to him. Let us therefore in the first chapter see the deep and profound way in which he understands the human person.

Basic Aspects of the Human Person According to Karol Wojtyla

In order to define the human person, Karol Wojtyla had recourse to the philosophy of St. Thomas Aquinas. He assimilated some fundamental concepts of him and integrated them in his own personalism. For him,

---

20 John Paul II, *Evangelium Vitae* (EV) (*On Human Life*, March 25,1995) (Trivandrum: Carmel International Publishing House, 2005).

21 Richard De Smet, *A Short History of the Person*. Abstract from *Indian Philosophical Quarterly* 4/1 (1976), 4/2 (1977), and 2/4 (1975), 8.

22 Donald G. McCarthy and Edward J Bayer, ed, *Handbook on Critical Life Issues* (Bangalore: Theological Publications, 1984), 7.

23 Kleetus Varghese, *Personalism in John Paul II: An Anthropological Study of his Social Doctrine* (Banglore: Asain Trading Corporation, 2005), 53.

> The person is a concrete man, the *individual substantia* of the classical Boethian definition. The concrete is in a way tantamount to the unique, or at any rate, to the individualized. The concept of the person is broader and more comprehensive than the concept of the "individual," just the person is more than the individualized nature. The person would be an individual whose nature is rational – according to Boethius full definition *persona estrationalisnaturae individual substantia.*[24]

The above abstract, from the book *The Acting Person* by Karol Wojtyla, defines the human person in a nutshell. Apart from having a rational nature, the person is also a concrete man, an individual and as an individual he is unique. It also gives the structure of this chapter. After dealing with the human person as an embodied subject with its rational and spiritual nature, we shall see how the body itself expresses the person and how he becomes aware of his personhood. One of the unique characteristics of the human person is the 'Image of God.' It will be further illustrated to show how the body itself is the part of *Imago Dei.* And in communion of persons man becomes the image of God. If the human person is the image of God, then he is necessarily a gift of God and a gift to the other. Lastly, we shall briefly examine the identity of the person in original solitude, consciousness, self-awareness, and subjectivity.

1.1 Definition and Meaning of the Human Person

The subject matter of my study is the human person. This study will certainly raise many questions for which one does not have proper and logical answers. In my study I have used different words to represent the human person – like man, subject, being, person, and many others. For Wojtyla, "Man is neither pure spirit, nor pure matter, but a compound of both, so it is customary to say that man is a union of body and soul." Man is an episode of this cosmic dialectic and lives in this antithesis. He has the consciousness which processes mind uniquely and a language of free will – 'I am what I am.' Existence is a unique quality of man; the word 'existence' contains notions of awareness, possibility, transcendence, openness, freedom and responsibility.

Man has always been aware of the incomparable worth of the person – an absolute unique destiny. "What does it profit a man to gain the whole world and lose his own soul?"[25] In this interpretation, the person finds a primary recognition of his destiny. In front of every rational reflection, the human person is the point of reference. The philosophy of Wojtyla was the fruit of metaphysical reflection on personal and communal life. The metaphysics of man and being born of his own reflection became the unifying force for his conscious personal action.[26] The human person is called to fullness of life. Development must be measured and

24 Wojtyla, *The Acting Person*, 73.

25 Mark, 8:36 (NRSV).

26 Varghese, *Personalism in John Paul II*, 20-97 passim.

oriented according to the reality and vocation of man seen in his totality, namely his interior dimension. For him, the very essence of humanism consists in finding man's dignity.

1.2 The Centrality of the Human Person

The heart of Pope John Paul II's philosophy can be summed up as a belief in the centrality of the subjectivity of the person. Human fullness comes through the authentic realization of the self through participation in humanity. The human person is an operating and determinant subject of all intention. The realization of the fullness of the human person is in becoming more of a human being. As a person, one is therefore the subject of one's action coming to realise one's humanity. The human person is called to fullness of life.[27] Development must be measured and oriented according to the reality and vocation of man seen in his totality, namely, his interior dimension. For him, the very essence of humanism consists in finding man's dignity. In Christ, the fullness of the possibilities of the mare revealed and we may have the model of who we might become. The person is a spiritual being subsisting by his adherence to a hierarchy of values so it helps in a return of a person and to a rediscovery of the person.[28] Let us view some aspects to the human person.

1.3 Some Aspects of the Human Person

1.3.1 *The Human Person as Unity of Body and Spirit*

Wojtyla, like any other philosopher of the contemporary era, believes in the unity of soul and body. He refers to the human person as an embodied subject. As he says, "A person is, of course, not merely an organism. A human body is the body of a person because it forms a unity of substance with the human spirit."[29] He further says that the body and spirit are indispensible in the person: In the willing agnet and in the deliberate act they stand or fall together.[30] This embodied aspect of the person is the unique quality of the person, says Karol Wojtyla, and it also explains the structure of the person as having the material and spiritual nature.[31]

27 Jonathan Kwitny, *Man of the Century: The Life and Times of Pope John Paul II* (New York: Hamy Holt, 1997), 137.

28 Varghese, *Personalism in John Paul II*, 102-153 passim.

29 Karol Wojtyla, *Love and Responsibility*, trans., H. T. Willets (London: Collins, 1981), 55.

30 John Paul II, *Veritatis Splendor* (VS) (*On the Church's Moral Teaching: Splendour of Truth*, August 6, 1993. Trivandrum: Carmel International Publishing House, 2005).

31 Jove Jim S. Aguas, "The Notion of the Human Person and Human Dignity in Aquinas and Wojtyla," *Kritike* 3/1 (June 2009), 51.

1.3.2 *The Human Person as a Rational Being*

In accordance with the philosophy of St. Thomas, according to Karol Wojtyla, the *persona estrationalinaturae individual substantia.*[32] Hence, the person is first and foremost an individual having a rational nature. This rational nature subsists in a person and does not have an existence of its own. It is the rational nature together with the spiritual nature that makes the person the perfect being. Aguas emphasizes agreeing with Wojtyla, says that 'man is a rational being'[33] and this differentiates him from the whole world of objective entities, which is man's distinctive character as a person. Further, we can add that will and freedom, are two properties concretized in the person. The person, therefore, is always a rational and free concrete being, capable of all those activities that reason and freedom alone make possible.[34]

1.3.3 *The Human Person has a Spiritual Nature*

From the rational nature, Karol Wojtyla goes a step further in acknowledging the spiritual nature of the person. Previously, we have mentioned that the person's perfectibility consists in the rational nature. This is highlighted when we consider the spiritual aspect of the person. As Wojtyla says,

> A person differs from a thing in structure and in the degree of perfection. To the structure of the person belongs an "inner" in which we find the elements of spiritual life and it is this that compels us to acknowledge the spiritual nature of the human soul and the peculiar perfectibility of the human person.[35]

As a result of his spiritual life, which is the basis of his rationality, and because of his inner being and interior life, man is a person and is therefore distinct from other entities. It is this spiritual life that allows him to be involved and related to the world of objective entities.[36] As Wojtyla emphasizes that A person is an objective entity, which as a definite subject has the closest contacts with the whole (external) world and is most intimately involved with it, precisely because of his inwardness, its interior life. The spiritual life indicates truth and goodness. It longs for truth and goodness. It asks two questions, 'What is the ultimate cause of everything?' and 'How to be good and possess goodness?' Having the spiritual

---

32 The English translation of the definition of the person is *an individual substance of a rational nature.* Wojtyla, *The Acting Person*, 73.

33 Aguas, "The Notion of the Human Person and Human Dignity in Aquinas and Wojtyla," 52.

34 Karol Wojtyla, "Thomistic Personalism," *Selected Essays: Person and Community*, trans., Theresa Sandok (New York: Peter Lang, 1993), 167.

35 Wojtyla, *Love and Responsibility*, 121.

36 Aguas, "The Notion of the Human Person and Human Dignity in Aquinas and Wojtyla," 52.

nature, the person not only communicates with the visible world but also with the invisible world, which is God.[37]

1.3.4 *The Human Person as Subject and as Object*

The human person has a complex constitution and is composed of the material and spiritual aspects that make him different from all other entities in the world. Although he can be considered as an object, but because of his nature, the human person is also a subject. As a subject, he is an entity that exists and acts in a certain way. At the same time, he is also an object, that is, an objective somebody. Wojtyla says, "As an object, man is 'somebody' and this sets him apart from every other entity in the visible world, which as an object is always only 'something'."[38]

As a subject, the person is endowed with the free will. He can decide for himself. He is also incommunicable and inalienable and is very much intrinsic to the person's inner self, to the power of self-determination, and free will. The person is the subject and he decides for himself. No one can desire for the person.[39] It must be perceived through his whole experience. As he exists and acts, the person constitutes himself.[40] Subject is constituted only upon the merging of consciousness and experience. Consciousness primarily allows man to experience himself as the subject.[41] And in the field of experience, the human being appears both as a particular *suppositum* (subject) and as a concrete self, in every instant unique and unrepeatable. On the other hand, object also can be seen on the basis of act. To take an example, in a sexual relationship, the woman is the object of activity on the part of man and the man is the object of activity on the part of the woman. So 'who' is the subject and 'who' is acted upon. And so subject is always the one who performs the act and the object is the one who receives the act. Person and his thought can be another example of the subject and object.[42]

1.3.5 *The Human Person as a Concrete and Unique Subject*

Karol Wojtyla who was influenced by Thomistic philosophy believed in the subjectivity of the person. This subjectivity of the person signifies the person's 'irreducibility' to the level of things and animals. He says that the person occupies a special place in the order of created beings and that the person is not an 'individualized humanness;' but actually consists rather in the mode of individual

---

37 Wojtyla, *Love and Responsibility*, 23.

38 *Ibid.*, 21.

39 *Ibid.*, 24.

40 Karol Wojtyla, "Person: Subject and Community," *Selected Essays:Person and Community*, 167.

41 Wojtyla, *The Acting Person*, 57.

42 Wojtyla, *Love and Responsibility*, 24.

being that pertains to mankind alone. The mode of being stems from the fact that the peculiar type of being proper to mankind is personal.[43]

The spiritual aspect of man is the core of his being, but the human person is not just a pure spiritual subject, he is also a concrete subject. The human person is a concrete 'I,' who exists and acts. In other words, man is not just a being specifically defined but as a 'concrete I,' he is a concrete living subject. Therefore, the person is a concrete individual. And as a concrete individual, all his actions and experiences become unique. Moreover, as a unique and concrete subject he stamps his own existence and utterances, actions and attitudes with uniqueness. The human person as a unique and unrepeatable subject possesses and dominates himself. He alone decides for himself and determines his own existence and actions, he alone thinks, wills and loves for himself.

The uniqueness of the person is further realized when man and woman come to the realization that they are man and woman. Karol Wojtyla attests, "Sex decides not only the somatic individuality of man but defines at the same time his personal identity and concreteness."[44] In the "one flesh,"[45] that is in their conjugal union when "a man...cleaves to his wife and they become one flesh,"[46] they come to become aware of themselves. In this sexual act in a unique way, the woman 'is given' to the man to be known and he to her.[47] Because of the fact that they are man and woman, each of them is 'given' to the other, as a unique and unrepeatable subject, as a person.

1.3.6 *The Body seen as an Expression of the Human Person*

First of all, we must remember that the body is composed of matter and spirit. Wojtyla says that there is a deep connection between the mystery of creation, as a gift springing from love and the existence of man as male and female. In the whole truth of their body and their sex there is the pure and simple truth of communion between persons. When the first man exclaims at the sight of the woman, "This is the bone of my bones, and flesh of my flesh,"[48] he merely affirms the human identity of both. This expression expresses that body is 'person.'[49] The 'body' reveals the 'living soul.' There came about life in the form of the body. It is the beginning of new life of soul. The beginning of new life is the beginning of solitude or 'aloneness' before all other living being. In this solitude, the man

---

43 Wojtyla, *The Acting Person,* 83.

44 John Paul II, *Original Unity of Man and Woman* (Boston: St. Paul's Edition, 1981), 151.

45 According to Karol Wojtyla, "one flesh" refers to the sexual union where the man and the woman give themselves completely in freedom. In the sexual act, they become one flesh. John Paul II, *Original Unity of Man and Woman,* 150.

46 Genesis, 2:24 (NRSV).

47 John Paul II, *Original Unity of Man and Woman,* 150.

48 Genesis, 2:23 (NRSV).

49 Karol Wojtyla, *Towards a Philosophy of Praxis* (New York: Crossroad, 1981), 78-79.

emerges as a gift to himself and he too becomes a gift to others.[50] On the other hand, masculinity – femininity, namely, sex – is the original sign of a creative force and of awareness on the part of man. And so, man is a subject not only because of his self-awareness and self-determination, but also on the basis of his own body. The structure of this body permits him to be the author of a truly human activity. In this activity the body expresses the person.[51]

1.3.7 *Man's Awareness of being a Human Person*

Man is 'alone' means that he is unique, exclusive and unrepeatable. We apply the term 'aloneness' to man in his totality. His body, through which he participates in the visible created world, makes him conscious of being 'alone.' Nevertheless, in this consciousness he reaches the conviction that he is 'alone.' Hence, we can link man's original solitude with the consciousness of the body. Through the consciousness of his body, man is distinguished from all the animal and is separated from them and also through it he is a person. And so, on the basis of 'original solitude,' the man becomes aware and conscious of the meaning of his body.[52]

The popular notion of 'solitude' is normally understood as calm, a silent retreat to a monastery on a hill. But, Wojtyla does not seem to refer to such kind of solitude. For him, original solitude refers to the internal and spiritual identity of the human person. It is the very humanity of the human person. To define original solitude, Wojtyla bases himself on Genesis, "It is not good for man to be alone; I want to make him a helper, similar to himself."[53] The 'aloneness' of man is not in the first instance a feeling of depression. The solitude describes man in his humanity, in the structure of his being.[54] Hence, the 'aloneness' of his solitude in man is the nature of his personhood, his identity. Man is basically alone. In his 'aloneness' or 'solitude,' man becomes conscious of himself. Wojtyla calls it 'man tilling the soil.'[55] From an external point of view, man digs and prepares the ground. Internally, he experiences loneliness or aloneness but he identifies himself in it, which we can call an internalidentity. In the creation story, man is commanded to 'till the soil' and as man does so, he realizes that he is 'tilling the

50 Wojtyla, *Towards a Philosophy of Praxis*, 79.

51 John Paul II, *The Theology of the Body: Human Love in Divine Plan* (Boston: Pauline Books and Media, 1997), 40-41.

52 John Paul II, *The Theology of the Body: Human Love in Divine Plan*, 38-39.

53 Genesis, 2:18 (NRSV).

54 John Paul II, *Theology of the Body: Man and Woman he Created Them* (Boston: Pauline Books and Media, 1997), 151.

55 Karol Wojtyla uses the phrase 'tilling the soil' to show the 'work' performed by Adam, the first man, after the first fall. The word is used here to refer in inclusive language to mean the different works performed by a person. Brian J. Bransfield, *The Human Person according to John Paul II* (Boston: Pauline Books & Media), 84.

soil.' He is also conscious of himself 'tilling the soil.' He is conscious of himself being conscious of the command to till the soil. Woznicki in supporting this says that man can realize his own existence only by relating to and communicating with other beings, in this case the otherness of the visible world.[56] The fact that man distinguishes himself from other beings as a being of consciousness is a hallmark of Karol Wojtyla's philosophy.[57]

Further, John Paul II is of the opinion that man's presence to himself is one in which he is 'aware' of his aloneness.[58] He tills the soil and is self-aware that his body has meaning in this human activity; this awareness of the meaning of his body in this activity reveals a structure to his consciousness.[59] The meaning of "original solitude"[60] is founded on man's experience of existence and being. This experience of himselfis what leads to self-awareness, and in the activity of tilling the soil, man is aware and he is 'acting.' For Karol Wojtyla, "Action reveals the person, and we look at the person through his action.... action gives us the best insight into the inherent essence of the person and allows us to understand the person most fully."[61]

1.3.8 *The Human Person as the Imago Dei*[62]

The fundamental message of the Sacred Scripture proclaims that the human person is a creature of God, for "God created man in His own image; in the image of God He created him; male and female He created them."[63] This message is further emphasized by Karol Wojtyla when he says, "To the human being, created in 'the image and likeness of God,' God communicates His own thought and

56 Andrew Woznicki, *A Christian Humanism: Karol Wojtyla's Existential Personalism* (New Britain, CT: Mariel, 1980), 6-7.

57 John Paul II, *Theology of the Body,* 150.

58 *Ibid.,* 152.

59 John Paul II, *Theology of the Body: Man and Woman he Created Them,* 153-154.

60 Man's awareness of being a person begins in his solitude, the "original solitude" as John Paul II asserts. This solitude has two meanings. Firstly, deriving from man's very nature, and secondly from the relationship between man and woman. William E May, *Theology of the Body: In the Context* (Boston: Pauline Books and Media, 2010), 74.

61 Wojtyla, *The Acting Person,* 11.

62 According to Wojtyla '*Imago Dei*' refers to the Image of God. The Image of God is to be understood on the basis of love, relation and gift. It is the love that the creator has for His creatures by creating him. The relation that is present in the Persons of Trinity: the Father's love begets the Son, of which the love between Father and Son brings about the procession of the Holy Spirit. And the gift that springs from love. And hence, it is God who loved the person and created him in the relation as a gift. Su Li Lee, "Person as Gifts: Understanding Interdependence through Pope John Paul II's Anthropology," *The Catholic Social Science Review* 14 (2009), 328. See also David V. Meconi, "Deification in the Thought of John Paul II," *Irish Theological Quarterly* 71 (2006), 131.

63 Genesis, 1: 27 (NRSV).

plan."[64] For him, the human person is the image of God. For Wojtyla, the person does not only posses the image of God but 'God also becomes a human being.' He enters into the drama of human existence through redemption and permeates the human being with divine grace.[65]

We can mention here the two tasks of *Imago Dei.* The first task is to explain the human person's need for loving communion. Men and women are called to make of themselves free gifts. Humanity's divine image is neither monadic nor static; it is rather rational and dynamic. As John Paul II expresses in *Crossing the Threshold of Hope* that "the fundamental dimension of man's existence...is always a co-existence."[66] The second task of the *Imago Dei* is to show that human communion can never suffice. The person exists together with the other in communion. In order to fulfill himself, the humanity needs something more than just the other person. In *Evangelium Vitae,* John Paul II asserts thus: "The life which God bestows upon man is much more than mere existence in time. It is a drive toward the fullness of life. It is the seed of an existence which transcends the very limits of time: For God created man for incorruption, and made him in the image of his own eternity (EV, 34)."[67] Thus, Wojtyla insists that the human person is called to go beyond, to transcend himself. Men and women are constituted to seek the transcendence. This transcendental aspect can be spoken of as the metaphysical aspect of man. Hence, the person is defined in a way that is more metaphysical than physical.[68]

> Man is the image of God not only as male and female, but also because of the reciprocal relation of the two sexes. The reciprocal relation constitutes the soul of the 'communion of persons' which is established in marriage and presents a certain likeness with the union of the three Divine Persons.[69]

Man becomes the image of God not so much in the moment of solitude as in the moment of communion. Right from the beginning, He is not only an image in the solitude of a person who rules the world, but also an image of an inscrutable divine communion of persons.[70] Hence, the person is not alone. He is always and everywhere or with someone or with somebody. 'Being a person in the image and likeness of God' also involves existing in a relationship, in relation to the other "I." The image and likeness of God is a quality of the personal being of

64 Karol Wojtyla, "On the Dignity of the Human Person," Selected Essays: *Person and Community,* 179.

65 Wojtyla, "On the Dignity of the Human Person," 179.

66 John Paul II, *Crossing the Threshold of Hope* (London: Jonathan Cape, 1994), 36.

67 Wisdom, 2:23 (NRSV).

68 John Paul II, *Original Unity of Man and Woman,* 24.

69 John Paul II, *God, Father, Creator: A Catechesis on Creed* (Boston: Pauline Books and Media, 1996), 232.

70 John Paul II, *Original Unity of Man and Woman,* 74.

both man and woman, and is also a call and a task. It is the 'call' and 'task' on the part of every person to share in this likeness and image of God and also to become the channel of this image. The foundation of the whole human 'ethos' is rooted in the image and likeness of God which the human being bears within himself from the beginning.[71] Being a person means striving towards self-realization which can only be achieved through a sincere gift of self.[72] To say that man is created in the image and likeness of God means that man is called to exist for others to become a gift.[73] This is so profound that as Pope John Paul II notes that the communion of persons is decisive for man as the image of God.[74] The body is also integral to this relation and communion for Wojtyla is the conviction that man is the "image of God" because of the soul has frequently been expressed. But traditional doctrine does not lack the conviction that the body also participates in the dignity of the "image of God" in its own way, just as it participates in the dignity of the person.[75]

1.3.9 *The Human Person as a Gift*

In his book entitled *A Theology of the Body: Man and Woman He Created Them* (1997), Wojtyla has unraveled the notion of the human person very well. Man does not simply receive a gift, he is a gift. And how does man know this gift? Wojtyla clarifies that the person realizes that he himself is a gift within the gift of creation and is able to understand the very meaning of the gift in the call from nothing to existence.[76] He is a gift in the creation. He realizes this the moment he is aware that he came into existence from nothing.

For Wojtyla, the gift can never be limited to one dimension. In the gift-of-self giving and accepting the gift interpenetrates in such a way that the very act of giving becomes acceptance, and acceptance transforms itself into giving.[77] The human person is meant to exist in a relation of reciprocal gift.[78] The gift is the help, of which God spoke when He said "It is not good that the man should be alone; I want to make a helper similar to himself."[79] The gift relieves man's 'aloneness,' because he is given a helper. It reveals the essence of personhood that both need to become the gift for each other. For Wojtyla says that these expressions, that is the adjective 'alone' and the noun 'help' seem to be the key for understanding the essence of the gift on the level of man, as the existential content inscribed in

71 John Paul II, *On the Dignity and Vocation of Women,* 450.

72 John Paul II, *Theology of the Body*, 165.

73 John Paul II, *On the Dignity and Vocation of Women,* 451.

74 John Paul II, *Theology of the Body,* 163, 168.

75 John Paul II, *God, Father, Creator*, 228.

76 John Paul II, *Theology of the Body,* 180.

77 *Ibid.*, 196.

78 *Ibid.*, 181.

79 Genesis, 2:18 (NRSV).

the truth of the 'image of God.' In fact, the concept of gift reveals a particular characteristic of human existence and of the very essence of the person who needs to become a gift.[80]

1.3.10 *Subjectivity*

Wojtyla uses the term 'subjectivity' to show the objective depth in every man. Subjectivity emphasizes the capacity of the person to grasp and internalize the objective meaning of existence, a meaning knowable by all. Thus Wojtyla says,

> Consciousness allows us not only to have an inner view of our actions (immanent perception) and their dynamic dependence on the ego, but also to experience these actions as actions and as our own. Thus, consciousness enables man to experience the intimate relationship between himself and his acts, thereby enabling him to take responsibility for his own acts and to share in the moral quality of the act as its subject.[81]

And so, it is the action of 'tilling the soil' which enables man to know himself and the objective meaning of his actions. Man takes responsibility for his actions and hence the subjective notion of the human person. As a subject, he is an entity that exists and acts in a certain way, and as an object he is an objective somebody. Wojtyla further says that as an object, man is 'somebody' and this sets him apart from every other entity in the visible world, which as an object is always only 'something.'[82]

1.4 Reflection

To set another step in our journey we need to reflect on one's own experience and one's own consciousness of being. Each man is unique and important with both great complexity and simplicity. Each one of us craves to know the two aspects within the human person, viz.,'who I am' and 'who I should be.' This is a very deep tenet of the human person and his inner life. It is not a deception but a reflection of reality.[83]

Conclusion

My journey has finally come to an end. However, it has actually begun. I have been fortunate enough to discover or rather have become aware of some profound truths, the awareness I speak of is with conviction of the human person during the course of this paper on the philosophical analysis of man. Before I end this epilogue on a personal note, I would like to conclude this paper with a reflection on a synthesis I have come to. To start with, I will briefly summarize the crux

80 John Paul II, *Theology of the Body*, 182.

81 Wojtyla, *The Acting Person*, 42.

82 Wojtyla, *Love and Responsibility*, 21.

83 O'Connor, *Universal Father*, 130.

of Wojtyla/Pope John Paul II's Philosophical Anthropology with a Christian perspective and from a subjective outlook.

Summary of the Paper

There is one idea or object that runs through the whole of Wojtyla's work like an ever recurring theme that is, of the human person. Many variations are played on this theme as his thought progresses but it remains always beneath or within them as the enduring subject. Indeed, the effort to explore it has taken Wojtyla himself into almost every part of Philosophy (and perhaps theology, too) it has become, as it were, a light to illumine the whole of reality. He regards this turn towards the person, and to the subjectivity and inwardness of the person, as a fundamentally positive and necessary development that must be embraced and pursued. And therefore, even in my paper I have followed a similar pattern keeping the theme of human person from a subjective point of view.

As I have said it before that, the prime concern of John Paul II was not to answer the question: "what is the human person?" but "who is the human person?" A human person is a unification of pure spirit and pure matter. Therefore, the first chapter consists of studying the basic understanding of the *human person*. It was a conscious experience, why do I say it so because of its intentional character is experience of a real external world and is itself the act or experience of a real human subject. Wojtyla turns to phenomenology as a conscious self. The objective reality of the self as a person subject is an immediate given of the subject's own experience. Thus, lead to the *experience* and *consciousness* of man. Wojtyla wants to explore from within the man because the human in its lived reality is precisely a within. The subject in being conscious of itself thus comes in a way to possess itself. In fact it thus first comes to be and constituted as self. And to constitute itself it turns to the will and freedom that lies within man. Therefore, was based on *will* and *freedom*. The lived experience of our personal subjectivity is simply the full actualization of all that is contained virtually in our subjectivity. The horizontal transcendence typical of intentional acts of awareness or affectivity we need the vertical transcendence of self realization in acts of willing and doing wherein we determine ourselves to choose and carry out the values we recognize in full freedom. It is in this transcendence one gets to the truth. Thus, I have elaborated on the theme of *transcendence* and *truth*.

A Personal Assessment: Critical Appreciation

After having briefly summarized the content of the paper, highlighting the philosophical anthropology of Wojtyla/ Pope John Paul II, I would like to critically appreciate the insights with a Christian background.

In my opinion, the whole of the philosophers (Wojtyla/ Pope John Paul II) thought regarding the human person has a very comprehensive and holistic approach, with a phenomenological care-fronting. He takes into account the whole truth about man. Precisely, because it is based on a rich synthesis of faith and reason, of a lived reality-experience, that gives the human person a centrality in the universe. His recurrent and insistent emphasis on each and every 'real,' 'concrete,' and 'historical' dimension of man intends to promulgate an understanding of man as a unique person. In this forceful declaration we gain an insight into the Personalism that enlightens both his philosophy and his anthropology.

I am well aware that this study has been a moment of growing and appreciating the human person in oneself as well as the other. I know that this study is not an exhaustive one, at the sametime; I feel happy and contended to have pursued my reading in studying the thought of John Paul II on the human person. It has definitely made me grow in my approach to life as a person and has enabled me to have more analytic, synthetic and dialectic with an understanding which is philosophical yet practical approach to life.

Bibliography

Encyclicals

John Paul II. *Redemptor Hominis* (The Redeemer of Man, 4 March 1979). Trivandrum: Carmel International Publishing House, 2005.

__________ . *Centesimus Annus* (On Work and Social Questions, 1 May 1991). Trivandrum: Carmel International Publishing House, 2005.

__________. *Veritatis Splendor* (On the Church's Moral Teaching, 6 August 1993). Trivandrum: Carmel International Publishing House, 2005.

__________. *Evangelium Vitae* (On Human Life, 25 March 1995). Trivandrum: Carmel International Publishing House, 2005.

Primary Sources

Wojtyla, Karol. *Love and Responsibility.*Translated by H. T. Willetts. New York: William Collins, 1998.

Wojtyla, Karol. *The Acting Person.* Edited by Anna-Teresa Tymienniecka and translated by Andezej Potoocki. London: Reidel Publishing House, 1979.

Secondary Sources

Accattoli, Luigi. *John Paul II – Man of the Millennium.* Translated by Jordan Aumann. Mumbai: St Paul's Publication, 2001.

Boadt, Lawrence. *John Paul II, Words of Certitude – Excerpts from his Talks and Writings as Bishop and Pope.* New York: Paulist Press, 1979.

Bransfield, J. Brian. *The Human Person According to John Paul II.* Boston: Pauline Books and Media, 2010.

Buttiglione, Rocco. *Karol Wojtyla: The Thought of the Man who Became Pope John Paul II.* Translated by Paolo Guietti and Francesca Murphy. Cambridge: Eerdmans, 1997.

O'Connor, Garry. *Universal Father, a Life of Pope John Paul II.* London: Bloomsbury, 2005.

Schall, V. James. *The Whole Truth About Man.* Boston: Daughters of St. Paul, 1981.

Simpson, Peter. *On Karol Wojtyla.* Belmont: Wadsworth Thomson Learning, 2001.

Varghese, K. Kleetus. *Personalism in John Paul II – An Anthropological Study of his Social Doctrines.* Banglore: Asian Trading Corporation, 2005.

The Wonder Years in Manila

(Bataan: 1990-1992)

I dreamt of belonging to a community
of refugees.
With people who have nothing
whose lives revolve around hope
in the direction of randomness
chance and mischance,
a system left to itself.
Where millions of flies
and cockroaches and mutant rats
compete with me.
Like the outcasts of India
where I can learn how fragile life is
how easily lost
how easily forgotten
to feel hunger
and to ask not when to eat
but, "are we eating today?"
To really taste ice-cream for the first time
and blood tastes sweet.
Never again tasting the same way.

7am, driving to the "U of I"
my dreams turned to ashes in my mouth.
Some kind of pain
like a lamenting philosopher
I have shed tears of sadness,
tears of September,
tears of failure and confusion.
I want to feel myself expanding,
not diminishing in this beautiful for spacious sky.

I am drowning in my own river of words
this intellectual life,
this academic competition to be recognized.
Can I explain my own Jargon?
I need an antidote for these illusions
of my own brokenness and mortality.
No one knows my fear and resentment
in these unforgiving consequences
of living, eating, sitting, dying like everyone else,
with background music and the eulogy.

This poem is somewhat biographical. I think we are living in a time where there are two dynamic forces pulling us together and apart as a group of people sharing a planet. Pulling together globalization and instant communication, on one hand and on the other separation or fragmentation of cultures into smaller groups, such as with the developing countries. Tragically, the current situation of refugees, migrant workers, humanity living below poverty line, those who are struggling for their basic needs which includes health and education is most heartbreaking. Ever since the Arab Spring that came about a couple of years ago, with hope and promise of toppling down regimes, now has turned into bitter years of uncertainty. We as people of the world must remember to relight candles that have gone out overnight by the wind of time. And allow ourselves to think of humanity with love and peace.

MINH DANG SDB is a perpetually professed member of the Salesian congregation belonging to the Province of SUE East USA but is a missionary in the Salesian Province of the Middle East. He has a Bachelor degree in Philosophy and Master Degree in Psychology. He is currently doing his Bachelor Degree in Theology at the Salesianum Theologicum Studium – Jerusalem Campus, Israel. As a person he inspires youth with his talents such as that of sketching and writing poems.

About the Compiler and Contributors

Michael, Manu is a member of the Salesian Congregation and belongs to the province of Kerela, India. He has obtained his master's degree in Philosophy at Divyadaan: Salesian Institute of Philosophy, Nashik, India on the theme Levinasian Subject (2013). His specialization is Contemporary Western Philosophy. He is currently a member of the faculty of philosophy at Vishwa Jyothi Don Bosco College, Karunapuram, Warangal, Kerela, India. To his credit, he has philosophical book reviews and has authored the book, *The Levinasian Subject: An Introduction to the Philosophy of Emmanuel Levinas* (2014).

Wanjal, Moses is a Ugandan Catholic Priest belonging to a Religious Congregation of the Salesians of Don Bosco. He accomplished his Licentiate in Sacred Liturgy (LSL) at the Pontifical University of Saint Anselm, Rome. He served as a Lecturer at Don Bosco Utume, Nairobi – Kenya, affiliated to the Salesian Pontifical University, Rome. He is currently a Professor in Israel at the *Studium Theologicum Salesianum*, Salesian Pontifical University, Faculty of Theology – Jerusalem Campus. To his credit, he has a book published*: Foretaste of Heavenly Liturgy: Commemorating, Celebrating and Living: An Anthropological, Theological and Liturgical Reflection on African Sub-Saharan Music through Saint Augustine and Sacrosanctum Concilium* (2015).

Alhadeff, Cara Judea (Writer/artist) engages embodied feminist theory. She has published essays in philosophy, art, gender, ethnic, and cultural studies' journals and anthologies. Her work is the subject of several documentaries for international public television. Alhadeff's first tome, *Viscous Expectations: Justice, Vulnerability, The Ob-scene* (Penn State University Press, 2014), explores vulnerability and the erotics of the uncanny. Her new book, Zazu Dreams, addresses eco-literacy and the diaspora of Jews-of-Color.

Storck, Thomas is an author and independent scholar who has written widely on questions of culture and Catholic social teaching in periodicals and collections in the United States, Europe and Australia. He taught history at Christendom College in Front Royal, Virginia, and philosophy at Mt. Aloysius College in Cresson, Pennsylvania and Catonsville Community College in Catonsville, Maryland. His books include *The Catholic Milieu* (Christendom Press, 1987), *Foundations of a Catholic Political Order* (Four Faces Press, 1998), and *Christendom and the West* (Four Faces Press, 2000).

Schall, James V. is a member of the Society of Jesus (Jesuit Congregation). He is an American Jesuit Roman Catholic priest, teacher, writer, and philosopher. Father Schall's interests include classical and medieval political philosophy, natural law, Christian political philosophy, and the nature of political philosophy. He earned his Ph.D in Political Philosophy Georgetown University in 1960. He is a Professor Emeritus in the Department of Government, at Georgetown University, Washington, D. C., USA. He is currently residing in California, USA. He has to his credit authored many books to name some of his works: *Reason, Revelation, and the Foundations of Political Philosophy* (1987); *The Modern Age* (2010); *Political Philosophy & Revelation* (2001); *At the Limits of Political Philosophy* (1996); and *Roman Catholic Political Philosophy* (2006).

Mwandha, Kevin Otieno is a Catholic priest from Kenya. He holds a doctorate in canon law from the Pontifical University of the Holy Cross – Rome. His area of specialization is Canon Law in the Catholic Church. He has been a visiting lecturer at the Institute of Youth Ministry, Tangaza College - Nairobi and at Don Bosco Theological Centre, Utume – Nairobi. He is an adjunct professor at the Salesian Pontifical University and a visiting professor at Studium Theologicum Salesianum – Jerusalem, Israel.

Göcke, Benedikt Paul is Doctor of Catholic Theology and Doctor of Philosophy. He specialises in philosophy of religion, philosophy of mind, metaphysics and German idealism. He is assistant professor at the Catholic-Faculty of Theology, Ruhr-University Bochum, and Research Fellow at the Ian Ramsey Centre for Science and Religion, University of Oxford. He is the author or editor of several books in philosophy and has published in numerous national and international peer-review journals. Dr. Göcke has lectured in Germany, Italy, Belgium, Macedonia, Austria, England, and the USA.

Golec, Jonna is a BA Student of Archaeology at the Warsaw University, and the member of Experimental Archaeology Club of Warsaw University and founder of Historical Cooking Project, at Poland. She is also an independent researcher passionate about the Archaeology of Hittites, Ancient Persia and concepts of the spirituality throughout ages. Furthermore, she designs historical costumes and administrates *I Love Archaeology* forum on Facebook and other social networking sites.

D'Costa, Marina has earned a Bachelor's degree of Arts in Sociology & Anthropology from St Xavier's College, Mumbai - India and a Masters in Anthropology from University of Pune – India. She is also a member of different associations worldwide such as Pax Romana – ICMICA (International Catholic Movement for Intellectual and Cultural Affairs), AICUF [All India Catholic University Federation], SYM - Salesian Youth Movement (Mumbai Province) and other associations in her networks. To her credit she also has scholarly articles written in the field of Inclusion and Anthropology. She is also an Innovator to champion the "power of dialogue" which has led her to conduct workshops, seminars and conferences to promote the culture of dialogue internationally. She has been a delegate for Asian Theology Forum, Panelist at the United Nations General Assembly, Cultural Exchange Programmes and has represented IMCS India for the World Council and Asia Pacific Council of Pax Romana IMCS (International Movement of Catholic Students).

Kumar, Albert has a Master's degree in philosophy from Divyadaan, Nashik - India. He was a professor of philosophy in Jnanodaya Salesian College, Yercaud - India. At present, he is pursuing his theological studies at the Salesian Pontifical University, Rome - Italy. He has articles like; *Conscience as a Way to Assent to God: A Study on John Henry Cardinal Newman* and *The Epistemology of Assent: A Study of Newman's Grammar of Assent* and some book reviews to his credit in philosophical journals and magazines. His area of interest is the epistemology of philosophy of Religion.

D'Souza, Romero is a perpetually professed member of the Salesian Province of St. Francis Xavier, Mumbai. He has completed his BA degree with a specialization in Sociology from the University of Pune, India. He has completed his Bachelor as well as Master in Philosophy from Divyadaan: Salesian Institute of Philosophy aggregated to the Faculty of Philosophy of the Salesian Pontifical University, Rome, Italy. He is currently doing BTh in Theology at the Studium Theologicum Salesianum, Salesian Pontifical University, Faculty of Theology – Jerusalem Campus - Israel.